EDUCATION AND CARE IN THE EARLY YEARS

AN IRISH PERSPECTIVE

SECOND EDITION

Josephine Donohoe
and
Frances Gaynor

GILL & MACMILLAN

Gill & Macmillan Ltd

Hume Avenue

Park West

Dublin 12

with associated companies throughout the world

www.gillmacmillan.ie

© 1999, 2003 Josephine Donohoe and Frances Gaynor

0 7171 3495 4

Design and print origination in Ireland by

O'K Graphic Design, Dublin

Illustrations on pages 65, 101, 102 and 251 by Rosa Devine

The paper used in this book is made from the wood pulp of managed forests. For every tree felled,
at least one tree is planted, thereby renewing natural resources.

AN IRISH

Second Edition

Dedication

This book is dedicated to the memory of Jill Molloy,
a valued colleague and friend who died on 28 September 2001.

Contents

Acknowledgments

T his book would not have been written without the support of our families, friends, colleagues and associates. In particular we would like to acknowledge the contributions of the following people:

Linda Hassett for the real life child observation and Rita Kwiotek, Equality Services Galway, for the section on disability in Chapter 5.

Thanks are also due to all the students, children and families with whom we have worked over the years.

J.D. and F.G.

Introduction

Since the first edition of *Education and Care in the Early Years* was published, a number of significant changes have taken place in early childhood policy, legislation and accreditation. The purpose of this edition is to reflect the above changes. It brings together at Level 2, material with a specifically Irish focus which is relevant to early childhood work. A practical rather than a theoretical approach is taken, and the activities and exercises throughout the book are clearly linked to FETAC Level 2 assessment work.

The material presented here is underpinned by a commitment to principles of quality and equality, which we believe should underpin all early childhood work. It takes as its starting point an affirmation of the child as a unique individual with rights, who is an active agent in his/her own learning. (In referring to the child and the early childhood worker, we have used the terms 'she' and 'he' in alternate chapters throughout the book.)

There are many excellent textbooks available which cover the general areas of child care and health, child development and early learning. We have not included these areas because we believe that they are adequately covered elsewhere.

A practical approach is taken in the presentation of the material. Activities, tasks, case studies and scenarios are interspersed at relevant stages throughout the text, and are designed to provoke discussion and reinforce learning. Many of these are suitable for use as research projects, and suggestions for child observations aim to facilitate the learner who is completing an observations portfolio. While making these links within the text, the suggested activities are not intended to be in any way prescriptive. They offer flexible options to both learner and tutor to adapt the material as they see fit. The aim is to maintain a balance between group discussion in the classroom and practical tasks which provide the opportunity for the individual learner to research or carry out activities alone.

Resources for further reading and useful addresses are included at the end of the book. These are not exhaustive, but are aimed at the learner who wishes to explore further a particular area; the majority of the suggested resources are readily accessible in Ireland.

High quality early years services require trained and qualified professional workers, and in Ireland more and more options are becoming available in this area. It is hoped that this textbook will be valuable to learners in all early years training at Level 2, such as the FETAC Level 2 Certificate in Child Care, the FETAC Level 2 Certificate in Community Care, as well as the FETAC Level 3 Certificate and the CACHE qualifications in early years work.

Although written primarily with the needs of the early childhood care and education student in mind, it is hoped that this book will also be of interest to parents and to early childhood workers engaged in in-service training — in fact to all those who have an interest in the care and education of young children in Ireland.

SECTION ONE

EARLY CHILDHOOD SERVICES

This section is designed to give an overview of issues which are of general relevance to early childhood workers. Chapter 1 gives an overview of the early childhood services, both publicly and privately funded, which are available to pre-school children in Ireland at present, and describes the most important policy initiatives of the past five years. It also looks at issues of employment in early childhood services.

Chapter 2 is concerned with the regulation of pre-school services under the Child Care Act 1991 and the Safety, Health and Welfare at Work Act 1989. The third chapter explores children's rights in an overall context of quality early childhood services.

1

DEVELOPMENT OF THE EARLY CHILDHOOD SECTOR

AREAS COVERED

▸ Early Childhood Services
▸ Recent Policy Initiatives
▸ Working in an Early Childhood Setting
▸ Employment Legislation
▸ The Role of the Trade Union

Introduction

Ireland provides a low level of State support for early childhood services, despite international recognition of the value of these services to children and families. A range of full-time and part-time services has emerged over the past twenty years to meet growing demand, largely outside of any legislative framework. This chapter outlines the range of early childhood services currently available in Ireland, and summarises the initiatives which support the continued development of those services. It looks at the work of the early childhood professional, outlines the main employee entitlements under current labour legislation and summarises the role of the trade union.

The term 'Early Childhood Services' is used here to denote only those services concerned with early childhood care and education.

Early Childhood Services

The past two decades have seen a rapid increase in the development of early childhood services in Ireland. There are two key reasons for this:

▶ Increased participation by women in the paid labour force

▶ A recognition of the value of play and socialisation opportunities for children's development.

In Ireland today, women with young children are forming an increasing proportion of the paid labour force, and it is now recognised that lack of childcare can act as a barrier to employment, training and education for women. Unlike several of our EU partners, Ireland has no state-supported mainstream early education system, and does not provide a service for the children of working parents, with the result that parents are increasingly turning to the private sector to meet their childcare needs.

There has, however, been some recognition of the value to children of participation in high quality early education programmes. On a community level, this is evident in the massive growth of the pre-school playgroup movement. On an official level the Department of Education and Science *Early Start Programme* was initiated to provide increased access to early education for children in designated disadvantaged areas, who are perceived to be at risk of educational failure. Altogether, a high percentage of under-fives attend some form of early childhood service, whether full-time or part-time, publicly or privately funded.

Early childhood services fall broadly into two categories:

▶ Services aiming to meet **children's developmental needs** — playgroups, naíonraí, parent and toddler groups, Montessori pre-schools. These are known as 'sessional' services

▶ Services aiming to meet the **needs of parents** who are employed, or in full-time education or training — crèches/nurseries, workplace nurseries and family day-care (childminding). These services are 'full-time'.

Sessional Services

Playgroups

Playgroups usually operate for up to three-and-a-half hours per day and cater for children aged between two-and-a-half years up to school-going age. Playgroups aim to promote the educational and social development of children through play and the involvement of parents. Privately operated playgroups are known as **home playgroups**.

Funded places may also be available in **community playgroups**, which are usually managed by parent committees. Most operate out of community centres, halls or school premises, and receive grant aid from local authorities or Health Boards to cover costs of equipment and/or premises, in addition to their own fundraising.

Playgroups are supported by IPPA, the Early Childhood Organisation, a voluntary body which offers advice, support and training to its members, through its network of regional advisers and tutors.

Naíonraí

These are playgroups which operate through the medium of Irish, and they cater for around 2,500 children. Naíonraí are supported by An Chomhchoiste Réamhscolaíochta Teo., which offers a similar service to that operated by IPPA, the Early Childhood Organisation. These are also mainly privately operated.

Parent and Toddler Groups

These are aimed at providing play and socialisation opportunities to babies and toddlers within the safe and secure environment of their parent's presence. They are mostly informal, often meeting in the houses of the parents involved or in local community facilities. These are also supported by IPPA, the Early Childhood Organisation.

Montessori Pre-Schools

These pre-schools are run according to the principles and methods devised by Dr Maria Montessori. Most operate on an academic year basis, and while the Montessori method is designed to offer a complete educational programme for the child up to twelve years, in practice in Ireland Montessori schools mainly cater for the three- to six-year age group.

The Early Start Pre-School Programme

This is defined as a compensatory/intervention programme designed to alleviate educational disadvantage, and to provide more widespread access to early childhood services in economically and socially deprived areas. The programmes are based within the primary schools, and take advantage of special grants to cover start-up and running costs, as well as developing parental involvement, thus making it 100% funded by the Department of Education and Science.

Pre-Schools for Traveller Children

Traveller pre-schools are run independently of primary schools, mainly by voluntary and religious groups, and are 98% funded by the Department of Education and Science to cover costs of tuition and transport. They may also receive a small grant for purchasing equipment. Funding is available at the discretion of the Health Boards to provide for assistant teachers/childcare assistants, but not all pre-schools can access the services of an assistant due to the uncertainty of funding. There is no provision for capitation or set-up grants.

Pre-Schools for Disabled Children

These services are mainly provided by voluntary organisations as part of their special school provision, and are funded by the Department of Health and Children and the

Department of Education and Science, and the European Commission, and supplemented by voluntary contributions. They are linked to special education primary schools.

There is no specific funding structure in place to cover the cost of integrating children with disabilities into mainstream services. These are either met by the parents or assisted by the voluntary organisations through the provision of back-up services such as visiting teachers.

Full-time Services

Crèches, Nurseries, Day Care Centres

Since these terms are often used synonymously and in fact there is no actual difference between them, it is convenient to deal with them all under one heading. These offer full-time care for children from about twelve weeks old to school-going age. Most nurseries offer a playgroup or Montessori-based curriculum for part of the day to the 3–5 year olds, and an increasing number are responding to the demand for after-school collection and care. This means in effect that a nursery can accommodate age groups as diverse as twelve weeks old up to 10 or 12 years. Many nurseries provide hot meals and snacks throughout the day for the children; in a minority of cases this is provided by the parents.

Nurseries may be privately or publicly financed, either through fees paid by parents, subsidies paid by employers or funding from Government departments such as the Department of Health and Children; the Department of Education and Science; or the Department of Justice, Equality and Law Reform. They are usually open for a minimum of eight hours per day and aim to meet the needs of parents who are in paid employment or in education. The National Children's Nurseries Association (NCNA) is the support organisation for nurseries and crèches.

Family Day Care

This is where children are looked after in someone else's home. Full- and part-time care is offered to a range of age groups, and hours are usually by negotiation. It is by far the most commonly used form of childcare; it is equally accessible to both rural and urban families and is considered to offer the nearest thing to a home environment for a child, where she can develop a one-to-one relationship with a single adult. The support organisation for family daycarers is Childminding Ireland.

TASK
Research what early childhood provision there is in the area where you live.
Group these under sessional services and full-time services.
This research could be used as part of a Social Studies project.

Table 1.1: Care Arrangements for Children Aged 0–5, 1997 (based on the use of services from 9 a.m. to 1 p.m.)

	0–1	2–3	4	5	Total
Total Population	**106,000**	**108,000**	**58,900**	**60,300**	**334,000**
At school	0 (0%)	300 (0.3%)	28,900 (49.1%)	59,900 (99.3%)	89,100
Mother and Toddler Group	0 (0%)	800 (0.7%)	0 (0%)	0 (0%)	800
Nursery/crèche etc.	3,300 (3.1%)	21,600 (19.9%)	15,100 (25.6%)	0 (0%)	40,000
Childminder's home	13,200 (12.5%)	11,000 (10.1%)	2,500 (4.2%)	0 (0%)	26,700
At home with non-relative	5,400 (5.1%)	2,100 (1.9%)	900 (1.5%)	0 (0%)	8,400
Relative's home	5,000 (4.7%)	3,400 (3.1%)	1,200 (2%)	0 (0%)	9,600
At home with parent/relative	79,00 (74.7%)	69,600 (64%)	10.400 (17.6%)	400 (0.7%)	159,400

Source: Commission on the Family 1998, 238. All figures rounded to the nearest hundred.

ACTIVITY

Aim: To summarise information on early years services in Ireland in an easily accessible format.

Compile a chart which summarises the range of provision of early years services in Ireland.

Use the headings:

▶ Type of service

▶ Who funded by

▶ Age range catered for

▶ Whether full time or sessional

▶ Support organisation, if any.

Recent Policy Initiatives

Ireland's economic success in recent years has resulted in a shortage of both skilled and unskilled labour. This has meant that attracting women back into full-time employment and retaining them there is essential if economic growth is to be sustained. The fact that the majority of early childhood services are still provided by the private sector and that fees paid for these services are not tax-deductible has made the option of full-time work less and less attractive to many women.

The general shortage of affordable, accessible, quality childcare and its overall impact on economic development has forced the Government to look at how services can best be developed and supported. In general it is this, rather than a concern for the child, which has driven the development of policy in recent years.

The principal policy initiatives since 1998 are as follows:

1998   — *Strengthening Families for Life*, the *Report of the Commission on the Family* (Department of Social, Community and Family Affairs)
— *The National Forum for Early Childhood Education* (Department of Education and Science)

1999   — *The National Childcare Strategy — Report of the Partnership 2000 Expert Working Group on Childcare* (Department of Justice, Equality and Law Reform)
— *Ready to Learn*, White Paper on Early Childhood Education (Department of Education and Science)

2000   — *The National Children's Strategy* (Department of Justice, Equality and Law Reform)

Strengthening Families for Life, the Report of the Commission on the Family
This report focused on the needs of families in a fast-changing social and economic environment. Its recommendations on supporting families in carrying out their functions are based on an approach which:

▸   prioritises investment in the care of young children
▸   supports parents' choices in the care and education of their children
▸   provides practical support and recognition for those who undertake the main caring responsibilities for children
▸   facilitates families in balancing work commitments and family life.

The National Forum for Early Childhood Education

This was set up by the Department of Education and Science with the aim of bringing together all interested groups to engage in an exchange of views on early childhood education. It also provided these groups with the opportunity to submit their own concerns and proposals for the development of a national framework for the sector. The report of the Forum was published in 1998 and informed the subsequent publication of *Ready to Learn*, the White Paper on Early Childhood Education.

The National Childcare Strategy — Report of the Partnership 2000 Expert Working Group on Childcare

The Expert Working Group on Childcare was established in response to the crisis in childcare provision which arose out of increased female labour force participation. Its membership included Government Departments, social partners, statutory bodies, non-governmental organisations and parents. The brief of the Expert Working Group was to develop a national strategy for the future development and delivery of childcare and early education services, which would be underpinned by the guiding principles of:

▶ needs and rights of children
▶ equality of access and participation
▶ diversity
▶ partnership
▶ quality.

The National Childcare Strategy was published in 1999 and made recommendations in relation to support for parents, support for providers, regulations, training, qualifications, employment, planning and co-ordination.

Arising out of the National Childcare Strategy, the National Co-ordinating Childcare Committee has been set up with the purpose of co-ordinating existing developments in the childcare field, and of informing national policy development. County Childcare Committees have also been established at local level, to co-ordinate new and existing services in the area, and to develop, implement and monitor county childcare plans. The County Childcare Committees offer a forum for all those involved in early childhood education and care — workers, providers and trainers — to become involved at a local level in influencing policy developments which affect them.

Ready to Learn, the White Paper on Early Childhood Education

This White Paper sets out a national policy framework for early childhood education in Ireland, which will build on existing provision and improve the extent and quality of service provided. The document acknowledges the value of early education both in terms of its impact on children's lives and its value to the community and to society in general. It highlights the crucial importance of quality of provision. Particular emphasis is placed on meeting the needs of children who are disadvantaged and children with special needs.

The National Children's Strategy is dealt with in Chapter 3.

Working in an Early Childhood Setting

Early childhood professional workers are qualified to work with young children in a variety of settings including crèches, nurseries, playgroups, primary schools and pre-school programmes. The key tasks and responsibilities of the early childhood worker have been set out by the Expert Working Group on Childcare. Included in these are the following:

The Childcare Worker

▶ Day-to-day responsibility under supervision for children attending the centre

▶ Implementing and reviewing activities appropriate to individual and group needs so as to provide for children's physical, emotional, social and cognitive development

▶ Observing all procedures as required in terms of care and control, safety and good childcare practice

▶ Choosing, organising and maintaining equipment and materials

▶ Contributing to the compiling and updating of children's records

▶ Delegation of tasks to childcare assistants

▶ Working as part of a team

▶ Liaising with parents.

The Childcare Assistant

▶ Undertaking routine tasks as delegated under the supervision of childcare worker/supervisor

▶ Maintaining equipment and materials

▶ Contributing to the updating of children's records

▶ Working as part of a team

▶ Liaising with parents.

Qualities of the Early Childhood Worker

As in all occupations, there are particular qualities which professional early childhood workers should strive to develop. First and foremost she needs to like children and enjoy being with them. Other qualities include the following:

▶ **Communication** — this involves being a good communicator, both verbal and non-verbal. This means also being a good listener.

▶ **Empathy** — having empathy toward others means being able to identify oneself mentally with them, to enter into their feelings in order to fully understand them. It is not the same as sympathy.

▶ **Sensitivity** — this requires being able to anticipate the feelings of others in order to be responsive to their feelings and needs.

▶ **Patience** — this means giving time to the child, parents and other team members, even when you are tempted to take over and complete a task yourself. It requires tolerance and awareness that your way of doing things is not always best.

▶ **Respect** — this comes from an awareness of the rights and personal dignity of each individual child and adult whom you come in contact with in your work. In practice it means a non-judgemental approach to dealing with people and an appreciation of the value of their contributions.

▶ **Self-awareness** — this means being able to perceive the effect your behaviour has on other people, and learning how to modify it when necessary. An early childhood worker who has a positive self-image is more likely to encourage and develop this in children.

▶ **Ability to cope with stress** — the work of the early childhood professional can be stressful. Awareness of this and finding positive ways to deal with it can ensure that it does not impact on one's work.

(Adapted from Bruce and Meggitt, 1999: 511–12)

Employment Legislation

Early childhood workers who feel valued in their work are more likely to create a warm, supportive climate for the children and team members with whom they work. This is explored further in Chapter 3. The European Commission Network on Childcare has identified good working conditions and appropriate salaries as factors which help to support the work of the early childhood professional. Membership of a professional early childhood organisation also provides support through access to local and national networks, as well as information and the opportunity to make an input into the development of early childhood policy and services.

Employee Protection

The early childhood worker has a responsibility to inform herself of her own rights and responsibilities under current labour legislation.

Ireland's EU membership has resulted in the introduction of legislation to protect the rights of employers and employees at work. State agencies to assist in resolving employer/employee disputes have also been established — these include the Labour Court, the Labour Relations Commission and the Director of Equality Investigations. Where disputes cannot be resolved through these agencies, cases may be taken to the civil courts. The main areas of protection in employment for workers are outlined below.

Contract of Employment

All full-time and regular part-time employees are entitled to receive a written statement of their terms of employment within two months of its commencement. A regular part-time employee is defined as one who has thirteen consecutive weeks' employment and works more than eight hours per week. Existing employees are entitled to a written statement within two months of requesting one. The written contract of employment must include the following:

1. Name and address of employer and employee

2. Job title

3. Job description

4. Date of commencement

5. Nature of contract, e.g. full-time/part-time

6. Duration of contract

7. Place of employment

8. Rate of pay

9. Method of payment

10. Hours of work

11. Holiday leave

12. Sick leave

13. Period of notice required by both parties.

Local information such as pension contributions and entitlements, grievance procedures, probationary period and specific company rules may also be included. There should be two copies of the contract, each signed and dated by both employer and employee, and a copy should be retained by both. An employer must advise an employee within one month of any changes in the terms and conditions of employment, apart from changes in legislation or national collective agreements.

Minimum Notice

Full-time and regular part-time employees are entitled to receive minimum notice of termination of their employment as follows:

Length of Service	Notice Required
13 weeks–2 years	1 week
2–5 years	2 weeks
5–10 years	4 weeks
10–15 years	5 weeks
More than 15 years	8 weeks

Employers are entitled to receive at least one week's notice from an employee, and both parties may receive payment in lieu of notice. The minimum notice requirement does not apply in cases of misconduct.

Holidays

Employees are entitled to 20 days paid holiday plus all public holidays for every year worked.

Maximum Working Time

Over a four-month period, an employee should not work in excess of 48 hours per week on average.

Rest Periods

An employee is entitled to one 15-minute rest period for every 4.5 hours worked, and to one 15-minute and one 30-minute break for every 6 hours worked.

Redundancy Payments

After 2 years of continuous service an employee is entitled to receive a lump sum redundancy payment which is calculated as follows:

▸   one half week's pay per year of service between the ages of 16 and 41 years of age
▸   one week's pay per year of service over 41 years of age
▸   one additional week's pay regardless of length of service.

Employees are entitled to two weeks' notice of redundancy, with time off during that period to seek other employment.

Unfair Dismissals

An employee may be dismissed if:

▸   she was not qualified or competent to the job she was employed to do

▸   her conduct contravenes company rules or constitutes a danger to others at work

▸   she is being made redundant.

Dismissal is considered to be unfair if it is due to:

▸   religious beliefs

▸   political beliefs

▸   gender bias

▸   racism

▸   trade union membership or activity

▸   pregnancy

▸   sexual orientation

▸   age.

An employee may take an Unfair Dismissal case through the courts, the Rights Commissioners or the Employment Appeals Tribunal. If it is found that an employee has been unfairly dismissed, the employer must re-instate the employee either to the original job or to an alternative job of similar standing, or pay financial compensation.

Minimum Wage

All employees (except apprentices, family members and members of the defence forces) are entitled to be paid at least the national minimum wage. From October 2002 the minimum wage is €6.35 per hour. Employees under 18 years are entitled to 70% of the minimum rate.

ACTIVITY

▸   Read the section on children's rights in Chapter 3 and the section on discrimination in Chapter 5.

▸   Discuss in your group whether there is any justification for paying 70% of the minimum wage to people who are under 18 years. Could this constitute discrimination on the grounds of age?

▸   List the reasons why people under 18 years should be paid the minimum wage.

Maternity Protection

The Maternity Protection Act 1994 provides protection for pregnant women and women who have recently given birth. It entitles a pregnant woman to:

▶ paid maternity leave of a minimum of 18 consecutive weeks, with an option of an additional 8 weeks unpaid

▶ time off from work, with pay, for ante-natal and post-natal care

▶ the right to return to her original job without loss of status or rights at work.

Expectant mothers whose health may be at risk in their employment are entitled to take health and safety leave during pregnancy, separate from maternity leave.

Parental Leave

This means that a parent who has been in continuous employment with one employer for 12 months can take leave without pay for up to 14 weeks in order to take care of a child. The entitlement is separate in respect of each individual child and may be taken consecutively or in blocks at any time over the five-year period, with the consent of the employer (see also Chapter 5).

Force Majeure Leave

This is a special, emergency leave which may be taken in the case of illness or accident affecting an immediate family member. It consists of 3 days in a 12 month period or 5 days in a 36 month period.

Adoptive Leave

This consists of 10 consecutive weeks' leave for adopting parents, from the date of placement of a child. This is paid by the Department of Social and Family Affairs. All employment rights (other than pay) are preserved during this time (see also Chapter 5).

Employment Equality Act

See Chapter 5.

The Role of the Trade Union

While workers are protected and can have their rights upheld in law, trades unions work to ensure that this continues to be the case. Unions aim to improve conditions for workers within their workplaces, to ensure that members get their entitlements and their rights and to act as representatives for their members in national negotiations such as pay deals. A trade union represents its membership on issues such as:

▶ better pay and conditions

- ▶ improved employment laws
- ▶ health and safety at work
- ▶ access to education for all
- ▶ improving industrial relations by negotiation, conciliation and resolving disputes
- ▶ supporting people who are likely to suffer discrimination at work
- ▶ improving conditions for part-time workers
- ▶ lobbying for fairer tax laws
- ▶ campaigning for childcare services
- ▶ ensuring that labour laws are properly enforced
- ▶ negotiating with governments and employers on national pay deals and partnership agreements
- ▶ showing solidarity with fellow-workers around the world who may experience exploitation, repression or infringement of their human rights.

(Adapted from SWAY Project, ICTU, 2000)

The Union Representative

Workers in an organisation who are members of the same trade union usually elect a representative who negotiates with management on their behalf. A full-time official from the union is available to give support and guidance to the local representative. Issues which arise at local level are usually dealt with according to agreed grievance procedures. This means that wherever possible the representative and the employer try to sort out the difficulties. If this is not possible, the issue will be taken up at a higher level in the union, usually through the local branch. All members have the option to become involved in their local branch, which meets regularly to discuss the issues that are relevant at both local and national level.

The trade union belongs to its members. Members pay an annual subscription fee, which can be either a fixed amount or a percentage of their wage — this is usually deducted at source. Members decide (through attending or being represented at annual congress) what matters the union will deal with in the forthcoming year. Members have the right to vote on all matters of national importance, such as acceptance or rejection of national wage agreements.

Trades unions in Ireland are usually affiliated to the larger parent body, the Irish Congress of Trades Unions (Congress).

Benefits of Trade Union Membership

Trade unions provide the following:

- A national support network

- Solidarity with other workers

- A more powerful voice in national negotiations

- Legal representation and protection

- Protection of employment rights

- Collective efforts to improve working conditions

- Protection of members through enforcement of safe work practices, pensions and entitlement issues

- Support of fellow members

- Representation at grievance and disciplinary hearings, and on bullying and sexual harassment issues

- Group insurance schemes.

TASK

- **Find out:**
  - Which trade union represents early childhood workers in Ireland?
  - Who is the local contact?
  - Are meetings held locally?
  - What is the cost of membership?
  - What would be the benefits of membership for yourself?

- **Discuss in your group**
  In what ways could unionisation help to improve the general working conditions of early childhood workers in Ireland?

SUMMARY

- A wide range of early childhood services is available to children and families; the majority of these are operated privately. Publicly funded services are mainly aimed at supporting disadvantaged families or children at risk.

- A number of policy initiatives have emerged in recent years, mainly aimed at developing the early childhood sector as a labour-force support measure.

- Good working conditions and appropriate salaries are factors which help to support the work of the early childhood professional. Membership of a professional early childhood organisation can provide support through access to local and national networks.

▶   Trades unions work to improve conditions for workers within their workplaces and to ensure that members get their entitlements and their rights.

References

Bruce, Tina and Carolyn Meggitt, 1999, *Child Care and Education*, 2nd edn., London: Hodder & Stoughton

Commission on the Family 1998.

ICTU, 2000, *SWAY — Skills, Work and Youth*, Dublin: ICTU

2

PRE-SCHOOL REGULATIONS

AREAS COVERED

‣ Regulation of Pre-School Services
‣ Role of the Health Boards
‣ Health and Safety at Work

Introduction

Since 1996, services offering early childhood care and education have been regulated by legally binding requirements. These are the Pre-School Regulations with which centres must comply in order to operate. The main focus in the regulations is to maintain standards in the physical environment. All employers and employees are also protected at work by the Safety, Health and Welfare at Work Act 1989, which imposes duties and responsibilities on both parties to maintain safe practice.

Regulation of Pre-School Services

Part VII of the Child Care Act 1991 relates to pre-school services. In interpreting its requirements, two documents need to be considered:

1. The Child Care Act 1991, Part VII
2. The Child Care (Pre-school Services) Regulations 1996.

1. The Child Care Act 1991, Part V11

This provides the legal framework within which regulations can be drawn up for the supervision of pre-school services.

The Act sets out two important definitions:

Pre-school child: A child under six years of age who is not attending a national school or a school providing an educational programme similar to a national school

Pre-school service: Any pre-school, playgroup, day nursery, crèche, day-care or other similar service which caters for pre-school children. These include sessional, full-time and drop-in services (see Chapter 1).

The main provisions of the Act which relate to pre-school services are as follows:

▶ Pre-school providers are obliged to notify their local Health Board that they are operating or intend to operate a pre-school service

▶ Pre-school providers have a duty to take all reasonable measures to safeguard the health, safety and welfare of children attending the service

▶ Health Boards are obliged to supervise and inspect pre-school services

▶ Health Boards are obliged to provide information on pre-school services

▶ Regulations drawn up under the Act must be complied with.

The following services are excluded from the provisions of the Act:

▶ Where children are looked after by relatives or their spouses.

▶ Where siblings or not more than three children of different families are cared for in the home of the carer, along with the carer's own children.

2. Child Care (Pre-School Services) Regulations 1996

These regulations set down specific requirements which pre-schools must comply with under the Child Care Act 1991, in the following areas:

▶ promoting the health, welfare and development of the child

▶ standard of premises and facilities

▶ record-keeping and general administration

▶ notification to be given to Health Boards.

Health, Welfare and Development of the Child
This general heading covers the following areas:

(a) adult/child ratios
(b) corporal punishment
(c) number of children to be accommodated
(d) food
(e) safety measures

(f)   facilities for rest and play

(g)   space.

(a) Adult/Child Ratios

The recommended adult/child ratios are as follows:

Sessional Services

Age	Adult/Child Ratio
0–6 years	1 : 10

A second adult should be on the premises at all times. The maximum number of children to be catered for in one room in a sessional group is 20.

Full Day Care

Age	Adult/Child Ratio
0–1 years	1 : 3
1–3 years	1 : 6
3–6 years	1 : 8

When a full day care service also caters for children who do not attend on a full day basis, the adult/child ratio for sessional services should apply.

Childminders

A childminder on his own should look after no more than six children including his own, who are under 6 years of age, and no more than three of these should be under 1 year. A childminder should have a telephone on the premises, or a second person available, to cope with emergencies.

Drop-in Centres

Age	Adult/Child Ratio
1–6 years	1 : 8
Under 12 months	1 : 3

It is understood that the majority of drop-in centres cater for children over two years of age. A second adult should be present at all times.

ACTIVITY

SCENARIO 1

Brendan is aged 7 months, and has been looked after on a full-time basis by Colette in her own home since he was 10 weeks old. He is an only child. Colette minds two other children, Sarah aged 2 years and Mark aged 3 years 8 months. She also has four children of her own of which the youngest, Grace is 8 years old and in primary school. The others range in age from 12 to 19 years, and all live at home.

SCENARIO 2

Barbara is aged 3 years. She has one older brother aged 5, who is in school, and her mother works part-time from home. Barbara attends a large crèche for three full days per week, usually for around 9 hours per day. On the other two days she stays at home with her mother.

Discuss:
▶   What are the advantages to the individual children and their parents of these arrangements?
▶   What are the disadvantages?

(b) Corporal Punishment
It is now strictly forbidden by law to inflict corporal punishment on a child in an early childhood service.

Inappropriate behaviour should be corrected in a caring, constructive and consistent manner. Positive methods of discipline which encourage self-control, self-direction, self-esteem and co-operation should be used.

(c) Number of Children to be Accommodated
The aim here is to prevent overcrowding in pre-school services. In the overall interests of safety and a quality service the maximum number of places for the different categories of services may be fixed by Health Boards.

(d) Food

▸ Pre-school providers should ensure that there is suitable, sufficient, nutritious and varied food available for children attending the service on a full-time basis.

▸ There should be appropriate facilities for storage, preparation, cooking and serving food.

▸ There should be appropriate eating utensils, hand-washing, washing-up and sterilising facilities.

▸ Food may be cooked on the premises or children may bring packed lunches.

▸ Prepared food may be purchased from a supplier whose premises is registered with the Health Board.

▸ Waste and refuse must be stored hygienically and disposed of frequently and hygienically.

(e) Safety Measures

General safety

General guidelines are set out in the Regulations to cover children's health and safety in pre-school services. These are as follows:

▸ Garden and external play areas should be fenced, and doors and gates secured.

▸ Ponds, pits and other hazards should be fenced.

▸ Hot water for use by children should be thermostatically controlled to a safe temperature.

▸ Childproof locks should be fitted on doors, windows, drawers and cupboards.

▸ Safety precautions should be in place on low-level windows, glass panels and patio doors.

▸ Windows on first-floor level should be fitted with restricted opening safety devices.

▸ There should be suitable handrails on steps and stairs.

▸ Gates should be fitted at top and bottom of stairs.

▸ Electrical sockets should be fitted with safety covers.

▸ Medicines and all toxic substances should be safely stored.

▸ There should be adequate and suitable storage for prams, pushchairs, carrycots, play and work equipment.

Fire Safety

▸ Adequate arrangements should be in place in the event of outbreak of fire.

▸ Staff and children should be familiar with evacuation procedures.

▸ Materials in furniture and bedding should have adequate fire-retarding properties and low levels of toxicity if on fire.

▸ All heat emitting surfaces should be protected or thermostatically controlled.

ACTIVITY

Aim: To become familiar with the practical application of the Pre-School Regulations in relation to safety

▶   Support organisations such as NCNA and IPPA, the Early Childhood Organisation, offer specific guidelines to their members on implementing safe practice in their centres. Find out what these guidelines are.

▶   Working in groups, draw up a specific list of safety precautions which could be applied in different areas of the early childhood environment, both indoors and outdoors.
  —   Write each one up as a checklist.
  —   Share the checklists among the group.
  —   Select one which could suit the environment in which you work, and ask permission to use it to carry out a safety audit of one particular area.
  —   Evaluate the checklist afterwards, adding to it if necessary.

(f) Facilities for Rest and Play
There should be adequate and suitable facilities for children to rest and to play indoors and outdoors during the day.

Rest Facilities
▶   The requirement for rest facilities is aimed primarily at children in full day care, and applies to nurseries, childminders and sessional services which cater for children under 3 years.

▶   Babies and children under 2 years should have sleeping facilities away from the general play area.

Play Facilities
▶   Equipment and materials for work and play should be suitable, non-toxic and maintained in a clean and hygienic condition.

▶   Furniture, work and play surfaces should be suitable, non-toxic and in a proper state of repair.

(g) Space Requirements

Adequate space should be provided per child, in accordance with the recommendations set out below. This relates to 'clear' floor space per child, i.e. the area available for children's play and movement, and does not include space taken up by furniture and permanent fixtures. Kitchens, toilets, sleep and other ancillary areas are excluded when calculating space per child.

Sessional Services

Age of child	Floor area per child
0–6 years	2.00 square metres

Full Day Care

Age of child	Floor area per child
0–1 year	3.70 square metres
1–2 years	2.80 square metres
2–6 years	2.32 square metres

Drop-in Centres

Age of child	Floor area per child
0–6 years	2.00 square metres

ACTIVITY

Aim: To assess the implications of the above space requirements for children in the different age groups in full day care.

▸ Measure out the different spaces per child on a clear floor space, for example in the classroom, and mark with chalk.

▸ Discuss whether each seems adequate for a child in the age groups as defined above. Consider the needs and characteristics you would associate with the different groups (e.g. toddlers like to move around frequently).

▸ If the spaces do not seem adequate, suggest alternatives.

Standard of Premises and Facilities

▸ The premises should be adequately lighted and ventilated.

▸ Sanitary facilities should be provided as follows:

— nappy changing facilities

— separate toilet facilities for adults where necessary

— wash-hand basins with hot and cold water, soap and suitable means of hand drying

— safe and hygienic storage and disposal of soiled nappies.

▸ Toilets and nappy changing areas should not communicate directly with any occupied room or food room except by means of a hall, corridor, ventilated lobby or ventilated space

Recommendation on toilets and wash-hand basins:

Number of persons	WCs	Wash-hand basins
For every 10 children	1	1
For every 8 adults	1	1

Record Keeping and General Administration

Record Keeping

The following records must be kept in a pre-school centre:

▸ A register of children attending (see sample below)

▸ Details of maximum number of children catered for

▸ Children's daily attendance records

▸ Details of staff, to include name, position, qualification and experience of the person in charge and all members of staff

▸ Details of daily staff rosters

▸ Staff/child ratios

▸ Details of medicine administered to children

▸ Type of care programme provided

▸ Details of accidents or injuries to children

▸ The facilities available

▸ Opening hours and fees

▸ Records of fire procedures, to include fire drills and fire fighting equipment.

The register of children should contain the following information:

Child's name and date of birth	
Date on which child first attended service	
Date on which child ceased to attend	
Name, address and contact phone number	
Authorisation for collection of child	
Details of illness, disability or allergy, with relevant notes concerning the provision of special attention for these	
Name and telephone number of child's GP	
Record of immunisation if any	

These records are open to inspection by:

▸ a parent or guardian of a child attending the centre, but only in respect of their own child

▸ an authorised person working in the centre

▸ a person authorised by the Health Board.

Insurance

Each child should be adequately insured against injury while in attendance. This should cover public liability, employer's liability, fire and theft, with additional cover as necessary for outings and transportation of children.

Notification to be Given to Health Boards

Local Health Boards must be notified in writing if a person is operating a pre-school service, intends to operate a pre-school service, and after the service has closed down.

Health Boards offer advice, guidance, support or information to service providers, and have a duty to inspect services for which they receive a notification. The inspection process provides regular monitoring of standards in the pre-school services. It is intended to reassure parents regarding the care provided to their children, as well as providing Health Boards with information on the availability of services. A list of services is available to parents on request.

Areas of Concern

Firstly, the implementation of the Child Care Act 1991 is an important first step toward regulating all early childhood services. Its requirements are mainly concerned with regulating the physical environment, and make only passing reference to provision for play and development.

Secondly, the emphasis is very much on health and safety issues, and while a hygienic and safe environment is important, it is not a primary indicator of quality care (see Chapter 3). Thirdly, there is no provision in the Act for regulating family day-care services. In view of the fact that a high percentage of the children in full-time pre-school provision are in family day-care situations this is a serious omission.

Finally, the regulations contain no reference to the area of training for early years workers, an area which is in need of co-ordination and regulation.

The Pre-School Regulations are under review at present, and all parties concerned have an opportunity to submit their views and make an input into the process.

Health and Safety at Work

The Safety, Health and Welfare at Work Act 1989 and General Regulations 1993

Under this Act, employers and employees have a duty and a responsibility to prevent accidents and increase safety levels at work. The Act also provided for the setting up of the Health and Safety Authority (HSA), which is responsible for enforcing the legislation, devising codes of practice and regulations, providing guidelines on Safety Statements and acting in a general advisory capacity on Health and Safety in the workplace. The Act imposes duties of care on both employers and employees.

Employers' Legal Obligations

▶ To provide and maintain a safe place of work, with safe access to and egress from the building

▶ To provide and maintain safe plant and equipment

▶ To reduce risks and prevent accidents by implementing, providing and maintaining safe systems of work

▶ To provide information, training and supervision to ensure that safety standards are met

▶ To provide appropriate protective clothing and equipment

▶ To produce and implement a Safety Statement which outlines safety procedures and emergency plans.

Employees' Legal Obligations

▸ To co-operate with employers in matters of health and safety, by following procedures and using protective clothing and equipment provided

▸ To take reasonable care to perform their duties safely so as not to adversely affect the health and safety of others

▸ To report unsafe conditions to a supervisor or safety representative.

A **Safety Statement** specifies how the organisation will implement safe practice in the workplace. It is the responsibility of the employer to ensure that the Safety Statement is implemented. The Safety Statement should:

▸ identify workplace hazards and levels of safety required

▸ identify the resources necessary to implement and maintain safety standards

▸ indicate necessary precautions to prevent accidents

▸ document names and responsibilities of safety representatives

▸ detail the co-operation required from employees to maintain safety

▸ document the consultation process between employers and employees

▸ specify the reporting procedures to be used in the event of an accident.

Incidents at work which result in minor injuries should be reported and recorded. The designated Safety Officer must report the following events in writing to the Health and Safety Authority, using the approved form:

▸ The death of any person as a result of an accident at work

▸ The death of an employee which occurs up to one year after a reportable injury

▸ An accident which prevents an employee from carrying out their work for more than three days

▸ Injuries requiring medical treatment to a person absent from work due to work activity

▸ Work-related accidents to members of the public, which require medical treatment.

SUMMARY

▸ The passing of the Child Care Act in 1991 means that the Department of Health and Children can now regulate pre-school services.

▸ The Child Care (Pre-school Services) Regulations were introduced in 1996. These set out the actual legal requirements which pre-school centres must comply with under the Act, and refer primarily to the physical environment rather than addressing the issue of quality care.

▶ Health Boards may now supervise and inspect pre-school services, and provide information to parents on these services.

▶ Childminders who look after fewer than six children including their own are exempt from the notification and inspection process.

▶ Corporal punishment may not be inflicted on a child attending a pre-school service.

▶ Under the Safety, Health and Welfare at Work Act 1989, employers and employees have duties and responsibilities in relation to safe practice at work.

References

Department of Health, *The Child Care Act 1991*, Dublin: Stationery Office

Department of Health, 1997, *Child Care (Pre-school Services) Regulations 1996* and *Explanatory Guide to Requirements and Procedures for Notification and Inspection*, Dublin: Department of Health

3

CHILDREN HAVE A RIGHT TO QUALITY SERVICES

AREAS COVERED

▶ Children's Rights

▶ Children's Needs

▶ Minimum Standards

▶ Quality Indicators

Introduction

In recent years, there has been a growing acceptance that children are entitled to civil and human rights independently of their parents/caregivers. This is most apparent in the *UN Convention on the Rights of the Child 1989*, which confers rights on children of all countries that are signatories to the convention. In Ireland, *The National Children's Strategy*, underpinned by principles of quality and equality, is our commitment to implementing the Convention.

International studies over the past twenty-five years have shown that participation in high-quality early years care and education programmes has long-term positive effects on the quality of life of the individual. It has a positive impact on educational achievement and social development and encourages a greater sense of responsibility and self-control in later life. Early childhood services have the potential to offer a rich learning environment to children; this potential can best be realised when there is a commitment to maintaining the highest quality in these services, based on respect for and implementation of the rights of the child.

This chapter looks at how all the resources of the early childhood setting, both physical and human, can best be used to meet the children's needs and validate their rights. It identifies a range of factors which contribute to creating a high quality environment and poses questions for the reader on how this can be achieved.

Children's Rights

The development of childcare policy in Ireland reflects the persistent tension between the rights of parents, the rights of children and the rights of the state to intervene in family life. The Irish constitution does not recognise any separate rights for children; they are defined within the context of the rights of the family. Laws and policies also reflect society's view on childhood and children; they are assumed to be covered by human rights generally and looked after in the context of the family.

However, during the second half of the twentieth century there has been an increase in the understanding of the needs of children as individuals and a recognition of the value of childhood. While the family is generally acknowledged as the fundamental unit of society and the natural environment for the development and well-being of its members, there has been a growing acceptance that children are entitled to civil and human rights independently of their parents/caregivers.

Evidence of this lies in the various international documents and charters which have been adopted.

The **UN Convention on the Rights of the Child 1989** is the generally accepted instrument which confers rights on children of all countries that are signatories to the Convention. Ireland signed the Convention in 1990 and ratified it in September 1992. The 54-article Convention is essentially a **Bill of Rights** for all children and is informed by four general principles:

▸ All the rights guaranteed by the Convention must be available to all children without discrimination of any kind (Article 2).

▸ The best interests of the child must be a primary consideration in all actions concerning children (Article 3).

▸ Every child has a right to life, survival and development (Article 6).

▸ The child's view must be considered and taken into account in all matters affecting him or her (Article 12).

The articles of the Convention can be broken down into four broad areas:

Survival Rights which cover a child's right to life and to basic needs such as nutrition, shelter, access to medical services and an adequate living standard.

Developmental Rights which include a right to education, play, leisure, access to information, freedom of thought, conscience and religion. The adult in an early childhood centre has a duty and a responsibility to ensure the provision of developmentally appropriate routines and activities for each and every child, which do not discriminate against the child on any grounds whatever.

Protection Rights which require that children be safeguarded against all forms of abuse, neglect and exploitation. Issues covered are care and rehabilitation for children who have been abused and/or exploited including special care for refugee children, safeguards for children in the criminal justice system and protection for children in employment.

Participation Rights which encompass freedom for children to have a say and to express opinions in matters affecting their lives. Adults have a responsibility to allow children control and choice in their lives and to acknowledge and act on the feelings and opinions expressed.

In general, no-one has any difficulty seeing how adults in an early childhood setting can provide for children's rights to survival and to protection. However, the area of developmental rights and participation rights may require more thought and effort. The idea of children having control and choice is a relatively new one in our society and brings with it some fears. If children were to choose their food does this mean we will have to prepare four different meals? Negotiation and discussion are the means by which we agree together as a group what is acceptable, appropriate and healthy. Several studies have shown that people — children and adults alike — are more likely to compromise and co-operate when they have had a part in decision making. Genuine respect for children is illustrated by adults' willingness to include them in the decision-making process. This is demonstrated in the Danish project *Children as Citizens* (Moss and Pence, 1994). The project aims to increase the amount of influence which young children have over decisions regarding their own lives, through consulting with them. In one Centre, children noted that fixed times for outdoor play and mealtimes were an unacceptable adult imposition. In response the adults agreed to build more flexibility into the daily schedule, for example staggering breaktimes and staffing the playground with one adult at all times.

ACTIVITY 1

Form four groups. Each group should select one of the Rights areas outlined above.

▶   Under the chosen heading make a list of specific rights which you feel all children should be entitled to, e.g. survival might include housing, water etc; participation might include a right to choose not to participate in an activity.

▶   Give examples of situations in Ireland where children may not be enjoying these rights.

▶   Join together with the larger group and discuss similarities and differences between the different lists.

ACTIVITY 2

Developmental and Participation Rights in the Early Childhood Setting.

List activities or ways in which early childhood workers could further children's rights in relation to development and participation in the setting in which they work. Make a separate list for 0–1 years, 1–3 years and 3–6 years.

Children's Rights in Ireland

The Child Care Act 1991 has affirmed the issue of children's rights, needs and the concept of 'the best interests of the child'. Although the Act has now been implemented in full and although most people would accept that children's basic needs should be met, some concerns have been expressed; for example, who decides what is in the best interests of the child — the authorities, the parents or the child?

Secondly, when one considers rights at a more general level (e.g. rights to education or health services) the question arises as to whether the unequal distribution of resources in Irish society means that society is denying many children their basic rights. For example, 7% of children live in consistent poverty, an estimated 5,000 children are homeless and over 1,000 children are on hospital waiting lists for inpatient procedures.

The introduction of sex education programmes in schools is a result of the recognition of the child's right to information and may even go some way to protecting them from abuse in the very families in which they live, but parents who are not happy about this can remove their children from such classes. Likewise the Irish Society for the Prevention of Cruelty to Children (ISPCC) campaign to end the smacking of children by their parents has caused concern for a variety of reasons. Many still hold firmly to the belief that parents own their children and therefore have a right to decide how to treat them. In fact they are responsible for their children and therefore have a duty to ensure that their child's rights are validated.

The UN Convention on the Rights of the Child has a monitoring system which reviews children's rights in any country that is a signatory to the Convention. A review took place in Ireland in 1998 and **The National Children's Strategy** which was launched in 2000 deals with most of the recommendations of the review.

The Strategy is a ten-year plan and is underpinned by six core principles. All measures taken under the Strategy will be:

Child centred: The best interests of the child should be served at all times.

Family oriented: Because families are seen as providing the best environment in which children should grow up, the aim should be to support and empower families.

Equitable: All children should have equal opportunity to access services and to participate in decision-making and planning. Those who are vulnerable or at risk should have the supports to facilitate their access and participation.

Inclusive: The diversity of children's experience should be recognised.

Integrated: Services whether statutory, voluntary or both should be co-ordinated and coherent.

Action oriented: Services should be developed and policies implemented without delay.

ACTIVITY

▶ Brainstorm and list all the matters that affect children in an early childhood setting.

▶ Select any one item from the list.

▶ Devise ways and means to incorporate children's views and participation in decisions and policies in relation to that particular matter.

The Strategy puts forward an holistic approach which will recognise the child as an active participant in any process that will have an impact on his life. It has identified three clear goals:

1.   **Children will have a voice in matters which affect them and their views will be given due weight in accordance with their age and maturity**. This is a core principle of the UN Convention on the Rights of the Child and should be a core principle in any establishment which cares for children.
2.   **Children and their lives will be better understood; their lives will benefit from evaluation research and information on their needs, rights and the effectiveness of services.**
3.   **Children will receive quality support and services to promote all aspects of their development.**

Implementation of the Goals
Goal 1
▸   The Government held one meeting of Dáil na nÓg (Children's Parliament), in September 2001. Dáil na nÓg is to be linked with local networks and at least one local meeting has taken place in 2002.

▸   The Ombudsman for Children Act 2002 has been passed. Appointing an Ombudsman for Children is a key feature in giving children a voice in their own affairs.

Goal 2
▸   A Children's Research Programme is underway, together with a unit designed to disseminate research results and information.

▸   A report will be made every two years on the state of the nation's children.

▸   A National Longitudinal Study of children in Ireland is to be undertaken and funding for this is already in place.

Goal 3
There are 14 objectives under this goal which include prioritising action on child poverty, children with disabilities, Traveller children, children in crises and homeless children. Recreation and play are key themes here along with accessibility of services and supports.

All of these goals involve the establishment of new structures to make them happen. A **Minister of State for Children** has already been put in place. The **National Children's Office**, although announced in 2000, was not fully funded or staffed until 2002. The **National Children's Advisory Council** which is made up of representatives from all interested areas (children, the government, the National Children's Office, social partners and researchers) has already met a number of times.

Figure 3.1: Children's Strategy Network

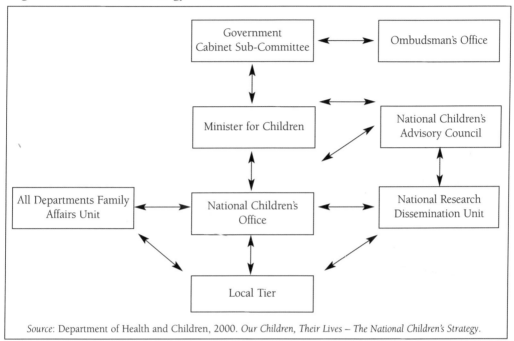

Source: Department of Health and Children, 2000. *Our Children, Their Lives – The National Children's Strategy*.

The Children's Rights Alliance

The Children's Rights Alliance is a national umbrella body comprising a wide range of organisations and individuals concerned with children's rights. It was formally launched in March 1995 and there are now over sixty member organisations. The aim of the Alliance is to promote the implementation of the UN Convention on the Rights of the Child in Irish laws, policies, practices and services.

Children's Needs

Children have a right to experience environments which meet their needs. High-quality early childhood programmes do not separate care from education, or education from care. They provide warm, caring and stimulating environments for children. Children are deeply involved in their own learning, supported by a knowledgeable, observant staff in an environment structured to drive exploration and discovery (IPPA, the Early Childhood Organisation, 2002).

In general, there is agreement about what children need to facilitate their all-round growth and development. In *Quality — a Discussion Paper*, IPPA identified the following core needs of children:

▶   A social environment that provides first-hand experiences to support their meaning-making

▶   Interaction with warm, responsive staff who 'scaffold' their learning

▶   Recognition of their development and cultural context

▶   Acknowledgement of their needs, interests and cultural strengths

▶   Accommodation of their varying abilities

▶   Learning experiences that they find challenging

▶   Opportunity to explore, experiment and solve problems

▶   Opportunity to learn through making choices, being actively involved and reflecting on their experiences and actions

▶   Experiences and materials that are meaningful, varied, open-ended, real and reflect everyday life experiences

▶   Experiences and materials that reflect inclusiveness and diversity.

(*Source*: IPPA, The Early Childhood Organisation, 2002: 15)

Any examination of quality in the early years setting must take into consideration how all the child's needs are being met on an ongoing basis, and at how this can be regularly assessed and evaluated.

Minimum Standards

The first formal attempt to set down minimum standards for the operation of early years services in Ireland came with the implementation in 1996 of the Pre-School Regulations set down under Part VII of the Child Care Act, 1991 (see Chapter 2). These regulations set down the minimum standards required by law, and concentrate on aspects of the child's physical environment such as health, safety and hygiene (static elements) in the early years setting, rather than on the quality of the child's experiences within that environment (dynamic elements).

Static elements of the early years environment are those that are relatively fixed and that can easily be measured. They include elements such as the number of children in the group, the minimum space requirements, the provision of materials and equipment for play and development or the provision for children's health and safety.

Adequate provision in all of the above areas is necessary for the delivery of a high-quality child care and education service, but these standards alone do not indicate that high-quality care is being provided. For example, it is possible for an early childhood centre to be adequately staffed and to meet all the requirements with regard to adult/child ratios. However, this does not guarantee that the children will receive adequate time and attention to meet all their needs, nor does it ensure that the quality of the interactions between children and adults will be positive and beneficial to the children or that their rights will be recognised.

Complying with the minimum standards set down in the Department of Health's Pre-School Regulations is a legal requirement, whereas meeting the quality standards of organisations such as IPPA, the Early Childhood Organisation, and the National Children's Nurseries Association (NCNA) involves a voluntary commitment on the part of the member group.

Standards can be measured relatively easily in the areas outlined above. For example, it is not difficult to determine whether a service meets a requirement to have a specified size of premises, maximum number of children in attendance, or that there are a certain number of qualified staff in attendance at any given time. Where the static and dynamic factors begin to overlap is in determining how that premises is used, what opportunities for exploration, discovery and learning are available to the children or what the staff do throughout the day. In other words, how does the setting use all its resources to meet all the needs of all the children?

An early childhood setting may have clearly defined policies covering a number of areas such as safe practice, children's nutrition or child protection, but may not have procedures in place for ongoing implementation and evaluation of those policies. The process of monitoring quality must take account of these kinds of factors, and must include all those involved — management, staff, parents, and where appropriate the children, in ongoing evaluation.

In arriving at a more inclusive definition of quality, it is necessary to try and pinpoint the **dynamic elements** which are less obvious and less easily measured. The static and dynamic elements are interdependent and it is a combination of the two which enables the delivery of high-quality services.

Quality Indicators

Factors which form the basis of high quality in an early years service are:

1.   the **ethos**, or underpinning values

2.   the **adults** and the relationships involved

3.   the **curriculum** and the **environment** within which it is offered.

1. The Ethos

This refers to the values and attitudes which underpin the service, and is reflected in the policies of the setting. It is important that these are clearly articulated, implemented in practice and reviewed on a regular basis.

The essential underpinning values of quality early years services are:

▸   Respect for the child as a unique individual with rights

▸   Acknowledgement of childhood as an important phase in its own right, and not as a period of waiting for a future stage

▸   Recognition of parents as the primary carers and educators of their children, involving a willingness to involve parents at all stages in the care and education process

▸   Commitment to the implementation of a planned curriculum based on a sound educational philosophy and developmentally appropriate practice, aimed at identifying and meeting the needs of each individual child

▸   An interactive approach to provision, welcoming and acknowledging the importance of input from all of the partners involved — children, parents, staff and community

▸   An acknowledgement that play is the means by which children learn; that play which is freely chosen and is process-driven is as important to the child as food and drink

▸   Recognition of the importance of keeping confidentiality with regard to children, parents and families

▸   A commitment to equality of access and participation for children and families, valuing and celebrating diversity and challenging stereotypes, discrimination and prejudice (see Chapters 4, 5 and 6).

2. The Adults

The relationships between all those involved in early childhood services — children, staff, volunteers and parents — are critically important in the delivery of high quality. The important indicators here are:

▸   interactions between staff and children

▸   interactions between the members of the adult team

▸   partnership between the centre and parents

Interactions between Staff and Children

All areas of children's development are integrated and interdependent — physical, cognitive, language, emotional and social. It is essential therefore that children's interactions with the adults in their lives should be positive and should support their development in all areas. Such adult-child interactions are evident when:

▶ Adults interact frequently with children, speaking and listening to them at their eye level, smiling, touching and holding them.

▶ Adults are available to children, they encourage them to share experiences, ideas and feelings; they listen to them with respect and practise **positive descriptive feedback** in order to reassure the child that real listening has taken place.

▶ Individual staff members remain aware of the activities of all of the group by positioning themselves strategically within the room, keeping all children, as far as possible, within view.

▶ Adults try to ensure that children do not have to wait for an adult response, and will show awareness of **developmentally appropriate practice** in their responses. For example, a baby's cry will be responded to immediately, while a four-year-old will be verbally responded to even if he has to wait a few minutes to have the adult's full attention.

▶ Adults ensure that children are as comfortable, relaxed and happy as possible, and involved in play.

▶ Adults help children deal with anger, sadness and frustration by comforting, identifying and **reflecting back** feelings, by helping children to name their feelings and to use words rather than actions to solve their problems.

▶ Adults are friendly, polite and positive when communicating with children. They converse frequently with them, speaking individually to them as much as possible and asking **open-ended questions** requiring more than a 'yes' or 'no' response, thus encouraging language.

▶ Adults involve children in **decision-making**, encouraging and responding to their suggestions and comments.

▶ Adults show awareness that children's communication skills derive from adults, and encourage this by engaging in one-to-one or small-group interactions whenever possible.

(Adapted from NAEYC, 1998, 15–19)

ACTIVITY

Over a period of several days, carry out three observations of a child in your placement as follows:

Observation 1: Observe the child during an adult-led large group activity such as circle time or lunchtime.

Observation 2: Observe the same child during a small-group activity with her peers, such as a co-operative play situation in which an adult is either not involved or only involved periodically.

Observation 3: Observe the child during a one-to-one interaction with an adult.

In each of the observations:

▸   Note the child's language interactions with the adult.

▸   In your evaluations, comment on the quality and value of the different types of interactions for the child's language, emotional and social development.

▸   Draw some conclusions based on the above.

The Adult Team

The adult team works together to meet the aims of the setting and takes collective responsibility for decisions made and implemented. To function well as a team the members must be:

▸   motivated toward common goals

▸   provided with the support and encouragement necessary to achieve these goals

▸   able to communicate effectively within the team.

French (2000) lists the following characteristics of an effective team, based on the High Scope model:

▸   Climate — people know what is expected of them and their roles are clear.

▸   Goal setting — team members work together to set goals. These include individual goals, centre goals and organisation goals.

▸   Communication — people are open and trust one another. Staff at various levels communicate often through memos, phone calls or talking. Communication moves up and down.

▸ Decision-making — many alternatives are discussed; there is time to think about an idea. Once a decision is made it is communicated clearly to all affected.

▸ Handling conflict — problems are recognised and dealt with openly and creatively.

▸ Relationships — there is co-operation and the sharing of ideas and energy.

▸ Use of resources — people know their own and one another's strengths.

▸ Regular evaluation of teamwork — regular times are scheduled for the team to evaluate personal contributions and team efforts, and to make new team goals.

Team Meetings

These are held regularly in an early childhood setting and are conducted according to an agreed agenda. In a formal meeting, the written agenda is ideally circulated to all team members in advance, and should include space for people to add their own items for discussion. Participants in the meeting should listen carefully to others, consider their ideas and offer ideas of their own. Discussion and decisions at a team meeting should be on the basis of their benefits to the children, setting, organisation or community. Team meetings offer the opportunity to discuss issues in an open way. Once decisions are reached, all team members work toward their implementation, whatever their personal feelings on the matter.

ACTIVITY

Role-play

You are working as part of a team in an early childhood setting which is planning an open day for parents and members of the local community. Role-play the meeting to include the following:

▸ Assign roles to different members of the team.

▸ Draw up an agenda.

▸ Through discussion, reach decisions on:

— when and how the open day will be organised

— how it will be advertised/promoted

— duties of different team members on the day

— how the children will be involved.

The Adult Role

The effectiveness of an early years programme is determined by the skills, attitudes and commitment of the adults involved. Adults play a key role in determining the quality of the experiences of the children, through:

▶   knowledge of child development

▶   regular, systematic observation of children

▶   use of observation outcomes to plan for the individual in a way that links learning to the individual's needs and abilities

▶   supporting and reinforcing the child's learning

▶   extending the opportunities for learning inherent in a given situation

▶   interacting with children in a way that builds trust, confidence, independence and self-esteem

▶   respecting the children and one another.

The Work Environment

Early years workers who themselves feel valued, are confident and enjoy their work will create caring, supportive environments where children's needs can be met. This happens when:

▶   their rights are recognised and upheld (see Chapter 1)

▶   they are trained in early childhood care and education

▶   adult-child ratios are adequate to ensure that staff members can carry out their allocated tasks without undue pressure

▶   roles and responsibilities are clearly defined and regularly appraised

▶   work schedules are planned to ensure task sharing among the team

▶   there is consensus about issues to do with the day-to-day running of the centre

▶   a forum exists for resolving conflicts and solving problems

▶   a system is in place to support and supervise team members in carrying out their work

▶   work conditions are adequate to ensure that there is a long-term commitment to the job. This includes salary structures, benefits, hours of work, a career ladder and an appreciation of their professionalism (see Chapter 1)

▶   there are regular opportunities for workers to take advantage of in-service training and to upgrade existing training.

Adults as Role Models

Children are receptive to messages in their environment, particularly messages from the adults who care for them. The attitudes and behaviours which adults bring to their work (often referred to as the 'hidden curriculum') should reflect, not contradict, what adults also want for the children — mixed messages can be confusing and distressing for children. Adults need to become aware of how they fulfil their own role in this area.

In a high-quality early childhood curriculum, the adults:

▶ provide a caring, encouraging environment, with a flexible routine and a curriculum that promotes independence, learning and self-esteem

▶ model good communication, both verbal and non-verbal, and appropriate ways of expressing feelings

▶ model fair and consistent behaviour with children

▶ value all children equally, and promote anti-discriminatory practice

▶ enjoy and value their work and that of their colleagues

▶ demonstrate good practice in their work at all times.

Partnership with Parents

Parents as the main educators of their children have to be involved in a meaningful way in the care and education process in the early childhood setting. Developing a working partnership with parents will benefit the children, the parents and the centre. It builds trust and confidence on the part of the child and the parents, helps to ensure that the goals of the centre are supported in the home and that the centre supports the parents' goals for the children. (Note: use of the word 'parent' here is meant to imply 'parent or carer', acknowledging the fact that many children are cared for by people other than their parents.)

High-quality early childhood programmes promote partnerships with parents by:

▶ ensuring open access for parents at all times, and providing an atmosphere where they are made to feel welcome

▶ involving parents in the decision-making processes of the centre, through management committees and input into policy formation

▶ involving parents in the activities of the centre; as rota helpers, on outings, involvement in fundraising activities, sharing a special interest or expertise with the group and sharing in celebrations

▶ providing a facility for nursing mothers

▶ involving parents in settling-in their child, and encouraging them to spend as much time on this as they feel is necessary

▶ respecting parents' wishes at all times, while keeping in mind the best interests of the child

▶ ensuring that clear systems for communicating with parents, both oral and written, are in place at all times, and that there is time for both listening to parents and sharing information about the child

▶ reaching agreement with parents on individual goals for each child, and ensuring that parents are clear on how these goals are met in the curriculum of the centre

▶ sharing all information about their child, including observations, assessments and any other written records with parents, and encouraging them to contribute to the compilation of these records

▶ respecting confidentiality of information about parents, children and their families

▶ encouraging participation by parents in workshops on child-related topics such as child development, play and behaviour management.

ACTIVITY

Suggest ways in which a private nursery could involve parents more in the running of the centre.

Discuss:

▶ areas where parent input and participation would be of benefit to the parents, the children, the centre

▶ how the participation could be implemented.

Communication with Parents
Good communication with parents helps children to sense the continuity between their home and the early childhood setting. The centre should encourage this communication, whether formal or informal, keeping in mind that not all parents may be able to read or to read the language that you use. Honesty and openness should form the basis of all communication with parents.

Formal Communication

Formal communication with parents can be facilitated by:

▶ a parent handbook which sets out the policies, ethos and procedures of the centre, and which is given to all parents as the child is enrolled

▶ a special noticeboard for parents, used for a calendar of events, meetings, menus etc

▶ a standard format for sending messages home regularly which makes it easier for parents to access information easily

▶ a regular newsletter to keep parents up to date

▶ a diary which is used by both centre and parents and goes back and forth in the child's bag to keep both sides informed

▶ parents being regularly invited to meetings with staff members to discuss their child's progress.

Informal Communication

The everyday interactions between parents and carers are usually informal, but are also used to show parents how their input is valued. These include:

▶ greeting parents by name

▶ sharing information about the child's day

▶ seeking advice from parents about the child

▶ supporting parents when settling in and saying goodbye to the child

▶ actively listening to parent's concerns about the child

▶ acknowledging the special nature of the parent/child relationship, and the intensity of feeling which this can lead to on the part of the parent.

ACTIVITY

In groups, discuss how the early childhood setting could best meet the needs of the following parents, both in terms of the service they themselves offer, and in their capacity as advisors about other services available in the community.

Máire and Joe: *'Our Nanny is excellent. She drops Chloë in to the playgroup every morning and collects her at 12.30. We both have to be at work by 8.30 and Joe often works late into the evening. We rarely get to talk to playgroup staff. We'd both like to be more involved in the playgroup but it's very difficult with our work commitments.'*

continued overleaf

Margaret: '*It's very difficult for me to leave my baby in the mornings. I phone the nursery often during the day to find out how he's getting on, and would love to call in sometimes to see him. Although I know he is being well looked after, I sometimes find myself in tears after these phone calls*'.

Seán: '*Since I split up with Jack's mother, I'm very conscious that he needs to have more female influences in his life. I'd like to get a bit more involved in the nursery too, but I can't face all those women!*'

Mr and Mrs Jawid: '*We came here to live six months ago, and Fettan has settled in very well to the crèche. She is now starting to speak English, and we are both concerned that she is not getting enough support in this from us, as we don't speak English at home.*'

Julia: '*I wish they could take the twins for more than three mornings a week. I really need to find a full-time job, and they get on my nerves sometimes when we're at home together all day.*'

3. The Curriculum

Active participation and involvement in spontaneous play provides the opportunities for exploring, manipulating and experimenting which enable children to construct knowledge. Providing quality experiences for children implies an acknowledgement and acceptance of play as the medium through which they learn. A high-quality early years curriculum:

▸ is based on sound knowledge about how children develop and learn

▸ promotes the development and enhances the learning of each individual child

▸ offers a range of learning opportunities while acknowledging that all areas of children's learning are integrated and equally important

▸ aims to develop positive attitudes to learning

▸ incorporates observation, assessment and record-keeping, recognising these as essential to inform effective planning for the child, as well as helping to identify best use of resources and gaps in provision.

The Learning Environment

Our physical surroundings affect how we feel, how comfortable we are, how we relate to others and how we achieve our goals. For young children, who learn by actively exploring and interacting with their physical environment, a well-organised and interesting environment is essential to enhance development and learning. In creating a high-quality environment for children, the following questions should be considered:

▸   Is the environment well designed and aesthetically pleasing, and laid out in a way that promotes independence and choice for the children?

▸   Is it safe?

▸   Is it accessible to all children and adults?

▸   Is it spacious, allowing for free movement, rest and relaxation and quiet activities?

▸   Does it contain a wide assortment of clearly displayed and easily accessible equipment and materials which reflect the developmental stages and learning needs of the children?

▸   Do the materials:

—   interest the children?

—   vary sufficiently in complexity to accommodate all types and stages of play and development?

—   reflect a diversity of cultural interests?

—   promote a range of learning opportunities, e.g. creativity, language, problem-solving? (See Chapters 6, 7 and 8.)

ACTIVITY

SCENARIO

The FLM Day Nursery is located in a Health and Fitness Centre, and caters for children aged from 1 to 7 years, offering full-time, sessional and drop-in services. Because there is limited access to outdoor space for the children, the nursery is equipped with a small gym. This is a large, airy room and contains a variety of materials for active play — large foam blocks, a ball pool, low-level balancing beams, slides, a child-sized vaulting horse.

However, the gym is mainly used as a rumpus room when children need to let off steam, and they spend around two hours per day in there, in mixed age groups. The time is mostly spent running around, sometimes wildly, jumping up and down off the equipment, and throwing the foam blocks around. Several of these are now torn and have had to be taken out of use. There have been some minor accidents too, especially to the younger children, with falling or being knocked over by older children or by flying objects.

Staff have not taken an active role in planning the use of the gym; while there are adequate numbers of adults on duty, their main roles seem to be supervisory rather than active participatory.

The manager has decided that the room will be closed down, since parents are starting to complain, and staff are unhappy at the lack of structure in this area.

▶   In a small group, identify the problems that have arisen about using the gym.

▶   List the causes of these problems.

▶   Plan alternative ways to use the gym, which would take account of all the children's needs, as well as safety considerations.

▶   Identify specific roles for staff members in implementing the plan.

Conclusion: It is neither possible nor appropriate to set down exact and unchanging quality standards which can be applied across the board in early years services. Each centre must formulate its own definition of 'quality', one which meets all the needs of the children and adults involved.

Such a definition must take account of agreed quality indicators, and must be arrived at through discussion and agreement with all the parties. This means that defining 'quality' is a process rather than an end, a process which is ongoing and which involves continuous self-evaluation.

SUMMARY

▶   A growing acceptance of children's entitlement to civil and human rights has informed thinking on childhood in recent years. These rights are set down in the UN Convention on the Rights of the Child 1989, which confers rights on children of all countries that are signatories to the Convention.

▶   In Ireland, The National Children's Strategy articulates a rights-based approach to children's issues.

▶   Minimum standards in the static environment can go some way toward ensuring that the conditions exist within which quality can be achieved.

▶   High-quality services base their provision on a knowledge of how children develop and learn, a recognition of their rights and needs and an awareness on the part of the adults involved of their own role in facilitating this.

▶ The ethos of the centre, the quality of the relationships between the adults involved and the curriculum are key factors in the development of quality in an early childhood setting.

References

Bredekamp, Sue and Carol Copple (eds.), 1996, *Developmentally Appropriate Practice in Early Childhood Programs Serving Children from Birth through Age 8*, New York: NAEYC

Department of Health and Children, 2000, *Our Children – Their Lives*, The National Children's Strategy, Dublin: Stationery Office

French, G., 2000, *Supporting Quality: Guidelines for Best Practice in Early Childhood Services*, Dublin: Barnardos NCRC

IPPA, The Early Childhood Organisation, 2002, *Quality – A Discussion Paper*, Dublin: IPPA

NAEYC, 1998, *Accreditation Criteria and Procedures of the National Academy of Early Childhood Programmes, Position Statement of the NAECP*, NY: NAEYC

Key Terms — Section 1

Chapter 1

Playgroup

Naíonraí

Parent and toddler group

Montessori Pre-School

Early Start Pre-School Programme

Pre-Schools for Traveller children

Pre-Schools for disabled children

Crèche/nursery

Family day care

Policy initiatives

Empathy

Labour legislation

Contract of employment

Minimum notice

Redundancy

Unfair dismissal

Minimum wage

Maternity protection

Parental leave

Force majeure leave
Adoptive leave
Trade union

Chapter 2

Child Care Act 1991
Child Care (Pre-School Services) Regulations 1996
Pre-school child
Adult/child ratios
Corporal punishment
Record-keeping
Notification to Health Boards
Safety, Health and Welfare at Work Act 1989 and General Regulations 1993
Safety Officer
Safety Statement

Chapter 3

UN Convention on the Rights of the Child 1989
Bill of Rights
Survival Rights
Developmental Rights
Protection Rights
Participation Rights
National Children's Strategy
Dáil na nÓg
Ombudsman for Children
Minister of State for Children
National Children's Office
National Children's Advisory Council
Children's Rights Alliance
Static and dynamic elements
Quality indicators
Ethos
Positive descriptive feedback
Verbal and non-verbal communication
Partnerships with parents
Broad, balanced, play-based curriculum
Developmentally appropriate practice
Equality of access and participation

SECTION TWO

EQUALITY AND DIVERSITY

This section is designed to promote awareness of the concepts of individuality, equality and difference. The chapters need to be read in sequence. Chapter 4 aims to enable the reader, through activities and exercises, to increase self-awareness, challenge assumptions which can lead to discriminatory practice and become familiar with the vocabulary used throughout chapters 5 and 6. The activities and exercises in Chapter 4 can be carried out individually but greater benefit may be achieved if they are undertaken in a group context. However, a word of caution — some of these exercises are of a personal nature. Groups and their tutors should be aware at all times of the need for sensitivity and confidentiality. In no circumstances should people be expected to reveal information unless they are happy to do so.

Chapter 5 examines the effects of prejudice and discrimination on people's lives. It identifies the groups in Ireland most likely to suffer these effects and focuses particularly on — social class, the Travelling community, race and racism and disability. The chapter looks at changes which have taken place and outlines the current legislative situation. Chapter 6 deals with the practical application of the principles of equality in early childhood work.

4

LOOKING AT OURSELVES

AREAS COVERED

▸ Individuals and Equality

▸ Definitions

Introduction

Each of us carries our own personal and cultural identity. This shapes our attitudes to ourselves, to others and to the world around us. People who are involved in work with children need to explore and understand how attitudes are shaped so that they will become aware of the impact that they may have on children.

This chapter aims to facilitate the development of an understanding of individuality, equality and diversity: to raise awareness of the issues involved, to challenge assumptions that we may have about ourselves and others and to introduce the terminology most commonly used in this area.

The first part is organised into a series of self-exploratory activities because any exploration of the area of equality and diversity must begin with oneself. While most activities can be done by individuals, greater benefit in terms of knowledge and insight will be gained if the activities are done in a group setting, followed by group discussion. People should not be expected to reveal personal information unless they feel comfortable doing so when working in a group. All participants must observe rules of confidentiality.

Individuals and Equality

A basic idea underpinning the concept of equality is the recognition of the dignity of individuals and their right to respect as human beings. A genuine acceptance of this ideal means that individuals should be enabled to participate in society to the best of their ability; this in turn would bring about some equalisation of power, wealth and resources. The acceptance and celebration of differences should lead to an overall balance and harmony among individuals in society. **This is not to say that people are all the same or that they should be treated in the same way.** It is obvious that an adult is not the same as a child or that a person who uses a wheelchair is not the same as a person who is walking. it is just as important to realise that one adult is not the same as another adult or that one child is not the same as another child.

Exercise 1: I Am a Unique Individual

Life may seem simpler when we classify and categorise, for example when we group people into 'toddlers', 'teenagers' or 'elderly'. In doing this, however, the uniqueness of the individual is lost.

Aim: To explore and describe the uniqueness of the individual. The list on page 57 is far from comprehensive but covers a variety of areas to show that our individuality is many faceted.

Using List 4.1 on page 57:

▶   Spend some time on your own filling out details about yourself.

▶   In a small group:

— identify what you have in common with one another

— identify what makes each person different and unique.

Exercise 2: Where Does Our Knowledge of Others Come From?

Using List 4.1:

▶   Fill in the details about other people, for example:

— Someone that you know well, such as a good friend or family member.

— A person with whom you are merely acquainted.

▶   In addition to the facts about the person, note down where your information comes from. Then consider the following questions:

— Do we make any assumptions about people whom we know well?

— Do we make any assumptions about acquaintances?

— Are there differences between the two in terms of where our information comes from?

List 4.1

First name
Family name
Colour of hair
Height
Birthday
Sex
Number of people in family
Place in family
Religion
Nationality
Talents
Temperament
Likes
Dislikes
Health
Hobbies
What makes me sad?
What makes me happy?
What makes me angry?

This page may be photocopied.

Activities for Work with Children

Aim: To help children to develop self-awareness and self-esteem.

Using the headings in List 4.1 (page 57) devise developmentally appropriate activities to help young children develop self-awareness.

These activities can involve the children in the use of a variety of different skills at all levels of ability, e.g. cutting out pictures and silhouettes, naming and using colours, drawing, looking things up, weighing, measuring, using family photos and using scraps to make collages and personal histories. Ask the child whether or not he would like to display his work.

Exercise 3: Being Positive about Myself

We have little difficulty identifying or acknowledging our weaknesses but are often less confident about doing so in relation to our positive/strong points. People who have a positive self-image are more likely to be happier, healthier, to learn more easily and to relate better to others. They respect themselves and command respect from others. In this activity you will have the opportunity to be positive about yourself in a supportive situation.

Materials needed: Several prepared sets of cards or slips of paper with one of the unfinished statements on List 4.2 (on page 60) written on each card.

▶   Divide into groups of four or five.

▶   Shuffle the cards and place them face down in the middle of each group.

▶   Take turns to select one card and complete the statement.

▶   Return the card to the bottom of the pile.

There are no right or wrong answers and a person can choose not to answer if he so wishes. While completing the sentence the others must listen and accept what is being said. Remember confidentiality and sensitivity; respect one another's contributions.

▶   When time is up or all cards have been used, all the groups should join together for a discussion to consider the following questions:

    —   Is it easy to make strong, positive statements about ourselves?

— Is it difficult to make strong positive statements about ourselves?

— Which statements were easiest to complete? Why?

— Which statements were most difficult to complete? Why?

— Suggest ways in which this activity could be adapted to suit children of various ages and carry out the activity in your place of work.

(Adapted from Canfield and Wells, 1976)

Exercise 4: Values and Roles

The beliefs and values which shape our behaviour come from our parents, families, friends, community and the society in which we live. The family has a primary influence on what we learn about social roles and behaviour, both our own and those of others.

Aim: This activity seeks to explore how roles are filled in families and if there are any identifiable patterns.

Read the tasks in list 4.3 on page 61 in the order of importance you believe society places on them.

▶ In the large group, chart the information from the whole group (e.g. bar charts, graphs etc.) showing which tasks have least/most value and who carries out each task (child/adult/male/female).

▶ Discuss why some roles/tasks are more valued than others.

List 4.2

I like...	I work best when...	I have always wanted to...
I am best at...	I see myself as...	I wonder...
I am good at...	I relax by...	I feel important when...
I am happiest when...	I am learning to...	I hope that...
I am confident when...	I will be good at my job because...	I believe that...
I enjoy...	I have achieved... in the past year.	My favourite activity is...
I am glad that...	I'm not afraid to...	My favourite book is...
My friends like me because...	I helped someone to...	My favourite CD is...
What makes me a good friend is...	I am improving at...	My favourite food is...
I know...	I am...	I would like to change...
When I am older I will...	I want to be...	The best thing that ever happened to me was...
A skill I possess is...	I can...	

This page may be photocopied.

List 4.3 Tasks carried out in households

▸ Cooking	▸ Setting the TV/video
▸ Cleaning	▸ Remembering birthdays
▸ Shopping for food	▸ Minding children
▸ Mowing the lawn	▸ Household decoration — indoor
▸ Weeding the garden	▸ Household decoration — outdoor
▸ Household repairs	▸ Christmas shopping
▸ Paying the bills	▸ Babysitting
▸ Looking after the car	▸ Organising holidays and outings
▸ Looking after people when they are ill	▸ Taking out the rubbish
	▸ Earning the main income

(Additional tasks may be added to the list.)

Exercise 5: Respect — Ourselves and Others

Aim: The aim of this activity is to learn to appreciate each other's understanding of respect rather than to reach a common agreement about the definition of the term.

Working on your own:

▸   List ways in which you show respect for others

▸   List behaviours in others that you personally find disrespectful.

Working with a partner, compare your ideas and consider:

▸   if any common ideas emerged

▸   if contrasting ideas emerged

▸   where our ideas of respect come from.

List 4.4

Name/nickname/petname
Where you are from
Where your parents are from
Type of family (small, large, extended, lone parent etc.)
A custom or tradition that is practised by your family. For example, how does your family celebrate birthdays, Christmas and other festivals?
Taste in clothes
Taste in music
Food preferences
What sort of partner are you attracted to?

This page may be photocopied.

Exercise 6: Celebrating Diversity

Diversity exists even in a seemingly homogenous group. Within any particular group, regardless of how much they may have in common, people will have different backgrounds and preferences.

Aim: This activity aims to provide an opportunity to explore diversity and to reflect on its implications.

▶ Prepare the answers to at least some questions from List 4.4 on page 62 (Remember you do not have to reveal anything about yourself if you do not feel comfortable doing so.)

▶ Share with the whole group:
— One thing that you think you have in common with the group
— One thing that you think makes you different from the rest of the group.

▶ List the differences and the similarities on a chart.

▶ Discuss how the group might celebrate these differences.

▶ Plan an activity appropriate to the children in your place of work to help them explore and celebrate diversity.

Definitions

This section will introduce and explore some of the main terms and concepts associated with equality and diversity.

Prejudice is defined as an attitude, judgement or feeling formed without any direct knowledge of the group or individual but based on preconceived ideas or stereotypes. Prejudice can be positive as well as negative and we all have some prejudices.

Stereotype is defined as a simplistic generalisation about or caricature of any individual or group. A stereotype is often derogatory, i.e. a put-down. It attributes characteristics to individuals on the basis of the group to which they are seen to belong and no allowance is made for individual differences.

Labelling means identifying an individual or group by reference to one characteristic or perceived characteristic of that person or group; the term 'classifying' can also be used.

Scapegoating occurs when someone (or group) wrongly blames another individual or group, against whom they are prejudiced, for their problems and difficulties. For example, when refugees from Bosnia began to come into Ireland, people who had poor housing conditions blamed the refugees for taking up good accommodation. In fact, people in Ireland had housing problems long before the arrival of the refugees.

Stigma refers to a name or stereotype to which shame, disgrace or negative connotations are attached. Some terms in common usage are stigmatising because they highlight an undesirable characteristic and devalue the individual, e.g. poor, mentally ill, criminal, handicapped etc.

Discrimination means policies, practices or behaviour which leads to the unfair treatment of individuals or groups because of their identity or their perceived identity.

Prejudice translated into action becomes discrimination.

There are three main forms of discrimination:

Direct discrimination: treating someone unfairly solely because of his perceived difference, e.g. 'Only two children at a time are allowed to enter this shop.'

Indirect discrimination: setting down conditions for something, such as a job or service, that automatically disqualifies certain people without good reason, e.g. 'Applicants must have fluent English.'

Unequal burdens: failing to remove obstacles that bar certain people, e.g. lack of ramps or lifts in a building automatically bars people who use wheelchairs.

EXERCISE 7

For each of the following statements identify which is an example of the terms explained above. Make up some more statements to help you apply the terms in practice.

▶   'You could not trust a woman to run a large business because she wouldn't be able to keep her head in a crisis.'

▶   'All Irishmen are drunks.'

▶   'Asthmatics must be careful to avoid undue stress.'

▶   'Room 3a is where the slow learners go for extra tuition.'

▶   'All red heads are hot tempered.'

▶   'Children must not play on the grass.'

ACTIVITY

We all have prejudices to some degree, being aware of these attitudes and prejudices and how they can affect us and others is an important step in developing a more just and equal society.

▶ Write about two instances of discrimination which you have personally experienced.

▶ Write about two instances when you have shown prejudice or discrimination toward another.

These can be related to age, gender, education or any other issue.

Under the Equal Status Act 2000 discrimination under the following grounds is prohibited:

▶ Gender

▶ Marital status

▶ Family status

▶ Religion

▶ Age

▶ Sexual orientation

▶ Disability

▶ Race Membership of the Traveller Community

Gender and sex are now often used interchangeably, but there are important differences in the meaning of the two words relevant to equality and diversity. Sex refers to biological differences which are used to distinguish males from females. Gender relates to society's ideas

Prejudice is the thought, discrimination is the action.

about appropriate masculine and feminine roles and characteristics. While the biological differences between men and women are the same the world over, gender differences may vary from society to society and in different eras. Gender roles in Ireland in the first half of the twentieth century were much more distinct than they are today. Childcare and housework were exclusively the woman's domain; being a family man then meant that the man worked hard to provide money to keep his wife and children.

Sexism means prejudice or discrimination in relation to a person's gender.
Example: *'Women drivers; they're a danger on the roads; too busy doing their make-up to watch where they are going.'*

Marital status refers to whether a person is single, married, separated, divorced or widowed.

Family status refers to whether a person is pregnant, has or does not have children.

Marital status and family status would in the past have been considered important in assessing one's suitability for a job. A married man was often thought to be more suitable for a managerial position because of having a supportive family behind him. 'Behind every successful man, there is a good woman' may be clichéd but it was a comment regularly used. Young women were often passed by in promotions because it was thought that they would soon turn their thoughts to having children and so could not be relied upon to give their full commitment to the job. Finding accommodation in the private rented sector is often more difficult for couples with children, because children are considered noisy, messy and undesirable.

Religion refers to one's religious affiliation or lack of it.

Age refers only to a person over 18 years in terms of equality legislation. The Child Care Act 1991 is the relevant legislation for persons under 18 years. Prejudice or discrimination in relation to a person's age is called **ageism**.

Examples of ageism in relation to children:

▶   not giving choices

▶   not listening to a child

▶   putting the rights and considerations of adults first.

Examples of ageism in relation to youth:

▶   being paid less for like work

▶   not being able to vote until 18 years

▶   not being represented in the Dáil.

Examples of ageism in relation to older people:

▸ having to retire at 65 years

▸ having to pay a higher insurance premium.

Sexual orientation refers to whether a person is attracted to men, women or both in their choice of sexual partner. A **homosexual** is one who is attracted to a person of the same sex as himself or herself (gay men, lesbian women). A **heterosexual** is one who prefers partners of the opposite sex.

Homophobia is fear and dislike of homosexuality and homosexual people. While sexual orientation in itself may not be an issue in early childhood work, attitudes toward homosexual people can be formed before children even hear the word. Negative attitudes which indicate homophobic reactions are shown in the name 'sissy' conferred on boys who cry, or in shock-horror reactions to boys who like to dress up in girls' clothing.

ACTIVITY

Many of the names used to describe gay men or lesbian women are extremely hurtful and derogatory.

Aim: To highlight the derogatory nature of some of the language relating to homosexuality and to explore underlying homophobic attitudes and beliefs

▸ Brainstorm all the terms/statements that you have heard used about gay men, lesbian women and bisexual people.

▸ List everything on a chart under these three headings — gay men; lesbian; bisexual.

▸ Spend some time in the group discussing the attitudes and myths that are associated with these terms/statements.

Membership of the Travelling Community, Disability and Race are issues which are covered in considerable detail in Chapter 5.

Whatever the grounds, discriminatory behaviour can be varied, ranging from the very subtle to the very violent and hostile. At its extreme this has often led to murder, e.g. genocide in the Second World War. Obviously discrimination in the form of violent behaviour will create a climate of fear resulting in serious limitations to quality of life for individuals and groups; children may not be able to play outside, adults may be afraid to go to work. But less extreme forms of discrimination which may be difficult to pin down may also seriously limit lives and expectations. Lack of affordable, good-quality childcare limits the access which parents, especially women, have to education, training, employment and promotion.

Power is essential to discrimination. No other person can discriminate against you, or in your favour, unless that person has the power to do so. Think of the individuals and groups who have power in our society and those who lack power. It is not politicians, bankers or bishops who suffer from prejudice or discrimination. It is those who are poor, who are Travellers, those who have a disability, i.e. those who lack power. During the latter half of the twentieth century many pressure and support groups emerged in an attempt by groups and individuals to take some control over their situations, to combat prejudice and discrimination through education and ultimately through equality legislation.

EXERCISE 8

Write down two examples of statements or behaviours that could be considered (a) racist, (b) sexist and (c) ageist.

ACTIVITY

Reflections: Defining Definitions.
The following are definitions of 'Black' and 'White' taken from the Encarta encyclopaedia which is now widely used.

Black: Being of the colour black
Without light
Soiled as from soot; dirty
Evil, wicked; black deeds
Depressing, gloomy
Angry, sullen
Of, or belonging to, a racial group who have brown skin.

White: Colour of maximum lightness
Light coloured, pale
Blank
Unsullied, pure; snowy, white Christmas
Incandescent
Of, or belonging to, a racial group who have pale skin.

Look up a thesaurus and other dictionary definitions, e.g. man/woman; disability/ability; old/young.
What might be inferred from the above definitions?
Reflect on the connotations of these definitions for people to whom the terms are applied.

(Exercises 5, 6 and this final Activity were adapted from Gorski, 1998)

SUMMARY

▶   Each individual is unique and it is important to appreciate, respect and celebrate diversity.

▶   Awareness of our own values and attitudes and how these are formed is an important part of the process of learning to recognise the dignity and worth of every human being.

▶   An understanding of the meaning and implications of prejudice, discrimination and associated terms is an equally important part of learning to challenge assumptions and raise awareness.

References

Canfield and Wells, 1976, *100 Ways to Enhance Self-Concept in the Classroom*, Hemel Hempstead: Prentice Hall

Gorski, P., *Multicultural Activities Archives*, Website: http://curry.edschool.virginia.edu/go/multicultural/activities/activity1.html

Microsoft Corporation, *Encarta 97 Encyclopaedia*, 1993–96

5

PREJUDICE AND DISCRIMINATION IN IRELAND

AREAS COVERED

▶ Social Class

▶ Poverty and Discrimination

▶ Irish Travellers

▶ Race and Racism

▶ Disability

▶ Equality and the Law

Introduction

In Ireland, prejudice and discrimination are most likely to occur because of a person's social class, age, disability, gender, ethnic group/race, religion, marital status, sexual orientation or membership of the Travelling Community. This chapter explores the effects of prejudice and discrimination on peoples lives, how attitudes and practices can be modified and changed and the effects and limitations of legislative change.

However, it is not possible to cover all aspects of prejudice and discrimination for all people so a number of areas have been selected for inclusion in this chapter, namely:

▶ **Social class** — focusing on the effects of poverty on people's lives

▶ **Ethnic groups** — focusing on race and racism and the facts and issues facing refugees and asylum seekers in modern Ireland

▶ **Disability** — focusing on the disability movement and disability awareness.

That is not to indicate that the experiences of people who are discriminated against on the basis of age, gender, religion or for any other reason are not important. Although individual experiences will differ and issues may vary in detail, the effects of discrimination and the strategies for change will be broadly similar for people in all groups. Activities included in this chapter and in Chapters 4 and 6 can be adapted to facilitate the exploration of prejudice and discrimination in other areas.

Social Class

Social Stratification

Social stratification describes how societies are divided into different strata or layers, where the people at each layer share similar levels of power, status and privilege. In pre-industrial societies slavery and estate were the dominant systems of social stratification. The caste system, practised by those of the Hindu religion, is another form of social stratification.

Social Class

Social class based on socio-economic status is the main form of social stratification in Ireland and in western industrialised societies today. Studies of social stratification and socio-economic status have differed in their detail. Various dimensions such as race, gender and educational attainment have been considered, but a classification by occupation tends to be most common. Officially in Ireland a person's social class is measured according to occupation.

The social class of children is derived from the occupation of their parent(s). Until the 1981 Census of Population women had their social class ascribed to them according to the occupation of their father or their husband. Now a woman's social class is derived from her own occupation but some difficulties remain, for example in relation to the classification of the role of mother/housewife/ homemaker.

The social class system is, in theory, **open** and one can move up or down the scale during the course of one's lifetime; this is called **social mobility**. A person might be born into a family where the father is a general labourer (social class 6); in theory that person could train, study, go to college and become a medical consultant (social class 1). However, the class into which we are born (**class of origin**) has a huge influence on how we live our lives and on where we end up (**class of destination**). It influences where we live, how we spend our leisure time, the papers we read, our educational prospects and our earning potential. The most significant aspect of the social class system is the inequality that exists between social classes in the distribution of wealth and income. It is estimated that 10% of the population own nearly half the wealth in the country; therefore 90% of the population share the other half — but not equally.

CASE STUDIES

CASE STUDY 1: Emma

Emma is four years old. She lives at home with her parents and her three brothers and two sisters and baby niece. Her father was made redundant two years ago from a factory job and is still unemployed; her mother works part-time, evenings and weekends in a city centre restaurant.

The family live in a three-bedroomed house on a large housing estate which has no playground for younger children; the parents are afraid to let their younger children play on the local green because of stray dogs, litter (including syringes sometimes) and gangs of older boys who, the parents feel, are up to no good.

Emma shares her bedroom with her two sisters. The eldest sister has a baby who is now nearly two; Emma and the baby sleep in the same bed.

She has just started school and is delighted with herself; she has shiny new books and loads of friends. Sometimes it is very hard to get up for school if the baby has been crying during the night. There are 32 children in her class. Sometimes she can't hear the teacher very well. Sometimes it is very hard to sit quietly at her desk for hours on end when she is not used to it. Her dad likes to help with her homework but she is not very good at reading. Her dad says you must work hard, learn to read and write so that you can get on better in life.

CASE STUDY 2: Mark

Mark is five years old. He lives at home with his parents and two older brothers. His father is an engineer and his mother is a nurse who works part-time.

The family live in a large four-bedroomed house on a new estate which has its own playground, but the house is in a cul-de-sac so Mark and his friends can play outside quite safely. At weekends his father and mother take the family out, to adventure playgrounds, museums, farms, theatres and all sorts of exciting places. At holiday time, the whole family goes to the seaside. The family has a small boat and Mark is learning to sail. He loves fishing too.

Mark shares his bedroom with his eight-year-old brother. His eldest brother has a room of his own. Mark doesn't mind sharing; they each have their own bed and their own locker and bookcase. Mark has loads of books and every night someone reads or tells him a story.

He is nearly able to read himself because he has just started 'big' school — a private school. He has attended a Montessori school for two years; he did not like the change at first but he is getting used to it. There are 15 other children in the class and his teacher is lovely. There is a huge gym hall in the school and he loves it when they go there. There are loads of toys and games in the classroom and once a week they get to use the computer. There is a computer at home so Mark already knows how to play lots of computer games. He is not allowed to spend as much time as he would like playing with the computer and he is not allowed to watch much TV either.

Mark's dad says you must work hard and then you can be anything you want when you grow up; Mark wants to be a solar engineer.

(Adapted from Combat Poverty Agency, 1991, *Fair Share*)

ACTIVITY

Aim: To highlight how social class can influence the life chances of a child from the early years

Read the case outlines above of Emma and Mark. Discuss:

▸ How might their early years affect how well they do in school?
▸ How might their lives outside school affect their development?
▸ How might the different school environments affect how well they adjust and learn?
▸ What are the main causes of the differences between Emma's and Mark's lives?

Poverty and Discrimination

Ireland has become increasingly wealthy over the past ten years; figures from the Economic and Social Research Institute (ESRI) show that consistent poverty has been greatly reduced, from 15% in 1994 to just over 6% in 2000. However, income inequality has increased and in the EU, Ireland (along with Spain and Portugal) has the highest level of income inequality; this means that we have the biggest gap between rich and poor.

Who Are the Poor?

Many different groups have been identified as being at risk of experiencing poverty, particularly the long-term unemployed, disabled people, women and Travellers. Lone parent families and families with four or more children are at particular risk. The percentage of children who live in consistent poverty has dropped from 24% (approximately one in four) in 1994 to 8% (approximately one in twelve) in 2001. Child poverty rates worldwide vary from 3% (Sweden) to 26% (Mexico). Ireland, with a rate of 17%, ranks sixth on a list of the 23 OECD countries.(See Bar Chart in Appendix 2, page 289.)

Trying to make ends meet incurs high levels of stress and anxiety and so living in poverty has negative implications for physical and mental health and affects every area of life. Poverty has many dimensions. Studies in various western countries indicate the following:

▶   Poor families tend to live in 'poor' areas which lack, or have inadequate, basic services and amenities such as housing, health services, transport, schools, recreational facilities and parks.

▶   A baby born into a poor family may have received less pre-natal care, may have a lower birth weight and is less likely to be immunised or breast fed.

▶   A child of a poor family is least likely to have access to early childhood care and education (see Chapter 1).

▶   Children living in poverty are more likely to have learning difficulties and behavioural difficulties.

▶   Isolation, stigma and helplessness are widespread.

▶   Where everyone is poor and over-stressed there is less support to go around.

Because of all this, poor children and families are caught up in what is termed the 'cycle' of poverty: poor housing, ill-health, inadequate education and fewer opportunities means that the children are likely to repeat the pattern and become 'poor' parents in the economic sense.

Strategies for Alleviating Poverty

In the past, strategies for alleviating poverty were related to ideas about why people were poor in the first place. A popular theory was that people who were poor had only themselves to blame; they were inadequate, unworthy and useless. According to the Human Development Report 1998 the idea continues to persist today that the responsibility for being poor is often assigned to the poor themselves. But the 'cycle' of poverty has been recognised and there is some commitment to breaking this cycle. In

Ireland, efforts to eliminate poverty have been haphazard. Examples include the following:

▸ The Department of Social, Community and Family Affairs has taken initiatives by allowing people who have been unemployed to retain some benefits while finding their feet in employment.

▸ Social welfare benefits have been increased, the detrimental effects of being on long-term benefits have been recognised and efforts made to address them; community employment schemes have been initiated.

▸ Legislation has provided some protection for low-paid, part-time workers.

▸ The Child Care Act 1991 empowers the Minister specifically to provide support services for families and children at risk.

▸ The Department of Education and Science has provided extra resources in designated areas and the Early Start programme provided in some disadvantaged areas is an attempt to provide a pre-school service to combat disadvantage (see Chapter 1).

▸ Local groups have attempted to address problems specific to their local areas, aiding and supporting employment and self-help initiatives, for example through area partnerships involving the private, public and voluntary sectors.

▸ NAPS: In 1997, Ireland launched the National Anti-Poverty Strategy (NAPS) as a co-ordinated and committed approach to eliminating poverty and has achieved a number of successes as shown by some of the figures noted above.

▸ 'Building an Inclusive Society' — the revised NAPS was launched in 2002 and aims to create a society where everyone will have the opportunity to participate and share in the benefits of economic and social development.

Targets of the revised strategy which are particularly relevant to children are:

▸ To reduce the numbers of those in consistent poverty to below 2%

▸ To have specific attention paid to vulnerable groups

▸ To achieve a rate of child income support set at around 35% of the minimum adult social welfare payment

▸ To eliminate long-term unemployment and to achieve the targets set out in the National Employment Action Plan

▸ To halve the proportion of pupils with serious literacy difficulties by 2006

▸ To improve the housing situation, and to have sufficient and appropriate emergency accommodation available to those who become homeless.

Irish Travellers

General Information

Travellers are an ethnic minority group. With a population of around 25,000, they are the largest ethnic minority in Ireland (0.5% of the population). They have a long history (over 1,000 years or more), lifestyle, customs, traditions and a value system which makes them a group recognised by themselves and others as distinctive and unique. Unfortunately they experience prejudice and discrimination which results in an ongoing struggle for survival and frequent physical harassment.

Traveller Culture

Some distinguishing features of the Travellers' culture are:

▶ nomadism, which basically means travelling or moving around

▶ a distinct language known as 'shelta', 'cant' or 'gammon' although use of this language has declined

▶ a high rate of inter-marriage; to be a Traveller you must have one parent who was/is a Traveller; you cannot become a Traveller by marrying one or by opting out of settled society and taking to the roads

▶ strong connections with extended families — in fact, the nuclear family as such makes little sense to Travellers because the extended family is such an intrinsic part of their lives and lifestyle.

Travellers and Discrimination

This section examines the effects of discrimination on Travellers in relation to the following:

▶ Economy
▶ Health
▶ Accommodation
▶ Education
▶ General lifestyle.

Traveller Economy

Up to thirty or so years ago, the Travellers were largely a rural people with an economy based on a wide range of activities that included tin-smithing (mending buckets, utensils, selling pots and pans), seasonal farming, recycling and flower-making. The advent of plastic, machines and industrialisation made these skills and occupations obsolete.

This forced many of the population to move to urban areas to try to change their traditional economic activities. Most Travellers are self-employed to some extent, dealing in scrap and recycling, but because this economy is marginalised the majority of Travellers live in poverty. Many are dependent on social welfare for survival.

Begging is engaged in by some of the women and children as a means of supplementing their income. Recently this fact has been used against the Travellers especially when children are involved. While not condoning the practice it must be pointed out that charities also use children to raise money. In advertising, images of starving and naked children are regularly used to make a point about the plight of some groups. Only a very small minority of families send their children begging alone on the streets, although the stereotype exists that nearly all these children are sent out under threat by Traveller parents and cannot go home until they have collected a certain amount.

Banks and building societies do not generally deal with Travellers, which as well as being discriminatory closes off a lot of financial options to them and leaves them with all the disadvantages and insecurities of a cash economy. Adult Travellers are fearful of approaching these institutions because of the amount of form filling that has to be done. Most Travellers who wish to borrow money have to go to a moneylender.

Travellers' Health

The health and welfare of Travellers is a sad reflection on the intolerable living conditions of the majority of the Traveller population. Health statistics clearly illustrate this, in comparison to the settled community:

▶   Still births are twice as likely among Travellers.

▶   Infant mortality rates are three times higher than in the settled community.

▶   Traveller children are three times more likely to be hospitalised in the first year of life.

▶   Less than 2% of Travellers live to be over 65 years compared to 11% in the settled population.

▶   Men's life expectancy is 10 years less; women's is 12 years less than that of settled people. In the settled community women tend to live longer than men, but in the Traveller community this is reversed.

▶   In all age groups Travellers have higher mortality rates.

▶   More Travellers than settled population die due to the following:

   — accidents
   — metabolic disorders in the 0–14 year age group

— respiratory ailments

— congenital problems.

Traveller Accommodation

Until the 1980s, the view was that the solution to Travellers' accommodation problems was to house or settle them so that they would become absorbed into the mainstream of society — **assimilation**. Sites were provided in areas where they would not be seen and often in most unhealthy and unsanitary areas, for example near to public dumps. Much of what was provided in the past was also of poor quality and with few services. These policies were driven by assimilation objectives. They were also driven by a lack of respect for the Travellers and their way of life, coupled with a denial of their separate ethnicity.

Travellers live in the following types of accommodation:

▸   standard housing (in mixed housing schemes)

▸   group housing schemes (all Travellers)

▸   official halting sites — permanent sites have full services, temporary ones often do not

▸   unofficial halting sites (on the roadside). This accounts for about 35% of Traveller accommodation.

Details of living conditions give some idea of the provision of accommodation or lack of it.

▸   16% of Travellers had no water supply.

▸   53% of Travellers had no electricity supply.

▸   36% of Travellers had no toilet.

▸   53% of Travellers had no bath or shower.

▸   10% of Travellers had no rubbish collection.

▸   100% of Travellers had no access to a phone.

(DACT Survey 1994 in O'Riain, 1997)

Little has changed since this research was undertaken almost twenty years ago.

Some sites developed in recent years have been designed to take account of the needs of the Travellers because they themselves have had some input into stating the needs of their own community.

The Housing (Traveller Accommodation) Act 1998 required local authorities to draw up a five-year plan in relation to Traveller accommodation and to have this plan in operation by 2002.

Traveller Education

The Task Force on the Traveller Community (1995) identified poor and inadequate education as one of the greatest barriers to progress in the community. The main feature of the Traveller Community in relation to education is that Travellers do not continue in education beyond primary school level.

▸ About 90% attend primary school.

▸ More than half of these are segregated into special classes or schools.

▸ Only 12% continue into secondary school and a mere handful proceed to do the Leaving Certificate.

The main reason for the lack of participation by the Traveller Community in education is that their distinct cultural identity is ignored within the mainstream education system. This is being addressed to some extent in early education services. Pre-schools for Travellers have been in existence since 1984 and are grant-aided directly by the Department of Education and Science. In addition, more Travellers are being trained to work in these early services, thus ensuring that the programme provided is more appropriate and meaningful for the children. Segregation in early childhood services and at primary school level continues to be a major obstacle to progress (see Chapter 1).

General Discrimination

On an individual level Travellers are often viewed as scroungers, thieves and dirty; names in common usage are distinctly insulting, e.g. 'knacker'. The practice of racism against the Travellers by the general population is very serious and damaging. It is the power and therefore the racism of the settled community that labels the Traveller way of life as deviant and unacceptable and is the root cause of the social, economic and political exclusion of Travellers in Ireland today (see Chapter 4).

Most of the difficulties and problems already outlined are caused not by ignorance and lack of education on the part of the Traveller but by ignorance, prejudice, discrimination and lack of education on the part of the settled community.

The effects of racism, prejudice and discrimination affect all areas of a person's life. The following give a flavour of the additional obstacles faced by the Traveller Community:

▸ Resident groups can prevent Travellers from coming into certain areas.

▸ Settled people can march on campsites and intimidate Travellers, often with the co-operation of the authorities.

▸ An elected representative can say at a public meeting:

'*The sooner the shotguns are at the ready and these travelling people are put out of the country the better. They are not our people.*' (Paddy Kenneally, April 1996, Waterford Co. Council meeting) and still retain his seat on the County Council.

▸   Racist and inflammatory articles can be printed in local and national newspapers.

Institutional racism also occurs in the actions and practices of our organisations and government institutions. Examples include the following:

▸   A voting system that excludes anyone who does not have a fixed address

▸   A social welfare system that segregates Travellers. In Dublin, social welfare provision for Travellers is administered from one office near to the city centre. Some unemployment offices continue to apply a rule that every Traveller must sign-on on the same day each week

▸   A local authority system which empowers local authorities to place boulders and overhead barriers obstructing any area that might suit as a temporary halting site

▸   A system which allows Travellers to be evicted or moved on without the provision of alternative suitable accommodation. Eviction in the settled community occurs usually only after a lengthy legal process and affects individual families rather than groups.

Beatitudes

I was hungry and you blamed it on my parents.
I was thirsty and you went to see the EC wine lake.
I was dying and you set up a Commission on itinerancy,
a Review Body on Travellers, and a monitoring body on what?
I was naked and you said so were my ancestors.
I had no job and you said we don't employ knackers.
I was all these things and you said it was the will of God.
I was homeless and you sent me a lorry load of stones and a bulldozer.
When did we see you hungry?

Anne Maughan

(From a collection of Traveller poetry compiled by Sr Patricia Lahiff)

Strategies for Change

There is no doubt that the voice of the Traveller Community is growing and that Travellers are being recognised as a distinct ethnic group. Travellers organising themselves into groups such as the Irish Traveller Movement and the Dublin Travellers Education and Development Group (DTEDG) have brought this about. Much more requires to be done in areas of combating prejudice and changing public attitudes toward Travellers and this will require not only willingness but also resources.

Their economic activities are to some extent limited by the following:

Mobility: Nomadism always had a basic economic function but it does not allow for the development of a trade, which requires storage facilities or heavy equipment. Even the improved facilities in the design and building of more recent halting sites do not accommodate this sort of economic activity.

Flexibility: When tin-smithing and repairing became largely obsolete Travellers were able to adapt their skills to recycling scrap and car parts. It is interesting that in a time of growing interest in and recognition of the value of recycling among the settled (particularly the middle class) community this is an area that is used to denigrate and criticise the Traveller population.

Self-employment: Although the Travellers engaged in seasonal farm work in the past, waged nine to five working is not a feature of their economic activity. Working under a boss, particularly a settled person who has little or no understanding or appreciation of their way of life, would not be easy for Travellers. Despite such limitations there has been some progress in the area of employment initiatives.

Examples of Employment Initiatives
The Traveller Resource Warehouse (TRW)
The TRW was set up by three Travellers in March 1989 and is an example of a thriving business initiative. Here all sorts of materials (paper, plastics and cloth) are recycled; a membership operates whereby a group pays an annual subscription and in return has unlimited access to the materials available. Many pre-school groups (also schools, drama groups etc.) collect materials here for their art and craft activities. Other businesses have been set up, one in Galway making flags and banners, and the Cara Park Laundry in Dublin. Such initiatives require support on two levels, financial support and a willing market among the settled community. The Traveller population is too small to provide a market sufficient to ensure success for any business.

Whole Community Initiatives

Whole community initiatives are where the settled community together with the Traveller Community join together to provide services and/or opportunities. It is a flexible system adapted to the needs of the community it serves.

The primary healthcare initiative is an example of one venture. Because they are a distinct cultural group with different needs and perceptions of healthcare, a different approach to service provision is required. The system which operates in the settled community, e.g. registration for free medical services with a named doctor, would not always suit a Traveller family.

Another area which is developing is that of the training and employment of Travellers in services aimed at Travellers, such as training of early childhood workers. Apart from providing much needed employment, these developments have a profound effect of empowerment.

Partnerships which are designed to support whole community initiatives are developing all the time.

ACTIVITY

Aim: To investigate media coverage of Travellers by:

(a)   *looking at the media image portrayed*
(b)   *examining the use of language*
(c)   *questioning the views and assumptions underlying the report.*

Material: Collect current news articles from the daily papers or from magazines. Tape a TV programme. If nothing is currently available seek out recent coverage in your library.

Analyse the content of the article or programme using the following guidelines:

Media image	Language	Opinion
Is the article critical or supportive, of Travellers?	Is the title negatively or positively worded?	Whose opinions are given in the article?
Is proof offered when claims or accusations are made?	What words are used to describe Travellers?	Have Travellers been given an opportunity to express their views?
Are visual images positive or negative?	Are these words negative or positive?	If this article was about you, your family or your community, how would you feel about it?

It is useful when doing this exercise to write down your results, taking note of relevant phrases and words used. If doing this in groups, then each group should discuss their findings and be encouraged to discuss their attitudes.

Race and Racism

In the biological/physiological sense it is not possible to divide human groups according to race. Attempts to do this are usually related to skin colour but are based on social attitudes. The term 'race' is commonly used to refer to groups who share distinctive cultural traits. It is more acceptable to use the term 'ethnic groups'. However, racism does exist. It seeks to justify and act upon ideas of inferiority and superiority based on characteristics ascribed to people who are supposedly biologically distinct.

Racism is prejudice or discrimination in relation to a person's ethnic group. It is based on the claim that racial or ethnic groups are inherently superior or inferior, implying that one group would be entitled to dominate another.

Ethnic group is the term used to describe groups of people who share common cultural characteristics, e.g. language, dress, food, religion, customs, beliefs, traditions etc. People in such groups perceive themselves and are perceived by others to have a distinct identity.

An ethnic minority group is a distinct ethnic group, which makes up a small proportion of a particular society. In Ireland, Travellers are an ethnic minority group as are the different groups of refugees.

Ethnocentrism occurs when one ethnic group (usually the largest one but not always so) sees its traditions and beliefs as the only important ones and therefore the only ones worth considering. In South Africa under apartheid white people made up only about one-fifth of the population but made the laws, controlled the resources and denied civil and human rights to the black population.

Xenophobia means a fear and dislike of strangers.

Asylum is a place of refuge for people in need of protection because of their beliefs, nationality, ethnic group, religion or political opinion. An asylum seeker is a person who is making an application to become a refugee.

Refugee is the term used universally to describe an individual who is fleeing persecution.

Programme refugees are groups of people who have been recognised as being in special need of protection. Usually this recognition is achieved in discussion with other countries, e.g. within the EU, and individual countries agree to take a certain number of refugees. The state plans for the arrival of programme refugees and should have accommodation, English classes and healthcare organised. On arrival, the programme refugee acquires the same rights as an Irish national and may apply for citizenship after three years living here.

Convention refugees are individuals whose applications are dealt with on an individual basis and judged according to criteria laid down in the 1951 Geneva Convention (see below).

A person who has been granted refugee status is entitled to work, study and receive the same social welfare and health benefits as any other Irish citizen.

Residency means that a permit is granted which allows a person to live in the country for a specified time. A child born in Ireland becomes automatically an Irish citizen. In the past the child's parents would have automatically been granted residency status. This system underwent review in 2002. This review is ongoing.

Leave to remain is granted to some people who cannot obtain refugee status and is granted totally at the discretion of the Minister for Justice, Equality and Law Reform.

Immigrants are people who choose to come and live in Ireland for personal or economic reasons. They must apply to the state for permission to do so and should obtain, in advance, the relevant visa and documentation if they wish to work here.

Illegal immigrants are people who arrive in the State without any documentation and who are not refugees or asylum seekers. Some illegal immigrants travelling from very poor circumstances are unofficially called economic refugees. Illegal immigrants can be deported immediately on being discovered.

Overview of the Legislation

The Universal Declaration of Human Rights 1948 assures people the right to look for and be granted asylum.

The Geneva Convention 1951 relating to the status of refugees sets down criteria and principles relating to war, famine and plague. It also states that no-one should be returned to a country where the person's life or freedom would be at risk.

The Dublin Convention 1990 aims to co-ordinate asylum policies within the European Union. The main thrust of the convention is to ensure that asylum seekers cannot 'shop around' within Europe for asylum by making application in several countries. Therefore, if persons travel to Ireland on a ferry from France, for instance, they cannot apply to Ireland for asylum; they must return and do so in France. The Convention also proposes to fingerprint all asylum seekers and refugees.

The Refugee Act 1996 which was implemented in full in November 2000 places the arrangements and procedures in relation to refugees and asylum seekers on a statutory basis. The main elements of the Act are:

▶ The setting up of an independent body to assess applications

▶ The inclusion of gender, sexual orientation and membership of a trade union as grounds under which people could apply for refugee status

▶ The requirement that the media get written permission from the Minister for Justice, Equality and Law Reform before they can identify asylum seekers.

The Immigration Act 1999 legislates for deportation from Ireland and includes the appointment of the Refugee Applications Commissioner, the setting up of an Appeals Tribunal and the Refugee Advisory Board.

The Illegal Immigrants (Trafficking) Act 2000 outlines penalties for trafficking, that is carrying or arranging the transport of immigrants, and deals also with appeals, detention and deportation of asylum seekers.

Historical Perspective

Until recently Irish people have tended to think of themselves as a homogeneous group but even a superficial glance over our history shows otherwise. Irish blood over the last few thousand years has been mixed with that of Celts, Normans, English, Scottish, Spanish, French, Jews and Huguenots to name a few. After the Second World War most people who came to Ireland did so to further their education and many experienced prejudice and discrimination. A study carried out in the mid 1970s found that a 'severe' degree of racial prejudice existed in Ireland with, for example, black people finding it extremely difficult to find accommodation.

In the latter half of the twentieth century Vietnamese, Hungarian, Czechoslovak and Cuban people came here as programme refugees. In the last twenty years, people of up to one hundred different nationalities, but mainly from Eastern Europe and Africa, have sought refuge and/or employment in Ireland.

The number of refugees worldwide has increased from 5.7 million in 1980 to 14.9 million in 2002, with a further 22 million internally displaced in their own countries. The increasing sophistication of armed conflict means that ever-increasing numbers of people are experiencing horror and devastation in their lives, but over 80% of refugees only get as far as a neighbouring country. Less than 5% of refugees get as far as Europe and only one in 50 of these, 0.06% of the total refugee population of the world, make it to Ireland. Until the late 1990s there was only a trickle of (mainly programme) refugees coming to Ireland.

Table 5.1: Programme refugees who were allowed to live in Ireland 1956–99			Table 5.2: Asylum applications made in Ireland 1992–2000	
Year	Origin	Number	Year	Numbers
1956	Hungarian	530	1992	39
1973	Chilean	120	1993	91
1979	Vietnamese	211	1994	362
1985	Iranian Bahái's	26	1995	424
1992–5	Bosnian	770	1996	1,179
1999	Albanian	1,000	1997	3,883
			1998	4,626
			1999	7,724
Total		2,658	2000	10,236

Of these 30,000 applications approximately 5,000 were withdrawn and 1,300 (4%) were recognised as refugees or granted leave to remain. Asylum approval rates in Ireland stood at 9% in 2002.

The Experience of Racism in Ireland

Various surveys since the 1973 study by Micheál McGréil have found that most non-Irish people in Ireland have experienced some form of prejudice and discrimination and that the proportion is consistently higher if the person is black, whether that person is Irish or not. One survey found that 78% of asylum seekers generally had experienced racially motivated verbal or physical assaults. Ninety-eight per cent of Africans compared to 14% of Eastern Europeans had experienced verbal abuse. Verbal abuse, stereotyping, staring, ignoring are the most common forms of discrimination. The Association of Refugees and Asylum Seekers has documented scores of violent physical assaults in recent years, and in 2001 one man was murdered in what was identified clearly as a racist attack.

Other forms of racism are difficult to quantify and research in the area is lacking. Many people are fleeing oppressive regimes and are understandably reluctant to give information or to complain about the country that they hope will give them asylum.

Institutional racism, that is racism in the actions and practices of organisations and government departments, is also evident. At immigration points people who do not appear to look Irish, European or white American have complained of receiving much more severe scrutiny from immigration officials.

The policy of **direct provision** of accommodation and food to asylum seekers instead of money (as is given to all other social welfare recipients) is a clear example of discrimination. This practice may in fact be illegal because there is no provision in Irish Social Welfare law which allows for such direct provision. In addition to being avowedly discriminatory it limits the control and element of choice in their lives. **Dispersal** which means that the State houses groups of asylum seekers in centres, segregated from the main community, is another clear example of whole groups being treated differently in terms of their accommodation requirements. Since April 2000 asylum seekers have been accommodated in 63 dispersed centres in 45 different towns. In effect these groups are living together in the same centre as others with whom they have little in common. In these centres people are not allowed to work or undertake training, recreational facilities are few and they are not allowed to cook their own food. Travelling is also restricted and an absence of more than three days means that they lose their place in the centre.

The overriding tone of the most recent publications from the Department of Justice, Equality and Law Reform is one of negativity — direct provision, dispersal, monitoring, tracking, deportation, finger printing are all terms which leap out from the front page of these official publications.

The main problems identified by the refugee/asylum population are:

▸ the long, slow process of decision-making in the Department of Justice, Equality and Law Reform. The Refugee Applications Commissioner and the Reception and Integration Agency are handling almost 800 applications per month, but there is a considerable backlog and people may wait months and even years for a decision. Two-thirds go on to appeal against unfavourable decisions

▸ living in dispersal centres with nothing to do, little or no access to English classes and little chance to integrate

▸ lack of support teachers/staff in schools which children attend

▸ Experience of discrimination and prejudice particularly for non-European people.

The Way Forward

Irish society needs to develop thinking and action in relation to multi-culturalism:

▸ Abandon discussion about whether a multicultural Ireland is a good thing or not; it is here to stay.

▸ Look at multicultural societies which are thriving and learn from them, e.g. Canada.

▸ Take a more proactive role in combating prejudice, stereotypes and discrimination.

▸ Speed up the processing of applications and differentiate completely between asylum seekers/refugees and immigrants.

▸ Abandon direct provision and long stays in dispersal centres.

▸ Allow access to education, training and employment.

ACTIVITY

In the first instance apply this exercise to yourself and ask yourself the questions listed below.

Talk to people casually about refugees/asylum seekers and take note (mental or written) of the attitudes and beliefs expressed. Follow this by attempting to probe how people formed their attitudes and where they got their information. You can do this by asking questions along the following lines:

▶   Have you ever had a refugee/asylum seeker as a friend?

▶   Have you ever been in a refugee/asylum seeker's home?

▶   Have you ever brought a refugee/asylum seeker to your home?

▶   Have you ever sought a refugee's/asylum seeker's opinion about anything?

▶   Have you ever read a book about a refugee/asylum seeker?

▶   Have you ever had a conversation with a refugee/asylum seeker?

▶   Have you ever been in a group that included refugee/asylum seekers?

▶   Where did most of your ideas come from?

Examine your findings to discover whether your interviewees were prejudiced; whether they had formed their attitudes and ideas based on direct experience or on labels and stereotypes.

These activities could be adapted to focus on any marginalised or disadvantaged group in our society such as refugees, people who have a disability, people who have a mental illness or people who are homosexual.

(Adapted from Combat Poverty Agency, 1991, *Fair Shares*: 63–4)

Disability

Who are Disabled People?

Disabled people are good, bad, ambitious, laid back, smart, silly, successful or unsuccessful. They are men, women, boys, girls, people of all ages, colours, religions or other kinds of beliefs, social origins (class), political opinions or non-political.

They are mothers, fathers, children, young, middle-aged or old people, people who are unemployed, employed, unskilled or professional. In other words they are the same kind of people you would normally find in any society. They are ordinary people who happen to be disabled because of an impairment. Although never counted before, it is estimated that in Ireland these ordinary people account for 10% of the population.

Impairments Fall into Four Groups

1. Physical and mobility impairments
2. Sensory impairments such as deafness and visual impairments, including blindness
3. Intellectual impairments or learning difficulties
4. Mental health impairments.

Recent History of Disability

In brief, the roots of the international disability movement are as follows: Throughout the 1960s and 1970s disabled people, mainly in Britain and America, began to look at their lives in relation to their place in society. Influenced by the women's liberation movement and the black people's civil rights movement, disabled people decided that disability should no longer be understood as a personal problem or a tragedy in a person's life, just because of the onset of a medical condition or an impairment. Consequently, they demanded human and civil rights; they demanded to be treated as equal citizens in society. Disabled people were no longer prepared to depend on charity, as they had been forced to do in the past — for them disability had become a social and an equality issue. In addition, disabled academics had begun to rethink disability and defined it as a social relationship.

The UN proclaimed 1981 the UN Year of Disabled Persons, and following on from this the UN Decade of Disabled Persons was launched in 1983. The pressures brought to bear by the international disability movement had succeeded in putting disability on the international political agenda. This had enormously important consequences not only for international developments but also for national and local developments, in bringing about changes in the lives of disabled people. These changes have been felt clearly by Irish disabled people in recent years.

Developments in Ireland

In Ireland the disability movement got underway in the late 1980s and became more and more powerful during the 1990s.

The 1990s — A Decade of Change

1990	–	Establishment of the Forum of People with Disabilities
1992	–	Establishment of the Centre for Independent Living
1993	–	Building Regulations requiring access for all in new buildings
	–	Establishment of the Department of Equality and Law Reform
	–	Commission on the Status of People with Disabilities
	–	UN Standard Rules on the Equalisation of Opportunities for Persons with Disabilities
	–	First European Disability Day
	–	First Disabled People's Parliament held in Brussels
1996	–	A Strategy for Equality: the Report of the Commission on the Status of People with Disabilities (402 recommendations)
	–	Fianna Fáil Policy Document on Disability
	–	Amendment of the Electoral Act
1997	–	Establishment of The Irish Council of People with Disabilities
	–	Review of the Building Regulations (Section M)
	–	Freedom of Information Act
1998	–	Employment Equality Act
	–	Establishment of Equality Authority and the Office of Director of Equality Investigations
1999	–	Human Rights Bill
2000	–	Equal Status Act
	–	Establishment of the National Disability Authority (NDA) and mainstreaming of services

Comprehensive disability legislation can be expected in the near future.

Toward a Definition of Disability

There are two main models or ways of looking at disability: the traditional **medical model** and the more recent **social model** of disability.

The Medical Model
The main characteristics of the medical model are as follows:

▶ It focuses on the individual's medical condition, illnesses or absence of bodily functions.

▶ It locates the 'problem' in the individual, seeing it as a personal problem and an individual limitation.

▶ It likens disability and impairment.

▶ It is based on a view of disability as a tragic occurrence in a person's life.

Responses/Solutions to Disability Informed by the Medical Model

▶ Cure of medical conditions

▶ Adjustment (to the non-disabled world), rather than access

▶ Rehabilitation in segregated institutions, rather than integration in mainstream environments

▶ Care, rather than liberating personal assistance.

The outcome for the disabled person is that she is forced into dependence on institutions and professionals, carers and social welfare. With such dependency comes poverty, passivity and apathy, resulting in disempowerment and inequality.

The Social Model
The main characteristics of the social model are as follows:

▶ It focuses on disability as being socially created.

▶ It sees disability as an oppressive power relationship.

▶ It differentiates between disability and impairment.

▶ It views disability as common experience of social disadvantage and exclusion encountered by all people with all kinds of different impairments.

▶ It focuses on barriers in physical environments and negative social attitudes.

▶ It recognises that these experiences of exclusion, discrimination and marginalisation are manifest on economic, social, cultural and political levels.

▶ It sees disability as a problem of social inequality rather than a personal problem.

Responses/Solutions to the Problem Informed by the Social Model of Disability

▶ Remove attitudinal barriers and dispel fear and myths, negative feelings and prejudices.

▶ Remove environmental and physical barriers.

▶ Remove economic and social injustices.

▶ Change social structures and organisation.

▶ Recognise disabled people as a social group of citizens entitled to equality.

The outcome would be positive not only for disabled people but for society as a whole. Disabled people would experience independence, access, inclusion, opportunities and equal life chances. In short — equality.

How Disabled People Experience Discrimination Because of their Impairments

▶   Many early childhood services still do not accept disabled children.

▶   Many primary and secondary schools are still not accessible, and do not have appropriate equipment and support services for disabled pupils, for example classroom assistants or lifts.

▶   At third level, despite many improvements in recent years there are still access and other barriers. For instance, people with visual impairments who read Braille or use audio tapes will still find it difficult to obtain study texts in these formats and deaf people will still have problems accessing sign language interpreters.

What is Disability Awareness and Why Do We Need It?

There seem to be no hard and fast rules for disability awareness. However, here is a comprehensive working definition developed by an experienced disabled disability awareness trainer:

> Disability awareness is a process of raising consciousness regarding the meaning and understanding of disability and impairment, the social relationships in which they operate and which they create, the impact and effects of these relationships on disabled people's everyday lives, the accommodation of disabled people's needs, to facilitate the realisation of their equal opportunities and their equal participation in society as a whole as equal citizens and as a matter of right. (Kwiotek, 2001)

The UN Standard Rules on the Equalisation of Opportunities for Persons with Disabilities, adopted by the UN Assembly in December 1993, puts awareness raising on disability at the top of its priority list. It is the first of four primary conditions for equal participation. 'Awareness raising' is given priority over medical care, rehabilitation or support services.

Disability awareness is fundamental to appropriate delivery of medical care and rehabilitation as well as to the effective delivery of support services. Disability awareness is essential in creating meaningful access to equal participation in education, employment, recreation, culture and sports. It is also equally crucial in disabled people's management of their personal and private affairs such as personal finance, including income maintenance and social security, their family life and personal integrity, their religion and freedom of expression.

To sum up, disability awareness should inform all matters relating to disabled people, whether in the public or the private sphere. It is relevant to partners, parents, siblings, friends, care or assistance givers, educators, employers, work colleagues, service providers and even to many disabled people themselves who need to become more disability and impairment aware.

Communicating with Disabled People — Do's and Don'ts

Do's

✓ Be approachable and offer assistance if appropriate.

✓ Be honest and do keep promises.

✓ Do remember that not all disabilities are obvious and not all can be seen.

✓ Do ask the person in a wheelchair how you can give assistance.

✓ Do talk to a disabled person directly, and never through a third person.

✓ Do offer your arm to guide a blind person.

✓ Do recognise a disabled person's right to privacy and independence.

✓ Do speak face to face with a deaf person, face the light, and don't move around while speaking.

Don'ts

✗ Don't treat a disabled person as your intellectual inferior.

✗ Don't gush pity, over-praise or fuss.

✗ Don't feel offended if your offer of assistance is turned down.

✗ Don't be overcurious — ask only necessary questions.

✗ Don't talk down to a person in a wheelchair, and if you are tall try to lower yourself a little to be more on a level with the person.

✗ Don't shout at deaf people — it only distorts lip movements and may affect hearing aids.

CASE STUDY

The Wheels Community

The Wheels Community is a purpose-built residential estate which is geographically isolated, and inhabited only by people in wheelchairs.

All the buildings are single storey, with ramped entrances and low, wide doorways. Ceilings are set at five feet high, as nobody living here needs more than that. All switches, handles and other controls are at a sensible height for the users. The same is true of counters, tables, work surfaces and so on. None of the cafés and restaurants has chairs, as all their customers provide their own. The same is true of the cinema and concert hall.

Many other facilities are drive-in, such as banks, supermarkets, fast food outlets, etc., in order to cater for the large number of vehicles specially adapted for the townspeople. Most of these vehicles are not equipped with seats, but with clamps to anchor the wheelchairs into position.

The system works well, and the first generation of residents continued to refine their environment to suit their needs. The community developed, and as is the nature of things, romances developed and marriages took place in the church without pews and the drive-in registry office.

Being moral and upstanding citizens, it was only after these marriages that children began to appear on the scene. It was not at first apparent, but as the children grew, the parents began to notice that things were not as they should be. These children only needed wheelchairs for the first year or two of life. While this new generation remained small, their problems could be managed at home and within the community. As they grew up, however, they suffered frequent bruising to the head as they tried to walk through the low doorways, or to stand up in the low-ceilinged rooms. There was also an increasing amount of toe damage as they would get their feet underneath some of the thousands of wheels about the town. Many also complained of back problems from having to bend down all the time.

Communication became difficult, as eye contact was lost with the children's increasing height and distance from the speaker. They began to be marginalised as they could not use the facilities at the youth club or join the basketball teams, or even sit in the coffee bar with their wheelie friends.

It became increasingly obvious that special provision would need to be made for them. Residential hostels were built, and social workers employed to counsel both them and their parents about their obvious differences from the mainstream of society. Areas were set aside especially to cater for them, with chairs available in cafés and the cinema, and separate entrances to allow for their greater height being built where possible.

Some parents even went as far as providing protective headgear for their children; charities were set up to help these poor able-bodied people who needed help. Money was raised to send them off to special schools where their problems could be catered for. Many suffered psychological problems, however, and there was an element in the community who shunned them and insisted that they should live a separate life. These people would give to the charities, but not let their daughter marry one (not their wheelie daughter anyway). An extremist group even went as far as raising money to be used for the amputation of the lower limbs of the able-bodied, but this was always a minority view.

Some of the 'able-bodied handicapped' reacted to this attitude and set up their own pressure group, organising marches demanding equal rights, adapted buildings suitable for their needs as well as everybody else's, and a guaranteed 'able-bodied' allowance from the town council.

They came to be seen as troublemakers, and the wheelie townspeople did not know how to deal with them. They came to feel uneasy in their presence, and then to avoid them if they saw them about, sometimes even crossing the street so that they did not meet.

(Source: Skelt, A., 1993, *Caring for People with Disabilities*, London: Pitman)

For discussion:
— Who are the disabled population in the Wheels Community?
— In what ways are they disabled?
— How could the problems of the non-disabled people be solved?
— Would it be a good or bad idea to create such a community? Why?

Equality and the Law

Martin Luther King, US civil rights leader of the 1960s, reflected on the fact that laws cannot change what is in a person's heart but they can change what she/he is able to do about what is in his/her heart. The law is there to protect people. It also serves a purpose in demonstrating society's opposition to intolerance and discrimination: it should promote positive action. The enforcement of laws may help to bring about some changes in attitudes as enforcement demonstrates a commitment to the values and concepts underpinning the laws.

Laws were often passed in response to pressure from certain sections of Irish society and were piecemeal in their efforts to eliminate prejudice and discrimination. When we examine Irish legislation closely and the order in which it came into force, it becomes evident that a lot of the changes to our laws were EU/internationally driven. Some Irish individuals went directly to Europe to appeal to the courts to have their human rights upheld, e.g. the Norris action in relation to the decriminalisation of homosexuality. Also, it is worth noting that in the absence of comprehensive equal status legislation individuals and groups had to use other laws to try to defend their rights and to fight discrimination. An example of this would be when members of the Traveller Community invoked the Incitement to Hatred laws to try and protect themselves although this law is not strictly relevant to equal status at all.

Another aspect of this piecemeal approach to equality legislation without a full commitment to the basic ideal of equality, is that the laws often act as stopgaps but do not address the fundamental problems. For example, equal pay for men and women is of little use in addressing problems of low pay for women in occupations that are predominantly female, as is the case in the childcare profession. Neither is it of any value to the many women who have to stay out of employment because of lack of affordable childcare. Currently the two principal pieces of legislation are:

▶ The Employment Equality Act 1998

▶ The Equal Status Act 2000

Employment Equality Act 1998

The Act outlaws discrimination by employers, collectives, advertising, employment agencies, vocational training authorities and vocational bodies (i.e. professional associations and trades unions). The Act lists nine distinct areas of discrimination:

1. Gender
2. Marital status
3. Family status
4. Sexual orientation
5. Religious belief
6. Age
7. Disability
8. Race
9. Membership of the Traveller Community.

The Act also:

▶   defines sexual harassment for the first time in Irish law and supports positive action regarding age, disability, gender and Travellers

▸ establishes a new statutory office of Director of Equality Investigations

▸ deals with requirements of the European Union Equal Pay and Equal Treatment directives in relation to gender.

Criticisms of the Employment Equality Act are that it:

▸ uses language which still allows room for discrimination

▸ is more to the benefit of those who discriminate against people

▸ does not clearly and unequivocally state rights for minority groups.

Equal Status Act 2000

The basic principle underlying equal status legislation is that people should, in general, be judged on their merits as individuals rather than by reference to irrelevant characteristics over which they have no control. The Act outlaws discrimination on the same nine grounds in relation to the provision of goods and services, accommodation, disposal of property and education. All services that are generally available to the public, whether statutory or private, are covered.

In order for the law to be truly effective both in changing attitudes and in protecting individuals, resources must be put in place to implement them.

In the first instance these resources must be sufficient for the enforcement of the law and the prosecution of those who break the law. Secondly, the law must be positively reinforced through the use of resources geared toward public education and changing of attitudes.

The Equality Authority

The Equality Authority is an independent body set up in 1999. It has four main functions:

1. To work toward the elimination of discrimination in employment, in the provision of goods and services, education, property and other opportunities to which the public have general access

2. To promote equality of opportunity in matters to which the legislation applies

3. To provide information to the public through a range of formats and media

4. To monitor and review the operation of the Acts outlined above but also the Maternity Protection Act 1994, the Adoptive Leave Act 1995, the Parental Leave Act 1998 and the Pensions Act 1990 (see Chapter 1).

The Equality Authority has an in-house legal service which provides a free confidential advisory service.

ODEI — The Equality Tribunal

This was also established in 1999 as 'The Office of the Director of Equality Investigations'. Its purpose is to investigate or mediate in claims of unlawful discrimination under both of the above Acts. Where it has been established that there has been discrimination, an equality officer may order one or more of the following: compensation, equal pay, arrears of wages, equal treatment, or a specified course of action. This order is legally binding.

SUMMARY

▶ Prejudice and discrimination are widespread in Ireland and are particularly relevant for some sections of the population.

▶ Change has come about through the efforts of pressure groups who raised awareness and lobbied for change; the change is limited.

▶ Laws have been passed which have helped to combat discrimination but much more requires to be done. Most of this legislative change has occurred since Ireland joined the European Union.

▶ Employment Equality Act 1998 should enforce some major improvements in the employment area.

▶ Equal Status Act 2000 extends from legislation against discrimination to the provision of goods and services.

▶ The Equality Authority and the Director of Equality Investigations are important structures which have been put in place in order to further equality in the State.

References

Combat Poverty Agency, 1991, *Fair Shares*, Dublin: Combat Poverty Agency

Combat Poverty Agency, 2002, 'Perspectives on Building a More Inclusive Society — NAPS', *Poverty Today* No. 54, Dublin: Combat Poverty Agency

Combat Poverty Agency, 2001, 'Richer But More Unequal: the Distribution of Income in Ireland', *Poverty Briefing* No. 11, Dublin: Combat Poverty Agency

Combat Poverty Agency, 2001, 'Child Poverty in Ireland', *Poverty Briefing* No. 10, Dublin: Combat Poverty Agency

Jolly, Richard, 1998, Principal author, 'Human Development Report 1998', *United Nations Development Programme*, New York: Oxford University Press

Kwiotek, R., 3 October 2001, 'What Is Disability Awareness and Why Do We Need It?', unpublished paper presented in NUI Galway

6

WHY FOCUS ON CHILDREN?

Introduction

The UN Convention on the Rights of the Child 1989 (see Chapter 3 and Appendix 1) sets out the right of all children to grow up in an environment that is free from prejudice and discrimination and one which enhances each child's self-image. It is in the valuing of differences and diversity that we embrace the real principles of fairness and justice for all regardless of gender, class, race, religion, age, marital status, ethnic group, ability and sexual orientation. This chapter raises equality issues in relation to development, care and education in early childhood. It explores how an environment committed to equality promotes an all-round positive attitude to oneself and others. The role of the adult is explored as it is central to the existence of such an environment. Finally a range of activities and materials for use in early years settings is suggested.

Developmental Issues and Equality

Children are aware of differences from a very early age.

By the age of 2 most children will have a sense of their own gender identity and will be able to distinguish girls from boys. This is not surprising because in most cultures, including ours, one of the first things asked about a new baby is whether it is a boy or a girl; from then on children are socialised according to their gender identity and they constantly see men and women in their families and communities behaving according to set social roles.

By the age of 3 children are able to recognise colours and different skin colour. They may also be aware of how different skin colour is perceived by people in the society in which they live. Between 3 and 4 years children also begin to recognise the different abilities and different roles that people have. They will ask factual questions about these.

By the age of 5 children are strongly influenced by social norms in how they behave toward others in relation to gender, race and ability. Additionally their cognitive development is such that they are ready for more complex explanations. They are also able to question attitudes and behaviour. (See Chapter 13 for information on roles and norms.)

ACTIVITY

Aim: To help you become aware of how children perceive gender differences

Give copies of the pictures on pages 101 and 102 to a boy and a girl aged approximately 5–6 years old.

▶   Ask the child to colour in the pictures.

▶   Observe the child during the activity.

▶   Record the following:

   —   Which picture does the child colour first?

   —   What colours are chosen for each picture?

   —   What is the child saying while doing the activity?

▶   Comment on:

   —   which picture was chosen to be coloured first and why you think this might be

   —   what colours were chosen for each picture. Are they typically 'masculine' and 'feminine'? On what do you base this opinion?

   —   what language the child used, if any, during the activity

   —   whether the child appears to be developing rigid ideas about what is appropriate for boys and for girls.

With the children's permission you could borrow the pictures and include them as part of an observation on social development.

This page may be photocopied

This page may be photocopied

Empowering Children

To empower children means to:

▶ develop their confidence, autonomy, independence and competence

▶ develop their skills and strategies for coping with discriminatory behaviour.

Young children's learning is experiential and exploratory and it is their right to learn in an atmosphere that is not only free from prejudice and discrimination but in an ethos which is anti-bias. How we relate to others is shaped by our life experiences. We can be encouraged to question and to challenge what we have learned. One of the aims of early childhood education should be to enable children to develop their awareness and understanding, to question false and unfair assumptions about the world and people around them and to challenge damaging attitudes and practices.

A child who feels inferior will fail to reach his full potential. A child who feels superior will fail to appreciate differences in a positive way and will not benefit from the richness inherent in the world. He will also be less able to cope with change. If his situation alters, for example, as a result in a change in the family's financial status or as a result of becoming disabled, he will be less able to adjust in a healthy and positive way.

Children are empowered when they feel good about themselves and their identity. Children will feel good about themselves and they will be comfortable in the early years environment if they feel:

▶ **Valued:** Adults know their names, their likes and dislikes, listen to them, show them respect.

▶ **Liked:** Adults give time to them, showing affection, smiling and generally showing that they (the adults) like being with them.

▶ **Secure:** Security comes from being accepted, the provision of routines and consistency, the setting of limits and being given some privacy.

▶ **Supported:** The child needs to know that nobody is allowed to put him down, tease or exclude him on the basis of a perceived difference such as in size, hair colour, skin colour or gender.

▶ **That their family type is included in the resources of the setting**: Visual images such as books and posters should show all types of families — large ones, small ones, one-parent families, extended families.

▶ **That their ideas and skills are used:** Offer to display all work not just that which the adult considers 'good'. Give all children an opportunity to help regularly with different tasks suited to the ability of each child; all children should have an opportunity to speak and have a choice about giving their opinions or news.

▸ **That assumptions are not made about them**

— Boys, as well as girls, like to be complimented on their appearance; both are equally good at cleaning and tidying if they get guidance and support.

— Girls as well as 'big strong boys' can help with fetching and carrying.

— A child who comes from a poor family may be hurt if not asked to bring in the same as everyone else, even though the adult may feel that it would put too much pressure on the parents.

— A child may, or may not, want to participate in Christmas or Easter because of his religious background.

▸ **That their emotions are acknowledged**

— Encourage children to recognise and acknowledge their feelings; go beyond sad, happy and angry to other emotions such as pleasure, frustration, fear, dislike, loneliness, pride, shame, embarrassment.

— Facilitate them in learning words to describe what they are feeling by drawing pictures, reading stories, using charts, naming their feelings and your own.

— Acknowledge your own feelings and be a positive role model on how feelings can be dealt with.

▸ **That they are allowed to take some control in their lives**:

Appropriate to their age and stage of development and without endangering their health and safety, children can be:

— given choices and allowed to make some decisions for themselves

— encouraged and facilitated to choose activities within the nursery/pre-school setting

— consulted about their likes and dislikes.

SCENARIO

A pre-school group are busy making Father's Day cards. The early years worker notices that one little boy is not participating very enthusiastically. When encouraged to do so he says, 'I have no Daddy at home.' The worker says, 'We'll just write Mammy instead.'

▸ How might the worker have avoided the situation arising in the first place?
▸ How would you have handled the situation as it arose?

Here the adult is stating that the child's fears are silly and unimportant.

Here the adult is taking the child seriously and asking what he would like and acknowledging his feelings.

Goals of an Environment Committed to Equality

Responding to the individuality of each person is the cornerstone principle in the provision of an environment committed to equality and anti-bias practice. This approach supports and affirms the child, the child's family, home background and community. It stretches the experiences of children to take account of the diversity that exists in their group, community and country.

An environment committed to equality aims to achieve the following:

▶ Free children from limiting stereotypical definitions which may close off aspects of their development.

A child who needs to use a wheelchair for mobility will increase his self-esteem and independence by being facilitated to fully participate in all activities, but will be undermined by having everything done for him.

▶ Promote the self-esteem of individual children by enabling them to feel positive about themselves.

Effort should be appreciated rather then results rewarded; what might seem like a mess to an adult may be the result of intense effort and concentration with paint and a brush by a small child.

▶ Promote and value individual development by facilitating each child's participation in activities necessary for physical, cognitive, social and emotional growth.

The individual should be catered for within the group. While some children will enjoy settling down to do jigsaws, a child who dislikes this activity or is unable to concentrate may be wrongly labelled unco-operative or disruptive.

▶ Develop each child's skill in questioning and challenging stereotypes.

Men and women, girls and boys, whatever their ability, colour or ethnic group should be shown in a variety of activities and roles. When involved in role-play children should be encouraged to take on non-stereotypical roles. Girls can be brave and protective, boys can be caring. Questioning and challenging should be encouraged.

▶ Foster children's curiosity, enjoyment and awareness of cultural differences and similarities.

Resources should be provided which will broaden children's knowledge and awareness of the world in which we live. Different religious festivals can be acknowledged/celebrated at appropriate times throughout the year. At Christmastime children could be introduced to the idea that not all people celebrate Christmas. Likewise not all children make 'First Communion'. Children can be introduced to different foods, clothing, music and languages.

▶ Enable children to stand up for themselves and resist and handle discriminatory behaviour.

Children will only do this if they feel supported. A clearly defined and implemented anti-bullying policy agreed by parents, children and the setting is an essential element of this type of support. Children could be encouraged to come up with their own ideas on change, as they are in the Danish project mentioned in Chapter 3. In mixed schools, for example, boys often tend to dominate the open space in the school playground and girls tend to play games like hopscotch and skipping on the periphery. Although girls may feel this to be unfair and will comment upon it, they are unlikely to try and even less likely to succeed in gaining equal access to this space unless backed up by school authorities.

▶   Imbue children with a sense of fairness and justice for all.

The stage of cognitive development is important here. Children are acutely aware of fairness at around 5 to 7 years. However, adults need to be aware of it at all times. If children are co-operating in 'turn taking' it is important to ensure that there is enough time/resource for each one to have a turn; if you do not do this then you cannot expect the child who has been left out to be so patient next time.

Young children love to take responsibility for doing jobs like setting the table or giving out biscuits — lists are a good way for the adults to ensure that no child is overlooked. This helps the group as a whole to appreciate the idea of fairness.

Adults as Role Models

The adults are the single most important resource in any environment. It is they who have the power to structure the environment, to buy the toys and books, to plan the activities and to organise the play space. If they are not aware of, and are not committed to, equality and diversity then all the equipment in the world will be of little use. In other words, the success or failure of an anti-bias curriculum depends on the adults involved.

 Do

Focus on differences and similarities that are, first of all, within the children's daily experience and that make sense to them. For example, in a group of five-year-old children an activity on hair could be used to highlight many differences within the group — colour, texture, curly or straight, short or long. The activity could be extended to focus on hair in the wider community, on styles in different cultures, fashions and many more topics.

Respond to questions, giving information, vocabulary and opportunities for discussion. Always try to be factual and if you do not know then say so, but make a point of finding out, including the child/children in the process if possible. Anti-bias education happens best in the context of interactions and experiences.

Provide challenging experiences for children so that they can learn about and explore the world through play.

Respond to each child's individuality and to each child's individual needs.

Use praise and affirmation to reinforce behaviour and attitudes that are desirable.

Provide a rich, varied and inclusive learning environment even if the group appears to be homogeneous, e.g. all white and able-bodied. Be careful not to add insult to injury here by having a token picture or book full of the very stereotypes you are trying to challenge (see the Resources section at the end of this book).

Intervene when difficult or hurtful incidents arise.

Set limits. It is never OK to be hurtful about another's characteristics.

Challenge sexist, racist and any offensive language or behaviour. If someone is hurt, insulted or discriminated against in any way the adult should step in immediately, let the offending person or child know that his behaviour/language is not acceptable. Explain what was offensive and give correct information. However, support for the offended child comes first; support and encourage the child to express his feelings and to speak for himself if he wishes to do so. An apology may also be appropriate. Depending on the age and size of the group these issues can be also addressed in the larger group through project work, discussion, role-play and puppets.

Model respect toward everyone, adults and children alike.

Constantly examine your own attitudes.

Draw up a policy and code of practice in relation to equality. This policy should include admission procedures, professional practice and what to do in the case of discriminatory behaviour. The basic premise of such a policy should be that every person is deserving of respect and the service should aim to facilitate each and every one to reach his full potential. No-one should be discriminated against on the basis of social class, age, disability, gender, ethnic group, religion, marital or family status, sexual orientation or membership of the Travelling Community. Parents and children should be involved in drawing up such a policy and it should be reviewed regularly. (The role of the adult in early childhood settings is more comprehensively covered in Chapter 3.)

Don't

Use hurtful or exclusionary language or behaviour.

Excuse such behaviour or language in others — 'She didn't realise what she was saying'.

Leave it to someone else to take action — 'The manager should be the one to deal with this.'

ACTIVITY

SCENARIO 1

John is three years old and has just started attending an early years setting. He was born in Ireland of Chinese parents. He is exposed to the English language, Irish culture and festivals. His immediate family also continues to honour and celebrate Chinese culture, so John has a wide experience spanning both cultures.

SCENARIO 2

The Tashita family has moved to Ireland just three months ago. Their daughter, Akane, is three years old and has just started attending an early childhood centre. Her mother who speaks no English brings her and collects her each day. Akane tends to observe what is going on or plays on her own. A trainee early childhood worker has begun a work experience placement and when she asks, 'What nationality is Akane?' she is told, 'Chinese or Japanese.'

Discuss

▸ Would it help to know where the child is from? Why?

▸ How could you improve communication with the mother of Akane?

▸ What difficulties might you encounter in your work with both children/families?

Exercise

▸ Make a list of ways in which you could help both children reach their potential, acknowledging all aspects of their background.

▸ Plan some activities that would help Akane to learn English.

▸ Plan activities that would help each of the children to settle in their environment.

▸ Plan activities to expose the children in your place of work to some words from another language; perhaps Irish if they do not already learn Irish.

Materials and Activities

Contact addresses and numbers are given in the Resources section at the end of the book to help you locate some appropriate resources. Much improvement is required in relation to equality in commercially available materials; many of the better materials are at present only available abroad. However, no-one should be discouraged by the lack of appropriate and affordable materials — you can always make your own! (See Chapter 8.)

Posters and Pictures

▸   Visual material should reflect the diverse community in which we live.

▸   Posters and pictures should depict one-parent as well as two-parent families.

▸   Flats, apartments, trailers and farmhouses as well as semi-detached houses should appear in visual and play materials.

▸   A variety of religions and ethnic groups should be portrayed.

▸   Gender stereotypes should be challenged by pictures of men and women in a broad variety of roles.

TASK
Find posters and pictures that you could use in your place of work.

Books and Stories

Books should be available to children in all age groups and not just to the child who can read. Picture books if carefully selected can be used at all ages to introduce the richness and diversity in society. Pictures of people with different skin colours eating a variety of foods, using household objects, as well as expensive shop items, should be on display.

In selecting books you should look for those that:

▸   build positive images, particularly of people who may not usually be portrayed in a positive manner

▸   challenge stereotypes

▸   show children and families in a world context

▸   help to develop children's autonomy and self-esteem

▸   depict children from a range of backgrounds and cultures playing leading roles.

Books and stories which present stereotypical images (and there are no shortage of these) can be used to help children explore various issues and develop their critical thinking, if the adult is aware of what the issues are. For example, in the Disney film *Pocahontas*, children are introduced to a Native American girl. In *Beauty and the Beast* or *The Hunchback of Notre Dame* they are introduced to people with a disability. With their interest already engaged, many other books and resources can be used to correct and broaden their view, and to explore the many issues that are raised in these very popular cartoon classics which children may see frequently. Likewise in many traditional children's stories the stepmother gets a very bad press (*Cinderella*, *The Children of Lir* and *Snow White*). With many families breaking down today, it is of the utmost importance to present alternative views of the step-parent. For some children their only exposure to disability may be through reading *Peter Pan* where Captain Hook is the 'baddie'; witches are invariably depicted as old women; the poor parents in *Hansel and Gretel* abandoned their children in the woods. The list is endless and these classics are probably going to be firm favourites for many years to come.

However, there are many new books coming on the market and these should be selected carefully in order to combat some of the stereotypes and present a more balanced picture to children.

The checklist on page 112 can be used to assess books (and other materials) with reference to equality and anti-bias content.

TASK

Use the Equality and Anti-bias checklist on page 112 to evaluate a selection of books that are available to the children where you work. Include books suitable for all ages.

Figure 6.1: Key for Filling In Table

Key to Equality Categories	
G	— Gender
M	— Marital Status
F	— Family Status
S	— Sexual Orientation
R	— Religious Belief
A	— Age
D	— Disability
E	— Ethnic Group
T	— Traveller Community

Symbols for Equality Rating	
++	Very positive images
+	Positive
o	Neutral
-	Negative Stereotype
=	Extremely Negative
If area is not covered leave blank	

Figure 6.2: Sample of an Equality and Anti-bias Checklist

Equality & Difference
Checklist for Assessing Books

A	Title	Suitable for: Age Range	Equality Categories									Comments
			G	M	F	S	R	A	D	E	T	
Civardi, A. + S. Cartwright	Going to the Dentist	1yr–6yrs	–	+		=	–					Middle class only All carers – female One token black child

Songs, Music and Games

Most children love activities in this area and simple enjoyment can increase each child's sense of well-being and self-esteem.

▶ Learn songs in different languages and accents; this will lead to an appreciation of different languages and dialects.

▶ Use various musical instruments; the percussion variety can be easily made from an assortment of household objects.

▶ Tapes are relatively cheap and children usually enjoy folk songs and music regardless of where they come from. At the pre-school stage it is not necessary for the children to be able to identify the language of the song or where the instrument comes from; it is important that the children enjoy the variety. Later on children can learn about the origins and history.

▶ Make puzzles and games from laminated pictures pasted onto lightweight cardboard and cut into pieces.

▶ Use photographs of children or their families to make jigsaws. This presents an ideal opportunity to bring up the whole area of difference and similarity. Keep a copy of the original picture stored with the puzzle.

▶ An added value here is that parents and children can become aware that you do not need to spend a lot of money to develop talents or enjoy yourself.

Dramatic Play

The imaginary play area should be as diverse as possible and boys and girls can be encouraged to explore a broad range of roles through dressing up. Arrange and stock this area so that it can be a home, a shop, an airport, a submarine or any number of scenes that children may opt to play.

▶ Provide large sheets of material and lacy bits and pieces, in addition to dresses, suits and briefcases in the dressing-up box. This helps develop children's imagination and creativity.

▶ Provide clothing from different cultures — these should be linked to visual material so children will connect them in a realistic way. However, remember some pictures can themselves promote stereotypes instead of the opposite. Would a picture of a child in an Irish dance costume be typical of what Irish children wear every day?

▶ Provide a variety of dolls, male and female; dolls with different hair and skin colour; some with a broken arm or a missing leg. These can be used to help children explore a variety of issues.

▶ Use dolls or puppets to tell stories and act out scenes. This can be an ideal way to introduce and explore a broad range of topics. They can also be used to help children learn how to cope with different and difficult situations, for example how to be assertive rather than rude or aggressive.

▶ 'Persona' dolls are used increasingly in early years work with children. For details about how to use these see Derman-Sparks (1989) pages 16–18 and pages 146–8; also Creaser and Dau (1996) Chapter 10. A number of sites are also available on the Internet.

In Ireland today many children will already have been exposed to different types of food; to add to their experience they could prepare some of these foods using the proper utensils. The Chinese wok and chopsticks are readily available in shops. Vegetables on the nature table could include okra and squash as well as potatoes and carrots. Organise outings to shops which sell Asian or African food.

Colour

Toys and equipment today tend to come in bright blues, greens, reds and yellows for older children and in pastel shades for babies. Various shades of blacks, greys and browns are rarely seen in toys, giving the subtle message that these colours are less desirable. It may sound far-fetched to state that this idea transfers itself to darker shades of skin colour, but children as young as three have learned to think that black is not a good colour! All colours should be used and face paints should include darker shades.

CASE STUDY

We often think of access solely in terms of children/people who have a disability but limitations on access are wider and more far-reaching as the case study below demonstrates. This is an important issue in the provision of equality and opportunity to **all** children.

Jane who is a lone mother has one three-year-old daughter, Deirdre. They live in a one bedroom flat. The family income comes solely from Jane's earnings from her part-time job as a nurse. There is no support or contact from Deirdre's father. Jane's own mother gives some emotional and practical support although this is limited.

Jane is anxious for Deirdre to get the best possible chance for a good start in education. Deirdre is on the waiting-list for the local Health Board nursery but she is unlikely to get a place. Meanwhile, Deirdre attends a private nursery while Jane is at work and Jane pays the fees out of her earnings.

Jane brings Deirdre to the nursery each day. Absences are infrequent but tend to occur when there are parties or outings. Jane depends on public transport and is often late collecting her daughter. Jane does not attend parent meetings although she always seems interested at other times to discuss her child's progress with staff.

In the nursery setting Deirdre is a very obedient child who is very willing to please. She tends to be a loner and does not mix easily with the other children. She has occasionally taken toys belonging to other children and this has caused friction with both the children and their parents.

On the physical side she is often tired and sometimes comes to the nursery having had no breakfast.

Read the case study above carefully and in a group discuss:

▶   issues of access for Deirdre and Jane

▶   how the nursery team might best meet all of Deirdre's special needs

▶   the friction that might arise regarding the child's and the parent's participation in the nursery.

SUMMARY

▶   Children learn attitudes and ways of behaving through the socialisation process.

▶   Diversity is all around us. Children become aware of differences and they learn to respond to those differences at a very young age.

▶   Prejudice and discrimination affect all children.

▶   The adult role is of crucial importance in the provision of an environment which is supportive to all and which celebrates diversity.

▶   Adults must be able to take action when offensive language or behaviour is used.

▶   Materials, resources and activities should be inclusive.

▶   A written policy on equality should be a fundamental part of any early learning establishment.

Key Terms — Section Two

Chapter 4

Equality
Values
Roles
Respect
Diversity
Homogenous
Prejudice
Stereotype
Scapegoat
Labelling
Stigma
Discrimination
Sexism
Ageism
Homophobia

Chapter 5

Social class
Gender
Marital status
Family status
Sexual orientation
Social stratification
Social mobility
Class of origin
Class of destination
Cycle of poverty
Ethnic minority
Race
Racism
Ethnocentrism
Refugee
Asylum

Direct provision
Dispersal
Institutional racism
Equal Status Legislation

Chapter 6

Opportunity
Equality of access
Culture
Empowerment
Self-image and self-concept
Socialisation
Assertiveness
Adult role

SECTION THREE

PROVISION FOR PLAY

This section covers some of the practical aspects of planning for children's play in an early childhood setting. Chapter 7 focuses on the role of the early years worker in planning the space for play, both indoors and outdoors, and considers some general safety issues in relation to the play environment.

Chapter 8 looks at the provision and maintenance of a learning environment for children aged from birth to six years, and also at the adult's role in planning for play.

7

THE PLAY ENVIRONMENT

States Parties recognise the right of the child to rest and leisure, to engage in play and recreational activities appropriate to the age of the child and to participate freely in cultural life and the arts.

(UN Convention on the Rights of the Child, Article 31)

AREAS COVERED

▸ Children and Play

▸ The Play Environment

▸ The Space for Play

▸ Safety at Play

Introduction

Children learn by doing, and play is what they mostly do; play therefore must involve active engagement on the part of the child with her environment in all its aspects. The richer the environment, the more opportunities it will offer the child to explore, discover and learn.

For a child there is no distinction between work and play — play is the child's work. Play is the child's means of discovery, learning, communication and expression.

This chapter is not concerned with the theory of play, but about the practicalities of providing play opportunities in a safe environment within the early years setting. It focuses on the role of the early years worker in planning the environment for play, both indoors and out.

Children and Play

Characteristics of Play

It is essential that the adult who is providing for play should have a clear understanding and acceptance of the play process and of its importance for children's learning and overall development — physical, cognitive, linguistic, emotional and social. This understanding enables the adult to implement a programme which is developmentally appropriate, i.e. in tune with the child's current stage of development. Play is best defined by describing its commonly accepted characteristics:

▶   It is pleasurable.

▶   It is spontaneous, though it may be initiated by an adult.

▶   It is intrinsically motivated.

▶   It is a process, and does not concentrate on a product.

▶   It has no explicit rules, and no right or wrong way of performing.

▶   Children have ownership of what takes place during play.

▶   The child is a willing and active participant.

▶   It builds on the child's first-hand experiences.

(O'Hagan and Smith, 1993)

ACTIVITY

Aim: To focus on the activities provided for children in early years settings, and to assess their play value

Use the criteria listed above to assess to what extent the activities you provide for children really are play activities.

The Play Environment

In the context of early years services, the play environment is where young children spend their time. It is the physical space in which they are cared for, the furniture and how it is arranged, and how the materials and equipment for play are presented in that space. Creating a play environment is an important aspect of the adult's work with young children. It is not enough to simply provide materials and equipment in an unsystematic way; children need to know where things are and be able to access them whenever they wish.

Creating a play environment involves organising space both indoors and outdoors to encourage play and exploration, as well as selecting and arranging materials and equipment in that space so as to maximise opportunities for learning and development.

When planning space for play, the basic requirements are that:

▶ there is enough space for each child

▶ each child or group of children has a 'home base' within that space which provides a sense of belonging

▶ there is access to outdoor play space, preferably attached to the centre.

Details on space requirements as defined in the Child Care (Pre-School Services) Regulations 1996 are set out in Chapter 2.

The Space for Play

Indoor Play Space

A well designed play space should:

▶ encourage involvement

▶ promote independence and responsibility

▶ foster decision-making

▶ acknowledge differences in ability, stage of development and play, likes and dislikes, general interests

▶ provide for spending time alone in quiet play, and in groups in noisy, active play.

Involvement, Independence and Responsibility

It is important to organise play space in such a way that it enables children to do things for themselves, and to take responsibility for their own activities and environment. This is encouraged through the following:

▶ Toys and materials are stored on low-level shelving, tables or boxes, depending on the need. For example, dressing-up clothes may be stored in a box or hung up on a low-level rail; materials for cutting and gluing may be displayed on a shelf or on a table; painting materials will probably stay partly on the easel and partly on a nearby shelf. Whatever the arrangement, children can see and reach everything that they need.

▶ Materials are logically organised and located in the areas where they are to be used.

For example, pencils, markers and crayons are kept beside paper and near a table. Shelves and containers are labelled with pictures or silhouettes to show the children where materials belong, enabling them to put things back when they are finished.

▸ Tables and chairs are light enough to be lifted and carried easily by the children if necessary.

▸ Children can take charge of tasks which enter into their play — filling and emptying water at the sink, washing and drying their own hands, cleaning utensils such as paintbrushes and playdough cutters, and hanging up their paintings to dry.

▸ Coats, bags, boots and protective clothing are accessible to the children and they do not have to wait to be given these by adults.

▸ Materials are not moved around without consulting the children and involving them in the move. Knowing where things are leads to a sense of security and ownership of the environment, and promotes independent action on the part of the child.

Encouraging Decision-Making

Children who learn how to make decisions for themselves are learning how to think for themselves — they are learning how to learn. A well-planned play environment offers children choices about how to spend their time and how to use the materials on offer. This is evident in the following circumstances:

▸ Children choose for themselves how they will spend their time. There is a rich and varied supply of play materials on offer at all times which reflect the range of interests and abilities in the group. Clearly visible and attractively displayed materials attract the child's attention and help her decide what to use. Grouping like materials together (e.g. art materials) creates interest areas which help the child to focus and ensures that everything she might need is within that area.

▸ Children choose for themselves how they will use the materials. Developing creativity and problem-solving are of critical importance here. Exploring, discovering and devising new ways to use materials is what creative thinking is all about. Adult-devised activities which require an end product contribute nothing to this process, other than that children learn what it takes to please the adults who care for them. Children need to be engaged in the process, for example in making their own playdough and discovering what actually happens when those very different wet and dry materials are combined in varying proportions. What may seem like a disaster to the adult who has a very fixed idea of what playdough should look and feel like can offer a new window of wonder to the child, a new opportunity to make a truly scientific discovery. The end product is rarely of interest to the child who is engaged in discovering. Adults spend long summer days building sand castles on the beach with their children, only to have the whole structure gleefully knocked down and jumped upon by a laughing child!

Acknowledging Differences

Each child is a unique individual. The play environment should be designed to encourage the expression of that individuality. Each child needs to discover for herself what she can and cannot do, and to feel supported in trying out new things. If she can practise these with success, she will perceive herself as capable, and develop positive attitudes to learning. A well-planned physical environment acknowledges and supports that expression of individuality:

▸ Materials and equipment are developmentally appropriate to the group being catered for. There is a range of materials within each area, offering different sorts of challenges. For example, the area containing construction toys should have simple wooden bricks as well as more intricate connecting bricks.

▸ There are some tables and chairs for children who enjoy working at a table, as well as space on the floor for the child who prefers this.

▸ There is enough space for children to comfortably move around and carry materials without bumping into things and feeling clumsy.

▸ The room arrangement is such that children with disabilities can be involved in all areas and activities. Consideration should be given to different kinds of disabilities, not just those which have to do with mobility.

▸ Cultural and language diversity is reflected in the materials and decoration of the room. There is a sense that diversity is valued and not just acknowledged.

▸ Interest tables and displays are used to reflect topics which are current (festivals, celebrations, changes in nature) as well as those which are of interest to the individual children. They should reflect what is happening in their lives and in the lives of their families and communities.

See Chapter 6 for more detailed suggestions.

Spending Time Alone and in Groups

Just like adults, children need to spend time alone as well as socialising in large and small groups. A well-planned play space takes account of this, and provides:

▸ space for group activities such as circle time, stories, music and movement sessions, and eating together. These activities help children to interact with others and learn to listen to one another. There should be space for this, even if it means moving furniture around

▶ opportunities for quiet play, alone or in groups, in areas set aside for activities such as reading, art, or table toys

▶ opportunities for active, noisy play, including dramatic play (home corner and dressing up), small world play (using vehicles and animals), and building blocks and bricks. These activities require more space, and this needs to be taken into consideration when laying out the room. It is a good idea to partly enclose this type of space, as it helps to avoid noisy activities creeping into quiet corners. See Figure 7.1 for a sample room layout.

TASK

Aim: Planning a play space on paper helps to identify the strengths and weaknesses in a room layout. The aim in the following activity is to enable you to plan the best use of play space in an early childhood setting.

▶ Draw a plan of the play space you are working in at present.

▶ Draw up a checklist of criteria for assessing play space which could be used in different early childhood environments. Early childhood organisations have guidelines in this area which you may find useful. See the Resources section at the end of this book for details.

▶ Use the checklist to assess to what extent the play space:

— encourages involvement

— promotes independence and responsibility

— fosters decision-making

— acknowledges differences in ability, stage of development and play, likes and dislikes, general interests

— provides for spending time alone and in groups, in noisy, active and quiet play.

▶ Draw a second plan showing where you would make changes and say why.

Figure 7.1: Plan of a Playroom for 3- to 6-Year-Old Children

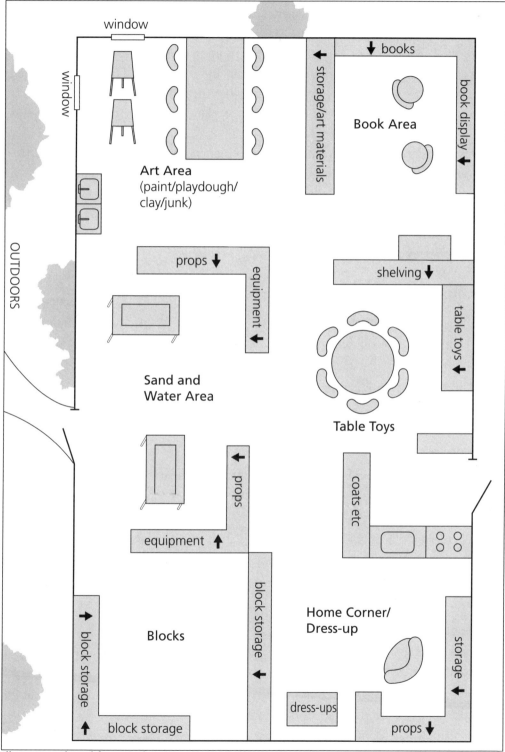

Illustration adapted from: Dodge, Diane T. 1989. *The Creative Curriculum for Early Childhood.* Washington. Teaching Strategies Inc.

Outdoor Play Space

This is often thought of as a place where children can go to let off steam, but outdoor play space is that and much more. Children's developmental needs do not change because they are outdoors. A child may enjoy running around freely for a short period of time, but the outdoor space should hold special interests too, and the time spent there should offer variety, stimulation and opportunities to explore, as well as fresh air and exercise. For this reason, most of the criteria for planning indoor play space will also apply outdoors.

Many of the activities which children enjoy indoors can be moved outdoors, weather permitting, e.g. playdough, paint, finger paints, books and stories, sand and water. An added bonus is that many of these can be extended outdoors in ways that are not possible indoors. Painting can be done with large buckets or bowls of water and household paint brushes (especially interesting on a hot day, when walls and paving slabs can be painted and observed as the water evaporates).

When planning outdoor play space, keep the following in mind:

▶ The Child Care (Pre-School Services) Regulations 1996 set down minimum safety requirements for outdoor play (see Chapter 2). These should be adhered to at all times.

▶ The surface should be partly grass and partly paved, if possible with impact-absorbing tiles. These are particularly important under play structures such as climbing frames or slides.

▶ Some part of the outdoor area should be shaded.

▶ Space and equipment should be organised so as to ensure that the children are clearly visible at all times and that they have the opportunity to engage in a variety of activities.

▶ There should be a quiet area for activities such as sand play, digging, or just sitting and chatting.

▶ There should be open space for active play.

▶ Adequate storage should be provided for equipment.

▶ Equipment should be versatile enough to allow for a variety of uses, for example a climbing frame can be used in many ways other than for climbing, and lends itself to imaginative play.

▶ There should be enough equipment to ensure that children do not have to wait for turns all the time. Time spent outdoors should be utilised fully.

▶ If babies and toddlers are cared for, they need their own space. Babies enjoy watching other children at play but should not be in danger of being knocked over or hurt. Toddlers enjoy pottering and exploring, and they should be able to do this in an unrestricted space, away from the potential hazard of older children. Alternatively they may use the outdoor space at a time when older children are elsewhere.

▶ The outdoor space affords a wonderful opportunity for children to plant and nurture seeds, observe them grow and harvest their fruits. Space should be set aside for this. Strong working tools and equipment should be available to the children — trowels, watering can, small forks, flower pots and containers, compost — so that they can actually participate in the planting and harvesting.

▶ A small part of the garden should be allowed to grow wild, so that children can observe weeds, seeds and insects in a natural habitat. This will in turn attract birds to the garden, and a bird feeder can be set up here in wintertime.

▶ Activities can be planned to use the outdoor space whenever possible. Themed activities to do with scientific learning such as growth, animals, insects, plants, mud, water can all be linked to outdoor play.

Equipment for Outdoors

The equipment provided should:

▶ Stimulate different kinds of **physical activity**.

Examples: climbing equipment such as a climbing frame with different attachments like a rope ladder, pole, platform, chute, bridge, slide as well as balls, balancing beams and wheeled toys for pushing, pulling and riding.

▶ Allow for children's exploration.

Examples: tunnel, large boxes or packing cases, water, earth and sand for digging, logs, bushes, wild garden area.

▶ Invite **co-operative play**.

Examples: rocking boats, skittles, dramatic play, space for group games for older children.

TASK
Having studied Chapters 9 and 10, observe a child at play outdoors.

▶ Note:

— what play areas the child uses

— what equipment she prefers

> — how long she plays in each area
>
> — areas or equipment that she avoids
>
> — who she interacts with
>
> — any conflicts that arise and how she resolves these.

▸ Evaluate her stage of development and comment on how outdoor play can enhance this.

▸ Make recommendations on how the child's outdoor play experiences could be enriched.

Safety at Play

General Safety

By its very nature, play involves taking risks. In an environment where children are encouraged to play in creative ways and to take risks, there will be some element of danger. Climbing those extra few rungs to the top of the climbing frame by herself, using scissors, or sitting without support for the first time all carry their own risks, but we cannot wrap children in cotton wool! What we can do is make sure that the environment we provide for them is as safe as possible, while retaining its possibilities for exploration, discovery and taking risks.

This does not mean that children are wilfully exposed to danger — on the contrary adults have to be vigilant at all times to ensure that risks to children's health and safety are kept to a minimum. When adults ensure that all measures to protect children's safety are in place, they can engage with the children instead of constantly 'policing' children's play with admonishments like 'Don't touch…!' 'Stay away from…!' 'Get down…!'

Children also need to be involved in keeping themselves and others safe — they should learn how to safely carry scissors, chairs, glass and crockery, to wash their hands properly, to open and close doors carefully, to wipe up after a spill, and in general to become aware about what constitutes danger to themselves and to others.

When providing for safe but challenging play, the following general guidelines should be observed:

▸ All activities should be carefully supervised, and correct adult/child ratios maintained (see Chapter 2). Adults should ensure that they have an unobstructed view of children at all times, particularly outdoors.

▸ Equipment and activities should be appropriate to the ages and stages of development of the children.

▸ Equipment and materials should be sturdy and well made, from non-toxic materials, and should conform with European safety standards.

▶ Equipment should be checked regularly; damaged items should be repaired or discarded.

▶ A strict hygiene routine should be followed for all play areas. Equipment should be washed and sterilised where possible. Particular attention should be paid to cleaning and sterilising play equipment for use by babies.

▶ There should be no sharp corners or points on furniture or equipment.

▶ Entry to and exit from indoor and outdoor play areas should be well managed at all times.

▶ Where the play area is shared with pets, stringent measures must be in place to ensure children's health and safety at all times.

▶ There should be safety rules about play which children participate in formulating and clearly understand.

Safety in the Indoor Play Area

▶ Floor coverings should be durable and of non-slip material. Loose rugs should not be used. Spills should be wiped up immediately.

▶ Curtain and blind cords should be inaccessible to children, and cords and strings on play items such as dressing-up clothes should be too short to present a danger.

▶ Electrical sockets should be covered, and there should be no loose or trailing leads.

▶ Potentially dangerous materials such as cleaning materials should be stored out of children's sight and reach, in a locked cupboard.

▶ Litter bins should be emptied regularly.

▶ Hot drinks such as tea or coffee should not be allowed in the play areas.

▶ Paints and glue should be non-toxic.

▶ Scissors should be safe for children, and stored safely after use.

▶ Small objects such as pegs and beads should be carefully monitored and should not be accessible to younger children.

▶ All early years workers and volunteers should be familiar with the safety policies of the setting as well as with the details of the Safety Statement (see Chapter 2).

ACTIVITY

Aim: To familiarise yourself with the practical application of safety in the play environment

▸   In a small group, choose an indoor activity area of a playroom, such as the art corner or the book area. Each group should choose a different area.

▸   Draw up a detailed safety checklist for that area. Present this as a checklist or a set of questions which can be ticked 'yes' or 'no'.

▸   Share the checklists among the large group, adding additional items if necessary.

▸   Use at least one of the checklists in your workplace.

Safety in the Outdoor Play Area

▸   An adult should be assigned to each area of play.

▸   Outdoor play equipment should be checked frequently for corrosion and weather damage.

▸   Walls, railings, steps and ledges should be made safe.

▸   The area should be checked before use for cat and dog faeces.

▸   The sand-pit should be covered when not in use.

▸   There should be enough space between pieces of equipment to prevent children running into one another.

▸   Slides should curve at the bottom to become parallel to the ground.

▸   Slide platforms should have protective railings.

CASE STUDY

Garrymore Community Playgroup has been operating for the past five years. It takes place in a prefabricated building at the rear of the community centre in an urban area. Children attend for morning sessions only, from 9.30 a.m. to 12.30 p.m. each day.

The children come from all sections of the local community, which is a mixture of private rented, owner-occupied and local authority housing, set around a busy shopping area.

Funding is an ongoing problem, and while staff and volunteers are enthusiastic and committed, there is usually quite a bit of improvisation as far as equipment is concerned. Lack of an outdoor play area is a particular problem. Children are taken on walks to the local park as often as possible, but not as often as the play leader would like. Several of the children live in a flat complex and have no outdoor space of their own. Staffing is heavily dependent on parents/volunteers, and this sometimes means that there are not enough adults to supervise the children on the walk to the park.

The committee of the community centre has been approached, and has agreed that the playgroup may have the use of a section of the outdoor space which is reserved for car-parking in the evenings. It is a tarmacadamed area, measuring around 500 square metres and fenced in on three sides. It is sometimes used on weekend nights by young people from the nearby housing estate, and on Monday mornings is often littered with beer cans, chip bags, condoms and even syringes. The playgroup have decided to accept the offer, but need some creative ideas on how to make the space suitable as an outdoor play space.

Discuss in small groups:

▸ What are the main health and safety issues which staff need to consider? List them under these headings:
  — Those which we can control
  — Those which we cannot control.

▸ Under each heading, suggest steps which could be taken to deal with these.

▸ How could materials and equipment already in use in the playgroup be adapted for use in this space?

▸ How could the physical space be adapted to make it suitable and attractive for children? Consider the play surface, walls/fences, the need for a space to dig and grow plants, attracting wildlife and general safety.

▸ Make a list of everyday items which could be used as outdoor play equipment, at small cost to the playgroup.

▸ Draw a plan of the play space as you imagine it could look when completed.

SUMMARY

▶ For a child there is no distinction between work and play — play is the child's work. Play is the child's means of discovery, of communication and expression and learning.

▶ Creating a suitable play environment is an important aspect of the adult's work with young children. This involves organising space both indoors and outdoors to encourage play and exploration, selecting and arranging materials and equipment in that space so as to maximise opportunities for learning and development, and ensuring the children's safety while they play.

▶ Well-designed play space should encourage the child's involvement, promote independence, foster decision-making, and accommodate differences in children's abilities, stages of development and play.

▶ Access to outdoor play space is important, and time spent there should offer variety, stimulation and opportunities to explore, as well as fresh air and exercise.

▶ Adults should ensure that the play environment is as safe as possible, while retaining its possibilities for exploration, discovery and taking risks. Children also need to be involved in keeping themselves and others safe.

References

Dodge, Diane T., 1989, *The Creative Curriculum for Early Childhood*, Washington: Teaching Strategies Inc.

O'Hagan, Maureen and Maureen Smith, 1993, *Special Issues in Child Care*, London: Baillière Tindall

UN Convention on the Rights of the Child, 1989

8

PLAY: AGES AND STAGES

Introduction

The provision of interesting and varied play materials is an important first step to facilitating children's early learning. Planning for play and supporting children's participation helps them to make best use of the opportunities offered by the environment and the materials. This chapter looks at the provision of materials and resources for play in the early years. In describing resources for play in the different ages and stages, it is not possible to include exhaustive lists of materials and equipment. Further information can be found in the Resources section at the end of this book.

Whilst taking account of variations in children's developmental stages, three broad age categories are covered. The term 'Babies' is used to indicate from birth to around 15 months, 'Toddlers' indicates from 15 months to 3 years, and 'Pre-school children' indicates from about 3 to 6 years.

Play for Babies

A baby comes into the world needing to find out what the world is like. Although he cannot perform the simple actions which we take for granted later on, like directing his eyes or taking his hand to his mouth, the reflexes evident at birth are quickly replaced by the planned, intentional actions that become evident as he progresses through the first year. His early experiences are sensory — sights, sounds, tastes, touches and smells.

Many of these experiences are mediated through the feeding process, when he is held and caressed by a caring adult who talks or sings to him, making it logical that once he is able to grasp things he will want to explore them using his mouth. His mouth helps him to discern how objects feel and what they are like. These discoveries must be made before the discovery of what objects can do. The baby cannot learn about the world just by looking at things; he must be an active explorer and discoverer. As he learns simple body control, he can more actively continue this process of discovery.

Time spent playing and talking with the baby in the first year is invaluable to him since he will learn more quickly at this time than at any other period of his life. Babies learn soon after birth to prefer the sight of a human face over other objects. By looking at him, smiling and talking as you hold him and responding to his sounds, you are encouraging him to respond in turn, and laying the foundations of human communication skills. Later on this interaction will include simple games, finger rhymes and looking at books together. These simple activities are essential for further developing communication skills, and the baby learns about the whole process of listening, waiting, responding — the turn-taking that is a necessary part of acquiring language. Play in this way takes place while the baby is feeding, being changed or bathed. It becomes part of the normal routine of adult-baby interactions.

TASK

Observe a baby's responses to an object which has been placed near him. Describe in detail actions such as touching, grasping, hitting and mouthing. Write up the observation using the format suggested in Chapter 10.

Play for babies in the first year should include a whole range of experiences in a form that is appropriate to them. Babies need stimulation which involves interaction with others, mainly adults, and they need opportunities to explore things by themselves. A baby's play during this stage is defined as **Solitary** or **Isolate Play**, which means that he does not play in a social way or interact with others while at play; he plays alone.

With adults, babies can play simple games, look at books, get involved in rhymes and songs, enjoy simple trips outdoors. Games, rhymes and songs played together with actions, such as *Round and Round the Garden*, *Roly-Poly* and *This Little Piggy*, all offer a chance for one-to-one activity involving pleasant physical contact and language. Time spent looking at books and telling stories helps the baby to associate these with a warm loving feeling, are calming and relaxing and stimulate language. Spending time outdoors stimulates the baby visually, and he will often be fascinated by things which adults no longer notice, such as leaves moving in the wind, flickering shadows or birds in flight. This is particularly relevant for the younger baby, whose body position when lying back in a chair gives him a different angle on the world outdoors.

All of these provide for the vital interactions through which babies develop a sense of security, language and responsiveness to others and to their environment. Variety is important for a baby, and while he will enjoy the familiar, he will also become bored. He needs variety in things to look at, new songs, different rhymes and a variety of objects to explore.

Exploring Objects

Babies enjoy being presented with simple objects to explore. Examples appropriate to the different ages are set out below:

0–6 months

A piece of card with one primary colour placed within his field of vision will help a new baby to focus. Later, objects hung above where he is lying will provide visual stimulation, e.g. mobiles made from coloured card or other light material will move in the air and attract his attention. Household objects such as cotton reels, clothes pegs or things that rattle or ring can be strung together on strong elastic within the baby's reach. These will encourage hitting and grabbing, and when one object is pulled it can set the whole lot dancing. Using household objects means that the whole selection can be changed often, giving plenty of variety. A baby can also hold onto objects such as rattles during this period, and will bring them to his mouth to explore.

Satisfying his curiosity at this stage needs careful consideration, and there is a wide range of equipment on the market for this purpose, in different sizes, colours and patterns with a variety of price ranges. A closer examination reveals, however, that most of this material is concerned with stimulating the visual sense, and to a lesser extent the sense of hearing. It is predominantly made from plastic, in very bright primary colours. In adults, the visual sense is so dominant that it gives us a lot of initial information about objects, and we do not need to handle and mouth them in the same way that babies do, to find out what they are like. These brightly coloured plastic toys appeal to the adult sense of what a baby will enjoy, because they are visually very attractive.

Babies, however, are developing all their senses, and during this stage their mouths give them more information about an object than their eyes can. Even if a child has a wide selection of bright plastic rattles to choose from, the information he receives about them will be broadly similar, since one plastic rattle tastes pretty much the same as another.

What the baby needs to explore is a variety of objects which vary in texture rather than colour. Examples are rubber rings, wooden objects such as wooden spoons, large curtain rings and clothes pegs, metal objects such as keys on a large ring, spoons or rounded lids, and fabrics in different textures. These everyday objects can be varied often in order to prevent boredom and, of course, what might appear ordinary and familiar to the adult is new and exciting to the baby.

6–12 months

Once the baby can sit up, household objects can be collected into a basket for selecting, investigating and discovering. This is known as the Treasure Basket.*

The **Treasure Basket** is a medium-sized, low, round or oval rigid-sided basket which contains up to one hundred natural and household objects. These can range from a pine cone, a lemon or a shell to a leather purse, a velvet jewellery box or an egg whisk — the only rules are that the objects should be non-synthetic and that the adult should feel comfortable about what is put inside. All objects should be checked for safety.

The Treasure Basket provides far richer sensory experiences for the child than sterile plastic. For example, the inclusion of a lemon in the basket can offer opportunities for the baby to discover about weight, smell and texture, as well as colour. The Treasure Basket offers choice and variety, and encourages exploration and independent activity. A six- to nine-month-old baby may spend up to an hour exploring the objects in different ways — mouthing, sucking, handling, waving, banging. Some babies will spend a long time exploring one object, while others will select and discard one after the other, constantly rummaging for something new. Each is meeting his own need, and when more than one baby is using the basket at the same time, there will also be some level of social interaction as they show awareness of one another's presence.

The presence of the adult is also important here, to give a sense of security to the child and freeing him to learn. The adult should, however, resist the temptation to intervene, as this can distract the baby from following his own ideas and will change the play from exploration to social interaction.

Toward the end of the first year, play changes again, and this is linked to the child's development of new physical skills such as crawling and standing, and the ability to use finger and thumb in a pincer grip. These developments in themselves take up a lot of time, and often the objects used will be connected to this new-found mobility, e.g. following a rolling ball, pulling himself up toward an object which is out of reach, or picking up small objects off the floor. His primary play requirement now is for a safe space in which to move around freely.

---

*   The *Treasure Basket* and *Heuristic Play* have been devised by Elinor Goldschmied (1994), and are described in her book *People Under Three — Young Children in Day Care*, published by Routledge.

Play at this stage typically includes the following:

▶ **Dropping objects voluntarily** — this involves practising a new skill and becomes a favourite occupation for a while. Objects to drop could include some that are heavy and light, roll and stay still. A large container to drop things into is also useful.

▶ **Emptying and filling** — posting boxes are often offered at this stage, but the different hole sizes make them somewhat complex. Typically at this stage, a baby will take off the lid and fill and empty the box over and over again. Simple variations on this theme can be offered, such as a saucepan and some oranges, or an egg carton with empty cotton reels.

▶ **Discovering cause and effect** — the baby enjoys a sense of power on discovering that his own actions have caused a particular reaction, and that he can cause it to happen over and over again. Examples here are toys which respond when a lever is pressed or a string is pulled. He enjoys repeating these actions, and in the process develops new skills and refines finger movement.

Play for Toddlers

The play needs of a baby change as he becomes mobile. Many of the objects which he enjoyed in the first year will continue to interest him, although he will probably use them differently. His main focus with objects now is not so much to discover what they are like as what they can do. Objects at this stage do not have a functional meaning, and are not played with symbolically during the early stages of this period, so their main purpose is to provide the opportunity to discover new properties, e.g. whether they will fit, bang, bounce, slide, roll, move — the possibilities are endless. Toddler play provision should be based on meeting this need, as well as on a recognition of their stage of social play, which is moving from **Solitary** to **Parallel** play. This means that the child will play alongside and will observe others at play, but is still not actively engaging with them.

When providing play for toddlers, the following should be kept in mind:

▶ The room should be laid out in such a way that children can move around easily, see what choices are on offer and make decisions about what they do. Toys should be easily accessible on low-level shelving or in boxes, or by placing larger toys on the floor.

▶ The toddler's need to move around constantly should be respected, and toddlers should never be expected to sit for long periods at a table. Sitting down to play for a toddler usually means sitting on the floor.

▶ Toddlers engage in solitary and parallel play and have not yet reached the developmental stage to understand sharing and turn-taking. For this reason, several of the same popular toys should be provided so they do not have to wait or take turns; in this way conflicts between children can be minimised.

▶ There should be opportunities for active, large muscle play both indoors and out. Practising newly acquired skills such as climbing should be safely encouraged, by the inclusion of small climbing equipment, ramps and steps. Push and pull toys as well as ride-on trucks and cars should also be freely available.

▶ Experimentation with materials should be encouraged. This includes the provision of natural materials like sand, water, playdough and paint and finger paints. Art materials such as large crayons and large pieces of paper should be available.

▶ Adults should never expect toddlers to use templates, colour in pictures or produce finished 'art products', and should respect the process involved for the child in using materials, rather than expect an end product.

▶ Toddlers also need play with adult involvement, e.g. reading and telling stories, making music, looking at pictures, finger plays, rhymes and puppets. These activities provide the adult with opportunities to observe and support the child's learning and development.

Heuristic Play

The term 'heuristic' derives from the Greek 'eurisko', implying discovery. Heuristic play offers opportunities for toddlers to explore objects and make discoveries within a safe environment. As with the Treasure Basket, commercially bought toys are never offered to children during a heuristic play session; rather a range of everyday objects is used to enable children aged around 12 to 20 months to do what they enjoy best — filling and emptying, slotting, selecting and discarding, recognising differences and similarities, building and balancing. Instead of the individual objects available in the Treasure Basket, there is a collection of each kind of object, as many as 40 or 50 of each. Material is abundant, and so conflicts between children are rare. Again, the adult does not become involved in this play, but sits nearby.

Suggested materials include the folllowing:

▶ **Large containers** of all shapes and sizes, such as biscuit tins, cans, plastic bottles, egg boxes, cardboard and wooden boxes

▶ **Objects which roll** such as small balls, pom-poms, tubes, reels and rollers

▶ **Assorted objects** such as lengths of chain, jar lids, pine cones, ribbons, keys, cheap bracelets, curtain rings and kitchen roll rods.

All of these objects can be explored in an open-ended way, with no right or wrong result, in contrast to many commercial toys. For example, bracelets can easily be slotted onto and taken off the kitchen roll rod, in contrast to the shop-bought 'rings on a peg' where graded rings will only fit in a particular order. Pine cones or shells can be put into and taken out of cans without having to first fit through a certain shape of slot. With heuristic play the child cannot fail, because there is always more than one way of doing something.

Play for the Older Child — Three Years Onward

Planning for children in this age group should recognise that play is now becoming **Shared** or **Co-operative**, which means that increasingly during this period the child enjoys playing with others, and has the linguistic ability necessary for negotiating in play. Play materials should be provided in clearly defined interest areas, where similar types of activities and resources are grouped together, for example:

▶ Pretend play

▶ Sand and water area

▶ Book corner

▶ Table toys

▶ Art area

▶ Interest table.

When organising the indoor play space for 3–6 year olds, the following should be kept in mind:

▶ Each area of play, or interest area, should be clearly defined using tables, shelves or different floor coverings, and as far as practicable should be cut off from other areas.

▶ Noisy and quiet activities should be kept separate and as far apart as possible. Similar activities should be grouped near to one another, e.g. the book area near to the area used for drawing, colouring, cutting and pasting. Both involve quiet concentration on the part of the child.

▶ Practical resources should be used to their best advantage, e.g. the art area and the water play area within easy reach of running water, and the book corner near a window.

▶ It is best to arrange furniture and equipment in such a way that children are discouraged from running in the room.

▶ Adults and children should not have to pass through the interest areas to get to somewhere else, so interruptions to play are minimised.

▶ Each area should be clearly visible to the adults, while giving children the sense of security that comes from being in a small, enclosed space.

The room plan on page 125 shows how these could be incorporated into a play area.

Interest Areas

The Pretend Play Area or Home Corner

Pretend play provides an opportunity for children to make-believe, to role-play and to dramatise, while planning, solving problems, using imagination, developing creativity and language, and refining social and physical skills.

The Home Corner should be in a clearly defined area of the room and should as far as possible resemble some

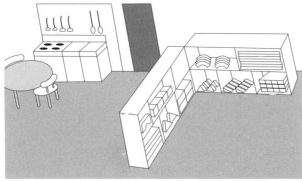

areas of the home, since children's play in this area is based on familiar themes and home life is familiar to all. This does not exclude the possibility of adding materials which will extend this play — dressing-up clothes can reflect a variety of occupations, both male and female, and the area can easily become a hospital, shop, car, train or a scene from a favourite story by the addition of suitable extra materials. Equipment in the Home Corner should include the following:

▶ **House Equipment:** e.g. furniture, kitchen equipment, variety of dolls and doll equipment, keys, large unbreakable mirror, telephones, ironing board and iron

▶ **Dressing Up:** a variety of clothes, shoes, hats, jewellery, handbags, purses, wallets, briefcases, and large scraps of material in different fabrics, which can be adapted for various uses such as cloaks and robes

▶ **Additional Materials:** to facilitate play in a shop, hospital, post office, train, aeroplane, boat or specific roles like mechanic, cook, teacher

▶ **Small World Play:** farm, zoo, doll's house, garage, small figures of animals and people.

The Sand and Water Area

Sand and water are familiar, soothing, relaxing, natural materials which are inexpensive to provide, and offer opportunities for children to explore and learn, make discoveries and solve problems. Although separate activities, they are related. They can be played with alone or combined. Dry sand can be poured, sifted, raked and scooped into containers; water can be poured, filled, splashed, bubbled and used to float objects. When combined, a third element emerges — wet sand, which can be used differently again. It can be built, shaped and moulded, and will change its texture as more water is added.

Play with sand and water provides an opportunity for children to explore safely the properties of natural materials, and to experience their calming, therapeutic effects. In doing so they can discover important mathematical and scientific principles, make plans, investigate and solve problems, understand cause and effect, develop language, as well as developing social and physical skills. While each should have its own distinct space, the two should be near enough to one another to combine easily when necessary.

The floor covering should be non-slip and easily wiped. Equipment for play should be stored in suitable baskets or basins, and not in the sand and water containers as they can become easily cluttered and this can disrupt play. Children may need protective clothing in this area. If so, hooks can be provided at their level for storing these items.

Sand can also be provided on baking trays or in basins to encourage small world play. These can be set up on a separate table and should be seen as supplementing rather than substituting for the main provision.

Equipment for Sand Play

▶ Sand and water trays, storage baskets for materials, dustpan and brush

▶ Sand — silver, coral or play sand

▶ Containers — buckets, plastic pots, empty cartons of different shapes, beakers, bun tins

▶ Sand wheel, shovels, scoops, spoons, rakes, sieve, funnel

▶ Weighing scales and measuring cups

▶ Shells, stones, twigs, leaves, small vehicles, play people.

Equipment for Water Play

Many of the items listed above are also suitable for water play, as well as the following:

▶ Bottles and bottle tops, dolls for washing, spray bottles, siphon, boats

▶ Straws, plastic tubing, corks, sponges, objects that sink and float

▶ Protective clothing.

The Book Area

Books should be part of every child's experience, and the early childhood setting can ensure this by:

▶   providing a wide range of high-quality books

▶   ensuring these are accessible to children

▶   presenting them appropriately

▶   using them regularly

▶   being seen to value them.

The book area should be quiet, comfortable and well lit, with a variety of books clearly visible and accessible to the children. It is a place where children can take 'time out' from busier, noisier activities, and where they may choose to spend time alone.

Books offer children an enjoyable way to:

▶   gain information about specific subjects

▶   deal with difficult events and transitions in their lives

▶   acquire new ideas

▶   discover different forms of literature such as stories, poems, rhymes and fairy tales

▶   lose themselves in other worlds

▶   find out about other people, countries and ways of life

▶   develop visual understanding and pay attention to detail.

Books stimulate imagination and help develop understanding of how other people act and feel. Through using books, children develop familiarity with the written word and its symbolic role. They develop an appreciation of the sequence in a story — the concepts of beginning, middle and end. Stories can be enjoyed alone or in groups. Enjoyment of books and stories in the early years lays the foundation for lifelong pleasure in reading. Membership of a public library provides access to around twenty books on special loan for playgroups and nurseries. This means a constant supply of books, as well as a regular outing for the children and the chance to make choices for themselves about what they read.

Equipment for the Book Area

▶   Low-level shelves, placed at a right angle to each other, can be used to form a semi-enclosed space.

▶   Books should be displayed with the front rather than the spine facing out.

▶   There should be comfortable seating, with space for an armchair, beanbags, cushions and room to manoeuvre a wheelchair.

▶ Remember that younger children will enjoy books which:

— reflect their life experiences and interests

— feature characters with whom they can identify

— have a simple plot

— are expressed in engaging language with lots of repetition

— contain clear, well-executed illustrations, filled with detail

— are well constructed, robust and easily handled

▶ Older children will enjoy, in addition:

— a more complex plot

— humour

— imaginative sequences

— more detail in the story

— factual books.

▶ Books for all children should challenge stereotypes — see Chapter 6 for further information.

▶ Books should be rotated regularly, reflecting the changing interests of the children, while keeping old favourites available.

▶ Reading and telling stories with children is an important feature of book provision in the play area, and should be incorporated into individual and group activities every day.

ACTIVITY

Aim: Books for children should be chosen with care. This activity aims to help you draw up and test criteria for choosing books for the different age groups. It will be useful to have read Chapter 6 before carrying out the activity.

▶ Draw up a checklist which sets out criteria for choosing books for:

— babies

— toddlers

— 3–6 year olds.

Include the criteria for promoting positive images set out in Chapter 6.

▶ Visit your local library to check out the children's books.

▶ Select one book for each age group above, and use your checklist to critique them. If the books meet most of your criteria, note the author, year of publication, title and publisher (see Appendix 2).

Table Toy Area

This area is set aside for play with toys which are suited to being used at a table, though many of them can equally well be used on the floor. Table toys can be grouped into two types:

▶ toys which are self-correcting, such as jigsaw puzzles

▶ toys which are open-ended like Lego bricks, threading cards or pegboards.

Play with table toys helps children to:

▶ develop concepts of colour, size and shape

▶ group, match and pair objects

▶ develop creative ways of using materials

▶ refine hand-eye co-ordination and visual discrimination

▶ learn how to work in cooperation with others, through shared projects

▶ develop concentration.

Equipment for Table Toy Area

Equipment in this area should be stored on open shelving near the tables, and some floor space should be allocated for more expansive projects. There should be a clear system to make it easy for children to return the materials to the correct place — plenty of shelf space so that materials are not stacked on top of one another, and a system of labeling and silhouettes to indicate where each item goes.

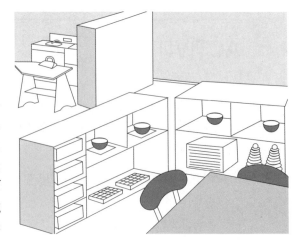

When selecting materials for this area, keep the following in mind:

- Children using this area will be at different developmental stages, and materials should reflect this.
- Both self-correcting and open-ended materials should be available.
- Materials need to be of high quality to endure constant usage.
- Materials such as puzzles should challenge stereotypes and reflect an anti-bias approach (see Chapter 6).

Equipment in this area should include:

- jigsaw puzzles, both interlocking and tray types, in a variety of sizes
- lotto games
- matching cards
- pegs and pegboards
- threading aids
- table bricks, such as Lego and wooden bricks
- activities for sorting, grouping and pairing objects, using shells, pasta, buttons.

The Art Area

Art is a very broad term but can be taken here to mean the activities that involve children in working with paint, paper, pencils, crayons, markers, scissors, glue, junk materials, playdough and clay. All of these involve children in a process of exploration and discovery — about the materials, about the tools and about themselves.

Play in this area promotes development and learning of a high order: children can represent their ideas creatively; learn about cause and effect; observe changes in properties of materials; become familiar with colour, shape and texture; compare and contrast; solve problems; make choices and develop an aesthetic sense, while developing fine motor skills, hand and eye co-ordination and using tools with increasing expertise and intention.

Children should feel in charge of their own activities here. A layout which enables this includes easy access to a range of materials, space and time to carry projects through, facilities for children to independently clean themselves and their environment. Constant replenishing of materials means that activities can be ongoing.

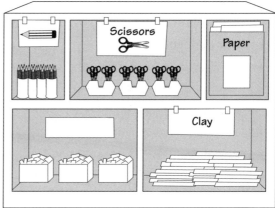

Adults should not direct children in what they may produce — play in this area is about process, not 'end product'. If a child is working toward an end product, it should be of his own choosing.

The art area should take up a large part of the room, since it incorporates many different kinds of activities. Space can be divided up for the different kinds of activities, e.g. drawing and colouring can be near the quieter, table toy area, while messier play can take place near the sand and water.

The art area should include:

▶   space set aside for painting, containing double-sided easels, and space for table painting and finger painting if children prefer this

▶   storage for painting materials

▶   tables for clay and playdough, along with storage for tools

▶   a table for junk modelling, and storage for materials

▶   a table for drawing

▶   protective clothing on low-level hooks

▶   hand washing and drying facilities accessible to children

▶   a facility for drying paintings, clay models and junk models.

Equipment for the Art Area
For Painting

▶   paper — different sizes, textures and colours

▶   paint — non-toxic poster and powder paint, in primary colours, black and white. Children discover other colours through their own exploration.

▶   non-spill pots

▶   brushes — variety of bristle sizes, blunt tipped.

For Drawing and Colouring

▶   large and small crayons

▶   pencils, both coloured and plain, and pencil sharpeners

▶   markers

▸   paper as for painting.

For Junk Modelling
▸   safety scissors, sharp enough to cut with

▸   non-toxic glue

▸   variety of scrap materials, e.g. paper, card, fabric, three-dimensional objects, wood shavings, feathers.

For Playdough and Clay
▸   ready-made playdough

▸   ingredients for children to make their own playdough

▸   clay

▸   working tools for cutting, rolling and making impressions.

ACTIVITY — CRITIQUE OF A PLAY ITEM

Aim: To assess the play value of commercial and home-made play materials.

▸   Using some toy catalogues, work in small groups to list toys which would be suitable for children aged 6 months, 9 months, 2 years, 3 years and 5 years.

▸   Based on the information in this chapter, draw up a list of criteria which you could use to assess the suitability of some of the items you have chosen.

▸   Assess the items using your criteria.

▸   For each item chosen, suggest an alternative that could be easily made or assembled either from household articles or from junk/scrap material.

▸   List all the groups' ideas side by side on a chart.

Interest Tables

These are used to display articles relating to themes or topics dealt with on an ongoing basis, e.g. seasons and festivals, concepts such as movement and colour, or practical topics such as transport or food.

    The Interest Table can include items brought from home, from outdoors or from within the nursery or playgroup. It is a useful way to help children develop observation skills and creates a link between home and the centre.

Interest tables should be attention-catching, relevant and attractive. The children should feel that all their contributions to the display are valued.

Planning Play Activities

In a well-planned environment, children will practise skills they have learned, while also trying out new skills. The sense of achievement and enhanced self-esteem that comes from mastering a skill brings confidence, a willingness to take risks and the ability to face new challenges. Children show most interest and concentration while engaged in child-initiated activities, but there is still a place for adult-initiated activities, where specific skills and ways of using materials can be introduced. Activities are planned by the observant adult to extend learning and to encourage this risk-taking by the child.

Planning for specific activities should be based on the following criteria:

▶ Use knowledge of child development to plan activities which are developmentally appropriate, that is, suited to the child's stage of development.

▶ Be aware of what the child's existing skills are, so that these can be reinforced and extended. This information is gained through regular observation of the child at play (see Chapters 9 and 10).

▶ Consider whether the activity will lay the foundations for future learning, e.g. pouring sand in and out of containers may appear merely as relaxation and enjoyment while refining hand-eye coordination, but it is also enabling the development of mathematical and scientific concepts such as weight, shape, volume and capacity, texture and gravity, and problem-solving.

▶ Consider whether the activity is best suited to an individual child or a group. Some activities such as stories, rhymes, songs and music-making are suitable as group activities. Small groups generally work better than large ones, since each individual has the opportunity to participate.

▶ Take account of the space available for the activity and ensure that children are not restricted.

▶ Allow enough time to carry the activity through to the end. This includes preparation and tidying up time, and children need to be involved in both.

▶ Check that staffing levels are adequate. Adults should be able to give their full and undivided attention to the activity.

▶ Check in advance that all necessary materials are available and in good order.

▶ Ensure that activities and materials used reflect an awareness of equality issues (see Chapter 6).

▶   Consider the health and safety of the children at all times.

▶   Link in to a current theme or topic if there is one.

Evaluating Play Activities

The cycle of '**Plan-Do-Review**' is the basis of the planning process. Having observed and assessed the child's stage and learning needs, an activity may be planned to reinforce or extend existing skills. The activity is carried out and should then be evaluated by the adult. Planned activities should be evaluated in terms of:

▶   their effectiveness in meeting objectives for the children

▶   the adult's own role.

Evaluating Objectives for Children
These can be defined as either learning outcomes or developmental outcomes.

Learning Outcomes are described in terms of the potential learning promoted — mathematical, scientific, creative, physical, linguistic, personal and social.

Mathematical learning is about developing an awareness of mathematical concepts through actively exploring shapes, patterns, relationships between objects, ordering, measuring, estimating quantities, problem-solving and becoming familiar with mathematical language like 'bigger or smaller than', 'the same as', 'long', 'short', 'equal', 'matches with' and so on.

Scientific learning is about exploring the properties of living and non-living materials. It is about investigating, questioning, experimenting, classifying and recording information.

Creative learning occurs when children have the freedom to express ideas and feelings, explore and experiment with materials through art, music, movement, dramatic play, stories, poetry.

Physical experiences are about using the whole body to develop confidence and expertise, learning how bodies work, developing a sense of self and cultivating positive attitudes toward a healthy way of life.

Linguistic learning is linked with early literacy and involves developing speaking and listening skills, communication, awareness of how language is used — thought, spoken, written, signed, read and listened to — understanding and being interested in the purpose of the printed word, exploring and using a variety of writing media.

Personal and Social learning is about developing awareness of oneself and others, self-esteem, developing confidence and autonomy, making choices, respect, moral and spiritual growth, developing relationships and forming friendships, interacting positively with others.

Developmental Outcomes are described in terms of the child's physical, intellectual, language, emotional and social development (see Chapter 10).

Evaluating the Adult Role

The adult is a facilitator and enabler of learning, encouraging children to consolidate skills and build on them, linking past and present learning. Adults guide and help children to make choices and decisions about their play, providing the scaffolding or framework within which learning can take place.

Evaluation of the adult role should consider all the points on the checklist of criteria for planning as previously outlined. It should also:

▶ **Assess** what has been learned from planning and carrying out the activity:

(a) about the child or children

(b) about oneself — strengths and areas where there is room for improvement

▶ **Identify** what could be done differently if doing the activity again, and why

▶ **Recommend** follow-on activities which would further extend the child's learning and development.

TASK

Aim: To apply the principle of Plan-Do-Review in early years practice.

▶ Observe a child at play. Use the information in Chapter 9 to help you decide on the most appropriate method.

▶ In your evaluation, assess what learning is evident in the play.

▶ Draw up a detailed activity plan for the child, based on your assessment. Plan specific learning objectives for the child, using the list of outcomes above.

▶ Carry out the plan.

▶ Evaluate the plan in terms of both the child's learning and your own role.

Making Play Materials

Even with a wide range of play materials available on the market, there are several reasons why early years workers need to be able to assemble their own on occasion:

▶ Cost — an item can often be made for a fraction of the cost of buying it, e.g. a simple mobile for a baby, or finger puppets to aid in story-telling.

▶ The need for variety and change — interest is maintained when new material is frequently made available.

▶ Extending learning — e.g. a collection of household items can be assembled to extend learning about the properties of water.

▶ Catering for specific interests — e.g. if a child enjoys spending time dressing and undressing dolls, additional simple clothes can be made from scrap material.

▶ Availability — items which are not locally available can often be reproduced, e.g. matching cards, simple percussion instruments.

▶ Personalising a play item — e.g. a book about a particular child can be made from photographs.

Making play items does not usually require any specific skills on the part of the adult; it is more often about assembling things than actually making from scratch. Early years workers often tend to collect scrap materials for children's use, and many of these can be converted into usable items. Examples of these are fabrics, paper, ribbon, wool, string, plastic bottles, yoghurt cartons, tins with lids — in fact almost anything that is safe. Some materials will need to be bought, e.g. clear contact, different kinds of paper and glue, as well as basic equipment such as a craft knife, steel ruler, and sharp scissors.

Examples of play materials you could make:

To Develop Sensory Discrimination
▶ Fabric box with matching squares of different textures
▶ Mobile
▶ Matching sound boxes.

To Develop Language
▶ Wall frieze
▶ Books
▶ Puppets — sock, finger, wooden spoon, felt, paper bag.

To Develop Imagination and Creativity
▶ Doll clothes
▶ Collection of props for dressing up — jewellery, hairdressing props, post office
▶ Collection of painting tools — sponges, corks, string, feathers.

To Develop Physical Coordination

▶   Threading aid made from pasta or large buttons

▶   Tiddlywinks

▶   Skittles made from empty plastic bottles.

To Develop Rhythm and Make Music

▶   Drums — coffee or biscuit tins covered with contact

▶   Tambourine — pie plates filled with grains or rice and taped together

▶   Maracas — small plastic bottles filled with seeds, pasta, sand.

ACTIVITY — USING A TOY YOU HAVE MADE WITH A CHILD

▶   Plan to make a toy or piece of play equipment for a child you know. In your plan include the following:

— description of the play item

— aim and value to child/learning outcomes

— materials needed and cost

— safety factors

— equality factors

— research carried out

— how the toy will be made.

▶   Having completed the toy, give it to the child to use.

▶   Evaluate the toy using these headings:

— suitability for the child's age and stage of development

— appeal: comment on how the child used it

— learning outcomes

— safety

— durability

— what if anything you would change if making it again.

SUMMARY

▸ When providing play activities for babies in their first year, adults should ensure that they meet the need for stimulation which involves interaction with others, particularly adults, and exploring things by themselves.

▸ Toddlers focus mainly on what objects can do, and provision for their play should focus on meeting this need.

▸ Play for children in the 3 to 6 years age group should be based on the provision of clearly defined interest areas, where similar types of materials are grouped together and children can freely choose what they want to play with.

▸ In the early years environment, specific activities may be planned to extend children's learning. These activities should be evaluated both in terms of their effectiveness in meeting objectives for the children and of the adult's own role.

▸ The adult is a facilitator and enabler of children's learning, encouraging children to consolidate existing skills and face new challenges in a safe environment.

References

Dodge, Diane T., 1989, *The Creative Curriculum for Early Childhood*, Washington: Teaching Strategies Inc.

Goldschmied, Elinor and Sonia Jackson, 1994, *People Under Three, Young Children in Day Care*, London: Routledge

Key Terms — Section Three

Provision for Play

Play as exploration, discovery, learning
Intrinsically motivated
Process and end-product
Creativity
Problem-solving
Adult-devised activities
Developmentally appropriate
Non-toxic
Child-initiated activities
Adult-initiated activities

Plan-Do-Review
Learning outcomes
Developmental outcomes
Sensory experiences
Solitary/Isolate Play
Treasure Basket
Parallel play
Natural materials
Heuristic play
Co-operative play
Interest areas
Self-correcting materials
Open-ended materials

SECTION FOUR

CHILD OBSERVATION

This section examines the subject of child observation, which is an essential professional skill for work with young children in an early childhood setting. Chapter 9 looks at what child observation is and outlines a range of observation methods. It gives examples for each of the methods described, analyses the advantages and disadvantages of each and suggests a format for use when writing up an observation.

Chapter 10 looks at completing an observation, writing it up and interpreting information gained through observation. It also examines observation as a tool for assessing children's learning and development through a child study. Suggestions are included for presenting an observations portfolio for assessment.

9

INTRODUCING CHILD OBSERVATION

Introduction

Observing children is a key element of professional work in early childhood settings. It is different from the routine work of watching and listening to children. It provides the key to understanding a child's development, play, behaviour and learning, and forms the basis of future planning for the child. A wide range of observation methods is used for recording information about children's play and development — it is important to be familiar with these. The method chosen will depend on the aim, the subject and the time available to the observer. In this chapter, the most commonly used observation methods are described (Narrative, Time Sample, Event Sample, Checklist, Flow Chart, Histogram), their advantages and disadvantages are considered and an example of each is given.

What is Child Observation?

Child observation is a professional skill which early childhood workers need to practise and perfect in order to enhance the quality of their work with children. Watching and listening to children is a routine part of early childhood care and education. We do this for several reasons:

▶   to ensure their safety

▶   to pay attention to meeting their different needs

▶   because it can be informative, interesting or even amusing to listen to their conversations

▶   to understand behaviour

▶   to report back to parents at the end of the session

▶   to make provision for play

▶   to keep ourselves informed in a general way about the child's developmental progress.

There is an important difference, however, between watching and listening in this informal way and actually observing children in a formal, structured way. There is no doubt that in the busy environment of an early childhood setting, the adults can become so involved in routine work that they miss the opportunity to really take in what children are doing. Yet if we do not learn how to observe children properly, we will have little more than vague memories to guide us when we need to interpret a child's behaviour or play, or assess a child's development.

The concept of developmentally appropriate practice means that our work with children is based on our knowledge of each individual child and awareness of different stages of development. This information is gained through observation.

For observations to be effective, the observer needs to know:

▶   who is being observed

▶   why she is being observed

▶   when the observation will take place

▶   where the observation will take place

▶   what format will be used to record the information

▶   how the information will be interpreted

▶   how the information will be used.

The observer sets time aside in which to observe a particular child and focuses her attention on that child only during that time. The information is recorded accurately by the observer, and will subsequently be used to help in assessing the child's developmental progress, and for planning the adult's future work with the child. The observer does not participate or interact with the child during this time, since it is likely that the child's awareness of being studied may cause unnatural or unusual behaviour and influence the outcome of the observation.

ACTIVITY

Aim: To help you identify situations where observation would be useful or informative

▸   In the large group, spend one minute brainstorming the things you would be interested to observe about children.

▸   Chart up the information.

▸   From this, compile your own list of what might be useful or achievable for you.

Descriptive Writing

Accurate and objective description is the key to effective observation. It is a skill that needs plenty of practice to perfect. This is one of the reasons why early childhood workers are usually required to complete a portfolio of observations while training.

Accurate Description

Everyday speech is rarely totally accurate, yet we are usually able to interpret what people are saying because many of the inaccuracies are accepted within society. For example, it is quite common to hear phrases such as 'I don't believe you!' or 'I nearly died!' used in everyday speech. While these are accepted common usage, it is essential that a more scientific approach is adopted when recording observations. The most common inaccuracies here have to do with assumptions made by the observer. Early observations are likely to contain such phrases as 'She is looking **at** the teacher' or 'She is pointing **at** the toy'. It is more accurate here to replace the word 'at' with '**toward**' or '**in the direction of**', since these do not make any assumptions about what is happening. It is easy to assume that you know what a child is looking at, but in fact you probably do not — she might appear to be looking at the teacher, while all the time she is watching a tiny speck of dust floating in the air!

The more information you have, the better equipped you are to make an assessment afterwards. It is important to note the small details, and not to assume that these are unimportant. For example, if you are observing a child using a pencil, note which hand she is using, as well as the details of her activity. While observing, use the present tense, as this helps to ensure accuracy. Even an hour later, you may have forgotten many important details.

Figure 9.1: Accurate Description

✓	✗
J is sitting at the table, holding a book in her left hand.	J was sitting at the table. She was holding a book.
She smiles and talks to herself as she turns the page.	She seems happy as she turns the page.
C is looking towards her.	C looked at her.
She is moving in the direction of the display table.	She walks over to the display table.

ACTIVITY - PAIRED OBSERVATIONS

Aim: To help you to judge the accuracy of your description

▶ Working with a partner or in a small group, spend around five minutes observing and recording in one or more of the following situations:

— an area where several people are gathered, e.g. the college or workplace canteen

— watching part of a TV programme such as a soap opera

— one of the group acting out a simple role-play such as entering the room, moving toward the window, picking up an object etc.

▶ Try to describe accurately body movements, facial expressions and if possible language.

▶ Take turns reading your descriptions to one another.

▶ Discuss areas where the descriptions seem to match and where they do not.

▶ Do your descriptions contain interpretations?

▶ Compare notes with the rest of the group.

Confidentiality

Respecting the confidentiality of information gained when carrying out observations is an acknowledgement of the rights of the child and the family not to have information about them used or made available to others in any way. This means in practice that:

▶ Permission is requested from the parent or primary carer before starting to observe a child and an explanation is given as regards who is involved and who will have access to the information gained. In the case of a learner who is observing, this is usually done through the workplace supervisor. It is still the responsibility of the observer, however, to ensure that the permission is in place.

▶ The name of the person whose permission has been given is clearly stated on all observations.

▶ The name of the child or the name of the centre where the observation has been carried out is never given on the observation of a student or learner. Abbreviations such as TC (Target Child), or the child's initials are used.

▶ All learner observations are signed by the learner and parent or workplace supervisor before being submitted for assessment.

▶ Observations are not discussed with outsiders. Any discussion which may be considered appropriate is carried out either with parents, in the workplace with colleagues, or in certain classroom contexts, e.g. in a discussion of what has been learned from carrying out a particular observation. It is essential that there is group agreement that information discussed in this way during class time is not referred to outside that context, and that even in the classroom situation the child's anonymity is preserved.

Carrying Out an Observation

Having established through discussion with parents/management and co-workers that you are ready to get started on your observations, there are a number of practical issues which need to be considered. These are:

▶ Finding time and establishing a routine for observing

▶ Identifying the necessary equipment and taking notes

▶ Writing up the observation (dealt with in Chapter 10).

Finding Time

Developing observation skills is an ongoing process, and needs to be integrated into the daily routine of the early childhood worker and into the practical work experience of the learner or trainee.

It is very important that the issue of setting time aside for observing is clarified at an early stage between all the parties concerned, be they learners, staff, volunteers, supervisors or course tutors, so that all can be quite clear about what is expected from them. It can happen that a learner or early childhood worker becomes so caught up in day-to-day routine tasks that time spent observing is seen as less important than time spent on other activities. However, the value of time spent observing is well documented, in terms of the insights it provides into the individual child.

From the point of view of the learner, the best approach is to establish a routine right from the start of each work experience placement. This should be negotiated with the work placement supervisor, as should an agreement on a routine for handing over the completed work for reading, discussion and signing. It is not recommended that you observe at the same time every day, since observations should cover the whole range of experiences that make up the child's day — arrival, free play and structured play times, both indoors and outdoors, care routines such as nappy changing, preparation for sleep-time, and transition times such as preparing for mealtime or going home.

Taking Notes — Necessary Equipment

The most essential tools for carrying out observations of children are your eyes and ears! Most often, the only other piece of equipment you will need is a notebook and a pencil. Learners should make sure to take these into placement every day, since opportunities to observe often present themselves unexpectedly. Observations can be carried out on individual children or on groups but the essential skills are mastered by focusing first on the individual. This is known as the 'Target Child' approach, first developed by the Oxford Pre-School Research Group, who also have devised the following code for recording information while observing:

TC	=	Target Child (the child who is being observed)
C	=	Other Child
A	=	Any Adult (such as staff member, parent, learner, observer)
→	=	Speaks to

Examples of how these can be used in noting use of language:

TC	→	C	'I'm the father and you're the mother'
C	→	TC	'You're not coming to my party'
A	→	TC	Comforts him
TC	→	A	'Will you tie my apron please?'
A	→	Group	Announces milk time
A	→	TC + C	Reads a story.

(Adapted from Sylva et al., 1986: 232)

Mastering codes such as these (or devising your own) will help you to capture as much detail as possible, and they can be used in all of the observation methods outlined in this section. It is important when using a code to clearly identify this on the observation, and to provide the code key for the benefit of the reader.

Observation Methods

The Narrative Method

At its simplest, this involves recounting exactly what the child is doing and saying while being observed. The narrative observation is written in the present tense and involves setting time aside to watch and listen carefully for the designated period, which can be anything from five minutes to half an hour. This written record of the child's activity is recorded in rough form and written up as soon as possible afterwards.

A shorter form of the narrative is the snapshot observation or anecdotal record, used to give a brief account of a specific incident. This is recorded as or soon after it occurs. While anecdotal records may be short, they can be collected in a series over a period of time and are used to build up a picture of the child. This method could be used, for example, over a week, to observe a child settling in on arrival in the nursery or playgroup. At the end of that time, all the anecdotes are put together in sequence and the information is evaluated. Anecdotal records may also form the basis of a child study.

Uses
▸ When beginning to develop observation skills, as it trains the observer to be observant!

▸ When it is possible to set time aside without interruption, e.g. in the case of a learner who is on work experience placement, or when there are enough staff in the room to allow for one person taking time out.

Example of a Narrative (see Appendix 3 for example of a full Narrative Observation)
J is sitting at the table, holding a book in her left hand. Both her feet are firmly planted on the floor. With the thumb and first finger of her right hand she is opening the first page of the book. Placing the book on the table, she is bending her head down toward it.

Advantages of the Narrative Method
▸ It trains the observer to become aware of the small details of a child's actions, interactions and language.

▸ No unusual equipment is necessary — just pen and paper, eyes and ears.

▶   It gives a comprehensive and detailed record to the observer. It is non-selective in that the observer writes down everything that she has seen and heard the child do and say, rather than picking out specific actions to note.

▶   The observer starts out with no preconceived ideas or expectations about what will occur; the observation is recorded in a naturally unfolding situation.

Disadvantages of the Narrative Method

▶   It can be difficult to catch everything which occurs during the observation time, particularly during the early stages when the observer is not skilled and will not have developed a system of note-taking or codes for speed writing.

▶   It may give an atypical picture of the child, since it does not take into account factors such as tiredness, hunger, time of day or other factors that may influence how a child behaves at a particular time. For this reason, it is very important to note as much relevant preliminary information about the child as possible.

▶   Because the observation time is limited, an incident may be taken out of context, and therefore may be misinterpreted.

▶   It can be difficult for the observer to find periods of completely uninterrupted time during a busy daily schedule.

Time Sampling Method

A Time Sample observation gives a picture of a child's activities, social group and language interactions at fixed periods throughout a session.
Since it is not always possible to observe continuously, this method enables the observer to take notes at pre-set, regular intervals, using pre-set headings, such as:

▶   **Actions** (what the child is doing)

▶   **Social Group** (who the child is with)

▶   **Language** (what the child is saying).

It is important that the time set for the observation is decided in advance, and can be for as little as half an hour or as long as a full day, depending on the aim of the observation. For example, an observation of a child's spontaneous play could be carried out over half a day, while a thirty-minute observation could be used to discover something about the child's interactions with other children. The observation intervals are also decided in advance, e.g. you could decide to observe the child at ten-minute intervals for an hour, or at half-hour intervals over a three-hour period. This would give a sample of the child's activities during that time.

Uses

▶   When there is a concern about a child who appears quiet or withdrawn, the Time Sample will provide evidence to either back up or disprove the concern. (It is important that this concern should be clearly stated at the beginning of the observation.)

▶   When there is a lot of activity, making it difficult for the observer to focus on a child for a long uninterrupted period.

▶   To observe a child's spontaneous play.

Time Sample

Figure 9.2: Time Sample to Discover More About a Child's Activities in the Playgroup

Time	Actions	Social Group	Language
9.30	sitting on floor completing a jigsaw puzzle	C	Hey - look! This bit looks funny here! Give me that!
10.00	working on puzzle. Pointing towards unfinished edge	C	Put it there! Put it there – No...there!
10.30	Sand tray. Plunging both hands into sand and churning it up.	E D	I'm going to pour some into this (cup)
11.00			
11.30			
12.00			
12.30			

(The child is observed every thirty minutes over a three-hour session.)

Advantages of Time Sampling

▶ It gives a good overall picture of a child's activities over a period of time.

▶ It can be completed without much interruption to the daily staff routine.

▶ There is a specific focus on the child's social interactions and language.

Disadvantages of Time Sampling

▶ The observer may miss out on specific behaviours which may be important to note.

▶ It is possible to forget to take the sample in a situation where the observer is busy with other tasks (a kitchen timer can be useful here!).

ACTIVITY

In the group, discuss and list examples of when a Time Sample observation could be useful in an early childhood setting.

Event Sample/Frequency Count Method

An Event Sample observation records events involving a particular child whose behaviour is causing concern. It is used to study the frequency of particular behaviours and the conditions under which they occur. This observation is carried out over a number of sessions or days.

The adults need to define first what their concerns are about the child's behaviour before carrying out the observation. Examples could include aggressive or disruptive behaviour such as hitting, biting, kicking or using aggressive language.

The observer documents the behaviour as it occurs, rather than at pre-set intervals as in the Time Sample. Influential factors such as time of day, social group, whether or not the behaviour was provoked, the antecedent (what happened just before the incident) and consequences of the behaviour are also recorded. This shows at a glance how frequently the behaviour occurs, and under what conditions. Event Samples can often show surprising results. A child who has been observed over several sessions may well show fewer incidents of unacceptable behaviour than the adults expected. There may be also be evidence of provocation by another which had hitherto gone unnoticed.

Uses

▶ To collect information when there is concern about aggressive or disruptive behaviour

▸   To help adults interpret children's behaviour in its overall context

▸   To form the basis of planning to manage the behaviour.

Example

Event Sample (Fig. 9.3) to document the behaviour of TC, aged 2 years 11 months.
CONCERN: TC has been attending the nursery for over two years. He has recently begun
to act aggressively toward some of the other children; in particular there have been
incidents with pulling hair, grabbing toys and kicking. Several children have become
upset as a result of these.

Figure 9.3: Event Sample

Date	Time	Duration	Provoked Unprovoked	Who with	Antecedent if known	Description of Behaviour	Consequence
Jan 3	9.20	30 secs	UP	Alone	None	TC walks over to the bricks and sweeps them onto the floor. Kicks them around.	A goes to speak to him. Asks him to pick them up. TC begins to cry.
Jan 3	10.05	1 min.	P	FJ	J has pulled the bowl of crayons over to herself. They had both been using them out of the same box.	TC pulls the crayons back. Reaches over and grabs J's picture, tears it up. Pushes her in the chest.	J cries. A walks over to comfort J. Asks TC why he has torn the picture. Tells him to leave the table.

Advantages of Event Sampling

▸   It helps to isolate the behaviour which is causing concern.

▸   It clarifies the context in which the behaviour occurs — who else was involved?
     what was the antecedent? was the incident provoked? In this way the behaviour
     rather than the child is seen as the problem.

▸   It helps to clarify whether or not the adult's concern was justified.

▸   It can show significant patterns in behaviour occurrences, e.g. time of day (are
     tiredness or hunger relevant?), which adult is present, which children are
     involved?

▶   It can help the adult to develop strategies to support the child.

Disadvantages of Event Sampling

▶   It is time-consuming.

▶   The child may notice that her behaviour is becoming a focus of attention, potentially causing further occurrences.

▶   As there is no time limit, it is possible for the adult to influence the outcome by allowing the observation to continue until she observes what she expected in the first place.

▶   The observation record takes no account of external or family factors which may influence the child's behaviour.

ACTIVITY

SCENARIO

TC is aged 3 years and 8 months. She started in playgroup three months ago, and attends for five mornings per week. She had previously been minded by her Granny all day while both her parents were at work; now she goes there in the afternoons. She has a brother aged 7 months who is still minded by Granny.

TC appeared to settle in well at first, but things have changed over the past month or so. She cries every morning on arrival, and regularly gets into a fight with another child within the first half hour. During the session she frequently fights with other children over different things, kicking, hitting, screaming at staff and children and pulling hair; this often ends in tears all round.

Staff are concerned about this and have decided to observe TC using the Event Sample method.

▶   In a small group, discuss the advantages of using an Event Sample observation in this situation.

▶   How could this observation method help staff to learn more about TC's behaviour?

▶   What further information could be useful to staff when preparing to observe? Consider family factors here.

Checklist Method

A Checklist is a bit like a shopping list! It shows at a glance a range of skills or behaviours, arranged in a logical order on a list, which the observer ticks off, if and when they are observed.

The skills or behaviours listed will be easily observed, e.g. physical or social skills. In addition to ticking off items on a list, the observer may indicate what evidence there is to justify the item being ticked. For example, if a tick has been placed beside 'Plays parallel to others, using similar materials', the evidence could be 'Sat beside P using Duplo™ from a pile in the centre of the mat'.

It should be possible to take in the information on a Checklist at a glance. The completed Checklist should indicate only those behaviours which have been observed. If it is not possible to observe certain behaviours, e.g. something which is not a feature of the child's day in nursery or playgroup, such as going to bed or certain mealtime rituals, these items should be indicated by some agreed symbol (e.g. N/O for not observed), rather than being left blank. As with all codes, this should be explained to the reader. It is possible to transfer data collected in a Narrative observation onto a Checklist if it is necessary to store and share the information in an easily accessible format.

Guidelines for Preparing a Checklist Observation

▶   Items listed should be short and descriptive using non-judgemental language (e.g. 'jumps over a 20-centimetre object' rather than 'jumps high').

▶   Items listed should be positive (e.g. 'separates from parent without difficulty' rather than 'clings to parent').

▶   The Checklist should be easily understood by all users.

▶   Checklists are drawn from recognised developmental guides and the source should be acknowledged on the observation.

Uses

▶   When it is only necessary to find out whether a behaviour or skill is present, rather than the degree to which it is present

▶   When focusing attention on a specific area of development

▶   When accurate baseline information is required.

Example

Figure 9.4: Checklist: Social Development/Self-identity, 3 Years

Name   S C
_____

Group   Pre-School
_____

Directions:
Put a ✓ for items you have observed. Put N/O for items you have not observed. Leave all others blank.

Item		Evidence	Date
Separates from parents without difficulty	✓	*She separates from mother at the door, says goodbye and walks in with A*	22/10
Makes eye contact with adults	✓	*Looks into A's eyes when speaking — comes over to stand in front of her*	22/10
Makes activity choices without help		*Says what she intends to do next. Tells B what she has chosen to do*	23/10
Plays confidently in dramatic play	N/O	—	—
Shows enthusiasm in doing things for herself			

Advantages of Checklists

▶   They are quick and easy to use, and give information at a glance.

▶   The observer is not limited to a short space of time to gain the information; the observation can be carried out over several days.

▶   Checklists can be completed in a variety of situations, both indoors and out.

▶   No specialised equipment is needed by the observer.

▶   Through regularly consulting developmental guides and the application of theory into practice, the observer becomes familiar with the range of normative development and its limitations.

Disadvantages of Checklists

▶ The information given is very limited; checklists lack detail on duration of activity and behaviour, and there is no description. Since they do not record everything that happens, they may leave out important information.

▶ It is possible that if a Checklist is drawn up with a particular child in mind, the list will only include those skills or behaviours which the observer is sure the child will 'score' positively on.

▶ It is tempting to view a Checklist as a kind of 'test' which a child has to 'pass'; the observer may therefore be inclined to place a tick against items which she has been told the child has done, or which she seems to remember having seen at an earlier stage.

ACTIVITY

Aim: To draw up a series of Checklists for practical use

▶ Use a developmental guide to draw up a Checklist which could be used to assess an area of development in a specific age range.

▶ Check it against the guidelines on preparing a Checklist observation.

▶ Different Checklists can be drawn up, ranging over a variety of ages and areas of development and these can be shared among the group.

▶ Use one of the Checklists to carry out an observation in your workplace. In a subsequent session, evaluate how useful it was in helping you to gain insights into the child observed. Include this in the 'Personal Learning' section of the observation.

Movement or Flow Chart Observations

A Flow Chart depicts the movements of a child through the play area over a specified period of time. The information is shown on a plan of the room or play area. Lines and arrows are drawn on to the plan, indicating the child's movements and giving the time of each. It is sometimes known as a 'Trail' or 'Tracking' observation.

It shows the child's use of the available space and equipment/materials, and indicates her play preferences. It can form the basis of an observation of an individual child or an analysis of the use of the play space.

Uses

▸   To show a child's use of play space and materials

▸   To plan for play provision.

Figure 9.5: Flow Chart Showing a Child's Use of Play Area During a Morning Session

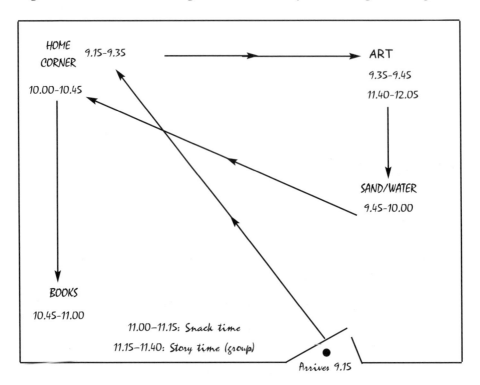

The Flow Chart gives a general picture of how the child has spent her morning in the playroom. The information can be summarised easily from the plan:

Self-initiated activity:

Sand/water	15 minutes
Art	35 minutes
Home corner	1 hour 5 minutes
Alone in book area	15 minutes

Adult-initiated activity in group:

Story time	25 minutes
Snack time	15 minutes

Advantages of Flow Chart

▶   It is useful for showing the play preferences of the child.

▶   It shows the extent to which different areas or equipment are being used.

▶   Different children can be observed on different occasions to show the play preferences within the group.

▶   It can be used in combination with other observation types, e.g. narrative, to build up a picture of a child's activity.

Disadvantages of Flow Chart

▶   The information collected is very general. For example even if you know that a child has spent one hour in the home corner, you have no information on what she actually did there, with whom she played or spoke to. It is not possible to make any kind of assessment of the quality of the child's experiences when using this method.

▶   It takes a considerable amount of the adult's time to complete, as the child's movements have to be followed and recorded.

▶   The information can be difficult to interpret if the child is very active and moves constantly from one activity to another.

TASK

▶   Draw up a plan of a play area in your workplace.

▶   Observe and record a child's movements during a play session, using a Flow Chart.

▶   Evaluate the observation.

▶   In the section on 'Personal Learning', evaluate the observation method.

Bar and Pie Charts/Histograms

Information about a group of children can be shown on a pie or bar chart. It is useful when compiling information about the group or the centre for use by the staff team, parents or managers.

Bar and Pie Charts can be used to collate information on topics such as:

▶   Which piece of equipment in the play area is most in demand at a given time?

▶   What is the nutritional content of the children's lunch boxes?

▶   Are there significant differences in the play choices of boys and girls at different ages?

This information can be collected over a period of time, and used in overall assessments of the centre's policies. For example, early childhood workers may be aware in a general way that dairy products are not appearing regularly in the children's lunch boxes, but may not be sure of the full extent of this. An observation carried out over a five-day period and presented on a chart can give concise information about this. This could then lead to a discussion with parents of the need to include dairy products in the child's diet and why, a promotion of dairy products on the noticeboard or a series of activities with the children on the same theme.

Uses

▶   To assess in a general way whether the provision is working effectively for all the children and parents involved,

▶   When easy-to-read information is needed, e.g. to present at committee or parent meetings.

Figure 9.6: Collecting Information on Children's Play Choices

Child		Equipment						
		Lego	Dolls	Farm	Kitchen	Blocks	Puzzles	Sand
Patrick	m	✓		✓			✓	
Aoife	f		✓	✓	✓	✓		✓
Sinéad	f		✓	✓		✓		✓
Conor	m	✓			✓		✓	
Seán	m			✓	✓		✓	✓
Barbara	f		✓		✓		✓	
Alice	f	✓		✓			✓	
Garbhan	m	✓			✓	✓	✓	✓
Awor	f					✓	✓	
Sophie	f				✓	✓		✓
Ngor	m	✓	✓		✓			✓
Elaine	f	✓		✓				✓
Adam	m	✓			✓	✓	✓	

Example

The aim of this observation is to record the play choices of a group of boys and girls aged between three and four years, and assess whether there are any significant differences between the sexes in their choices.

The children are observed over a period of one week, and rough notes are taken about who played with what. A simple way to do this would be to list the children's names, indicating whether male or female, list the equipment being observed, and place a tick against the child's name whenever a particular piece of equipment is used. The notes would look something like those in Figure 9.6.

The information can then be presented using a Pie Chart to show the overall picture, and Bar Charts to show the gender preferences.

Figure 9.7a: Pie Chart: Play Choices

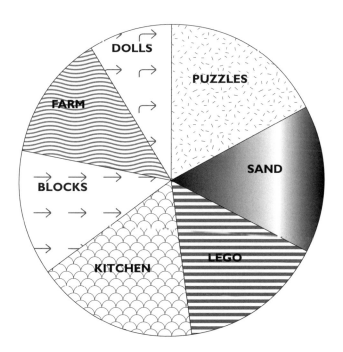

Figure 9.7b: Bar Chart: Play Choices — Boys

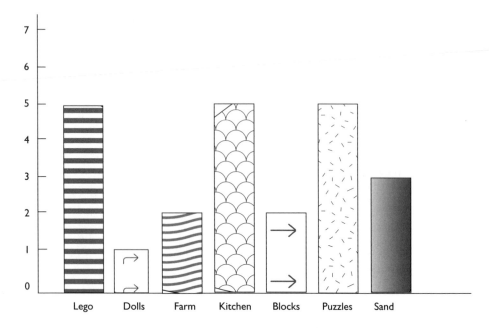

Figure 9.7c: Bar Chart: Play Choices — Girls

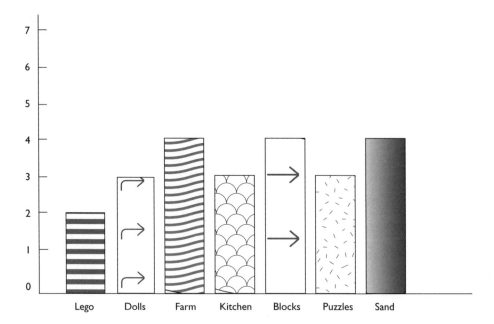

TASK

Aim: To use Bar Chart and Pie Chart observations to compile information about an early childhood centre

Plan and carry out an observation of this type at work. Discuss possible themes with your supervisor in order to make sure that the completed charts will be of use to the centre.

ACTIVITY

Discuss and list the advantages and disadvantages of using Pie and Bar Charts for observation purposes.

Audio/Video Taped Observations

Audio tapes are a useful way of capturing the richness and complexity of a child's language, when it is not practical to attempt to write it all down.

Some important points to note when using a tape recorder are as follows:

▶   Children have a right to know that you are recording them and to be involved in the discussion about this.

▶   The child should feel comfortable in the presence of the tape recorder; it is not unusual for children (as with adults) to overreact to being recorded, giving an atypical picture to the observer.

▶   Permission should be sought from the parents, who should clearly understand why this observation method is being used.

▶   As with all observations, preliminary information including the purpose of the recording and where it took place should be entered on the tape or on an attached sheet along with the evaluation. For learners who are completing an observations portfolio this information should be included in the file.

The above also apply when using a video recorder, and in addition the observer should note:

▶   Video recordings can be useful when a detailed observation is required in special cases, e.g. if there is a serious concern about a child's behaviour and specialist help is being sought.

▶ It is not possible to protect the identity of a child on film. This should always be clarified with parents/carers when seeking permission to carry out the observation.

SUMMARY

▶ Child observation is an essential skill for work with young children. It involves careful, systematic watching and listening to a child for a specified length of time and with a particular aim or purpose in mind, and accurately recording what the child does and says during that time.

▶ Observation enables the early childhood worker to assess a child's developmental progress and to interpret needs, interests and behaviours. It helps in planning to meet these identified needs through evaluating workplace provision, routines and procedures, and provides accurate records for sharing with parents and if required, with other professionals.

▶ Confidentiality should always be maintained.

▶ Several observation methods are commonly used for recording information about children's play and development. The method chosen depends on the aim, the subject and the time available to the observer. There are advantages and disadvantages to each of these. Learners need to practise using different methods in order to refine their skills.

References

Sylva, K., C. Roy and M. Painter, 1986, *Childwatching at Playgroup and Nursery School*, Oxford: Basil Blackwell

10
OBSERVATION IN PRACTICE

AREAS COVERED

▸ Why Observation Is Important
▸ Writing Up the Observation
▸ Interpretations and Judgements
▸ Observation as Assessment — a Child Study
▸ Presenting a Portfolio of Observations

Introduction

This chapter describes how an observation may be written up. It examines the interpretation of information gained through observation and looks at observation as a tool for assessing children's learning and development through a child study. Guidelines on presenting a portfolio of observations for assessment are offered, in accordance with the requirements of the FETAC Certificate in Child Care. The activities suggested in the chapter may be used as a basis for compiling such a portfolio.

Why Observation is Important

It is through carrying out observations that you will be able to relate the theoretical to the practical elements of your training course — in fact, this is where much of the theory comes alive and is memorable, simply because it becomes evident in the behaviour and play of individual children with whom you are working. Observation reveals to us and helps us to understand and interpret the varied and complex ways in which children play, develop and learn.

Systematic and regular observation enables the observer to:

▸   Make assessments of children's developmental progress, and maintain accurate written records for use within the workplace setting, for sharing with parents, and if required, with other professionals.

▶   Record interactions between the child, other children and adults.

▶   Interpret and assess a child's needs, interests and behaviours.

▶   Plan a high-quality curriculum for the child, based on the outcome/analysis of the observation.

▶   Assess workplace routines on an ongoing basis, to determine how they meet the changing needs of the children.

▶   Determine the effectiveness of curriculum provision, and room and equipment layout.

▶   Initiate and maintain practice which is developmentally appropriate.

Observation should therefore be seen as part of a cycle, which includes the following:

—   **Observation:** observe the child while engaged in activity.

—   **Analysis:** evaluate the outcome, identifying skills, strengths, difficulties, needs.

—   **Planning:** plan experiences to consolidate and extend existing areas and help develop others.

—   **Implementation:** carry out the plans.

—   **Observation:** observe the child again and evaluate the outcomes, starting the cycle anew.

Figure 10.1: Observation Cycle

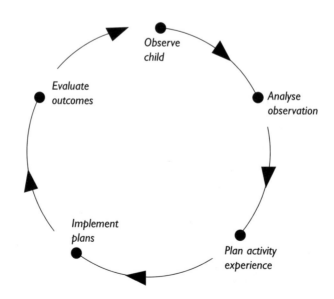

Writing Up the Observation

When writing an observation it is advisable to use a format which clearly sets out the necessary background information and clarifies for both the observer and reader who is being observed, where, and why. This could contain the following information:

1.	Observation Number	10.	Child Observed
2.	Date	11.	Brief Description of the Child Observed
3.	Method and Media used	12.	The Observation Aim and Rationale
4.	Time Started/Finished	13.	The Observation
5.	Number of Children Present	14.	The Evaluation
6.	Number of Adults Present	15.	Personal Learning Gained
7.	Permission Sought From	16.	Recommendations
8.	The Setting	17.	References and Bibliography
9.	The Immediate Context	18.	Signatures

Observation Number and Date (1, 2)

When observations are carried out regularly in an early childhood setting as part of care and education practice, it is important that they are numbered and dated, as this can help to give both staff and parents a picture of a child's progression within a particular area, and can clearly indicate a sequence being followed. This can:

▶ facilitate continuity in the event of staff changeovers

▶ provide accurate information for sharing with parents

▶ provide clear records where there are concerns about child abuse (see Chapter 12)

▶ show the outcomes of play planning and provision

▶ form part of the assessment of the adult's work with the child.

In the case of a learner who is presenting a portfolio of observations for assessment, it is usual to number and date them in sequence. This helps when preparing an overview of the portfolio contents and indicates which criteria have been met within the work.

Method and Media Used (3)

The method chosen should be appropriate to the information being sought in the observation. Observation methods are detailed in Chapter 9. The media used will vary depending on the particular observation being carried out. The most commonly used medium will be pen and paper, particularly in the early stages of developing observation skills. Other media would be audio tape, which can be useful, e.g. when recording children's language, or video tape, e.g. where there is a specific problem with a child's behaviour (see Chapter 9).

Time Started/Finished (4)

This should be indicated precisely. In some cases, e.g. a Narrative, the observation will last for a number of minutes only, a Time Sample may take place over half a day, while a Checklist or Event Sample may be carried out over a number of days.

Number of Children Present (5)/Number of Adults Present (6)

This is important for several reasons. If the ratio of children to adults is high, it may affect the observer's ability to remain uninvolved, either because a child is interacting with the observer or because the observer may have to set the observation aside and become involved with the children.

Permission Sought From (7)

It is essential that permission is sought either directly from the child's parent/carer, or indirectly through the workplace supervisor. In this section, the person's role rather than name should be used, e.g. The Child's Mother, or The Nursery Supervisor, rather than Mr O'Reilly or Ms Smith.

The Setting (8)

This refers to the type of centre in which the observation is to be carried out, e.g. a Primary school, Playgroup, Nursery etc. For example, a description of the setting could read:

The observation took place in a Community Playgroup which is open for three hours per day, four days per week, and caters for twelve children of both sexes, whose ages range from 3 years to 4 years 6 months.

The Immediate Context (9)

This is a description of exactly where in the setting the observation took place. It defines the context in which the child is observed, and should contain information on what she is doing, who she is with and if necessary what has just occurred. For example:

The child J is playing in the kitchen corner with two other girls, F and C. J has invited the other two over to play with her, and has just announced that she will be the Mammy and the others are the children. The three girls are sitting at a table with some cups, saucers and plates. There is a large cardboard box on the floor beside them, which J has referred to as the dishwasher.

Child Observed (10)

When a learner is completing an observation, the child's actual name should not be used, for reasons of confidentiality (see Chapter 9). Either an initial or the code TC (Target Child) are acceptable.

Brief Description of the Child Observed (11)

This should include details of the child's age in years and months, sex, and any other factual information which will be relevant to the observation. This could include details of the child's health, family details (if known) such as place in family, number of siblings, how long she has been in the centre, and staff concerns if any. For example:

J is female, aged 3 years and 4 months. She has been attending the Nursery for five mornings a week since she was 2 years old. She is in good health generally and rarely misses a day. She lives locally with her mother, father and her younger brother who attends the toddler section of the Nursery twice a week. She drops in to see him from time to time. Both her parents are in full-time employment, and she spends the afternoons along with her brother in the house of a local childminder who collects her at around 1.00 p.m. It is planned that she will start primary school in September of next year.

The Observation Aim and Rationale (12)

This should explain what it is that you hope to learn from carrying out the observation and why. It should clearly relate to the child being observed and to the specific situation the child is in at that particular time. For example:

My aim is to assess the language development of the child J while she is involved in a role-play in the kitchen corner. I am doing this because J seems to spend a lot of time in role-play situations at the moment and has been pointed out to me as a child who enjoys being with other children of her age. Role-play offers many opportunities for language and I hope to assess both her verbal and non-verbal communication, as well as noting how she uses language to socialise.

The Observation (13)

The main body of the observation should be focused on the child. Write down everything that you see and hear the child do. You will need to mention what the carer is doing only if it directly affects the child and what is happening during the observation. Essentially, you are recording in detail the actions, interactions and language of the child.

The time the observation lasts will depend on the child, the aim and the observation method chosen, as well as on unforeseen circumstances. If starting off with the Narrative method, five minutes is probably enough initially, but this should increase to ten or fifteen minutes and upwards as the technique becomes more familiar; often the child will dictate the time as an activity may finish naturally. For an example of a Narrative observation, see Appendix 3. For other observation methods see Chapter 9.

The Evaluation (14)

This is where you analyse what you have observed. Essentially you are asking three key questions:

▶   What was I looking for?

▶   What did I find?

▶   What does it mean?

It is useful to start by briefly summarising your aim, i.e. what you were looking for — this will help to focus the evaluation. You then need to ask what you found during the observation. This involves careful re-reading of the observation with the aim in mind. For example, if you had aimed to observe the child's physical development, then you would look for examples of where this is demonstrated, including both gross motor and fine manipulative skills.

The next stage is to ask what all this means in terms of the child's present stage of development. The usual way to make sense of what you have observed is to compare it with what is considered appropriate for the age, using a developmental checklist or guide. It is essential that you use acknowledged sources which are clearly referenced, and not what **you** think is normal. Most textbooks which deal with holistic child development contain such information, giving a detailed guide to expected developmental milestones at each stage, helping you to make valid assessments and demonstrating that there is a wide range of behaviour, learning, skills and development within the norm.

Depending on what source is used, the information may be organised in different ways, but essentially will cover one or more of the areas of development:

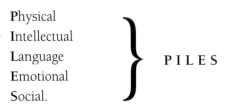

Physical
Intellectual
Language   PILES
Emotional
Social.

Physical Development includes gross motor skills such as walking, running, climbing, riding a bike, as well as fine motor skills like using bricks, completing puzzles, threading beads or using a pencil or crayon — the skills which involve co-ordination of eye and hand movements.

Intellectual or Cognitive Development covers the development of the child's thinking and includes sensory development, concept formation, problem-solving, memory and concentration, the development of creativity and imagination.

Language Development includes a child's non-verbal and verbal communication, expressive language, understanding of spoken language, vocabulary acquisition and understanding of the rules of language.

Emotional Development includes the expression of feelings, development of self-esteem, self-confidence, autonomy and responsibility.

Social Development covers the forming of relationships, social play, interactions with others, both adults and children, and the development of social skills such as eating, dressing and undressing.

Children's Behaviour is usually included within the last two areas.

Detailed information on a child's development in each of these areas gives us an all-round picture of the child's development at a given point in time. There is, however, a danger that in using guides of this type we may build up an expectation about the child, and therefore perceive the observation as a kind of 'test' which the child must 'pass' or 'fail'.

No child demonstrates all the skills and behaviours 'on cue'. It is important to note the pattern and sequence of development. It is also important to remember that development is holistic. One area of development may be well 'on target' while another may be slightly delayed. This is quite common in young children. For example, during the period when a child first begins to express language clearly, another area of development may be put 'on hold' so to speak, while the child's whole being concentrates on developing language.

Reference to child development theory is important here. Look for examples of where your observation appears to either agree with or contradict a theory that you have studied. For example, you have observed that a child of 18 months has put an object in and out of the same container several times. Your reading of child development tells you that children learn through repeating actions. Your evaluation here could refer to Jean Piaget, whose cognitive development theory was based on the notion of the child as an active learner, who needs first-hand experiences of objects to inform him of what they can do, and what he can do with them. You have seen evidence of this in the child's repetitive actions.

You could also examine aspects of whatever play the child is engaged in. Your discussion could include consideration of why a particular activity is provided for the child, whether it is suitable for the child's stage of development, the type of play and stage of play the child is engaged in. This can provide the observer with a clear insight into the child's interests and abilities. It shows the child's play progression, where support from the adult needs to be provided and to what extent the available equipment and materials are meeting the child's learning needs. This can form the basis of future planning for the child.

Personal Learning Gained (15)

In this section the focus is on what the observer has learned by carrying out the observation. This can cover learning about:

▸   the individual child being observed

▸   child development in general, and the application of theory in practice

▸   the play provision available to the children

▸   the difficulties and distractions encountered in carrying out an observation

▸   the advantages or limitations of the observation method used.

In fact, it can cover just about any kind of learning which has taken place. It is important that it does not repeat information which was previously known about the child, but should be seen as an opportunity for the observer to reflect on his own personal learning, and to use this as a basis for future observation work.

Recommendations (16)

This section offers an opportunity for the observer to make recommendations or suggestions about how the child's development could be supported. This could include areas such as the provision of specific play materials or equipment to enrich play or to enhance learning in a particular area, opportunities for specific experiences such as outings or outdoor play, or the application of a particular behaviour management strategy.

References and Bibliography (17)

See Appendix 1.

Signatures (18)

The work should always be signed and dated by the observer. In the case of a learner presenting a portfolio of observations, the work should also be signed and dated by a workplace supervisor or parent — usually from whomever permission has been sought.

This authenticates the work, and verifies that it has been carried out as stated by the observer. After it has been assessed, it is also signed by the tutor.

Interpretations and Judgments
Interpreting Information

When observing, there is always a likelihood that you will interpret what you see rather than simply record it. The most obvious example of this is the way in which we interpret the feelings of another. Your observation record should contain only facts and not opinions. For example, when recording the details of a child who is leafing through a book, you might find yourself writing something like 'He seems happy as he turns the pages.' This is your interpretation of what you see. It would be more appropriate to simply state 'He is smiling as he turns the pages.' Other common examples of this are:

'He is delighted to see his mother walking in.'
'He is getting hungry now — it is almost dinner time.'
'He is upset because she won't sit beside him.'

In all of these examples, the recorder has made some assumption about how the child is feeling and why. If an observation is to contain an accurate record of what the observer has seen and heard during the observation period, then statements like these are clearly out of place, since they have not been either seen or heard, but assumed by the writer.

Making judgments

Judgments can be influenced by your own childhood experiences and memories of how you felt in particular situations. For example, seeing a child standing alone may bring back memories of a lonely time in your childhood, and lead you to assume that the child is lonely or forlorn, thus causing an emotional reaction in you which is likely to influence the outcome of your observation.

It is also possible that your work will contain some value judgements based on preconceived ideas you may have about a child's background. This could include family type, social class or culture. For example, because you know that a child lives in a small flat with no garden, you might assume that he gets little physical exercise, and you use this as an explanation for his lack of competence in vigorous outdoor play. An observation of a Traveller child might contain the assumption that his language development was delayed because he used some vocabulary which you did not understand. Judgments are also easily made on the basis of comments you have heard made about the child by fellow workers, for example:

'He can be very aggressive at times.'

'She's a real little attention seeker.'

'I know for a fact that he never gets to bed in time.'

'I heard Sheila say that she's a TV addict — it's no wonder her attention span is so bad'.

Comments like these can influence the observer without his realising it. An observation may appear to confirm what you thought you already knew about the child, simply because you were influenced by the opinions of others and were selective in what you recorded.

Objectivity

Even the most experienced observers have difficulty in remaining objective at all times. The fact is that as you get to know a child better, you will have certain expectations with regard to his abilities and behaviours, and will sometimes deny the evidence of your own eyes. Your expectation that a child will perform a task in a particular way will probably be based on your knowledge that he has done it in this way many times before. The danger is that you will carry this expectation through into your observation, and instead of recording what you actually see happening you record what you think is happening, i.e. what you have seen happen on previous occasions.

Factors Which Can Influence Objectivity

▶   Previous knowledge of the child — you may feel that you know this child so well that you have nothing new to learn here, or that you can predict how the child will behave based on previous experiences.

▶   Emotional responses to the child — how you feel about him. This can be either positive or negative, and is an area that you need to explore regularly and frequently, either with work colleagues or in your class group, so that you can identify and deal with possible bias on your part either toward or against a child.

▶   The aim or purpose of the observation — are you looking for something and determined to find it? When learning to become a child observer, many people perceive the observation as a sort of 'test' which the child has to 'pass' in order to make it appear that the observation has 'succeeded'. It is important to become aware of this and remain open — simply record what you see and hear, not what you expect to see and hear.

▶   Previous experiences — experiences you may have had, either of this child or of an earlier observation with the same aim but carried out on a different child.

A Child Study

A **Child Study** is a series of observations carried out on the same child over a period of time, examining the different areas of his development. Several observation methods may be incorporated into the study, since the child will be observed at different times in a variety of situations. The study is used to:

▸ create an integrated developmental picture of a child at a particular point in time

▸ identify the child's abilities, strengths and areas which need strengthening, for the purpose of promoting and supporting the child's future development, to enable him to grow and develop to his fullest potential. This is informed by an analysis of the observations, and an understanding and application of child development theory.

The child study should help you to pinpoint the following:

What are the child's strengths?

What does he do well? What developments are particularly noticeable? Remember that development will be uneven, so there will always be areas in which strengths are more obvious. For example, a child who is particularly interested in playing with construction toys may, during that period, show limited interest in other play materials. His strength however is in his interest in construction, and he is developing skills of manipulation, dexterity, matching and classifying, learning about shape and size and the relationships between objects.

Are there areas which are developing but need help?

Always think of these in a positive way — they do not show lack of achievement. They are areas in which skills are still developing, and indicate that the adult needs to make provision to facilitate the further development of emerging skills.

How can the adult help the child improve in his developing areas?

Observations should help the adult to plan to provide further opportunities for the child to use his strengths and build on them. The child already referred to could, for example, be encouraged to use his interest in construction in other areas like the sand tray. The adult could encourage him to talk about what he is doing and in this way use his strength/interest to help develop his language. Further observation of the child while engaged in these activities will enable ongoing assessment based on the model outlined here.

Observations help the observer to make discoveries about individual children and about child development in general. This knowledge must always form the basis of planning opportunities for the child's learning and development. Acknowledgement of the stage of development a child has reached means that planning for that child will be developmentally appropriate, i.e. suited to the developmental and learning needs of the child.

Presenting a Portfolio of Observations

A portfolio of observations should reflect a range of children's ages, activities, areas of development and observation methods. This information is shown on a matrix chart, which reveals at a glance what criteria have been met.

Figure 10.2: Example of Observations Matrix

Area of Development

Age Range	Physical	Cognitive	Language	Emotional	Social
0–1	obs. 3				
1–3		obs. 5	obs. 2		
3–6				obs. 1	obs. 4

The portfolio may also contain an index, which gives an overview of the contents.

Figure 10.3: Example of Observation Index

Observation Number	Area of Development	Age Range	Method
1	Emotional Development	3-6	Narrative
2	Language Development	1-3	Checklist
3	Physical Development	0-1	Checklist
4	Social Development	3-6	Trail
5	Cognitive Development	1-3	Narrative

SUMMARY

▶   Observation forms the basis of effective planning for each individual child. It is an integral part of the cycle of observing, evaluating, planning, implementing and observing.

▶ Accurate and objective description is the key to effective observation. Accuracy comes with practice and with regularly reviewing what has been written. Objectivity can be influenced by several factors, and it is essential to become aware of what can potentially influence one's objectivity.

▶ Interpretations should be based on the known facts and not on assumptions about the child. Judgments should be avoided.

Key Terms — Section Four

Child Observation

Observation as a professional skill
Developmentally appropriate practice
Children's developmental progress
Children's needs, interests and behaviours
Relating theory to practice
Accurate description
Objectivity
Paired observations
Judgments
Interpretations
Confidentiality
Permission
Observation and the planning cycle
Observation as assessment
Target Child (TC)
Codes
Observation format
Observation methods: Narrative, Time sampling, Event sampling, Frequency count, Checklist, Movement chart, Flow chart, Trail, Tracking, Bar chart, Pie chart, Histogram
Audio-taped observations
Video-taped observations
Child study
Antecedent and consequence of behaviour
Developmental guide/checklist
Observations index
Matrix chart

SECTION FIVE

LEGAL ISSUES

This section covers the main aspects of the legal framework relevant to the child and the family. Chapter 11 initially outlines, very briefly, how government works and how laws are made. It then covers aspects of Irish law relating to marriage, marriage breakdown and partnerships that are not based on marriage. Chapter 12 is about the issues and procedures involved in child protection as set down in the Child Care Act 1991, and the professional role of the early years worker in protecting children.

The Child Care Act 1991

Key Points of the Act

▶   The child's welfare is of paramount importance; safeguarding and promoting this welfare is a priority.

▶   Health Boards have a duty to ensure that support services for children 'in need' are provided; unnecessary intrusion into family life should be minimised.

▶   Delays in court proceedings and provisions of services must be avoided.

▶   Service providers must listen to and work in partnership with children, parents, those who have parental responsibilities and any relevant others.

▶   Needs arising from race, culture and language must be taken account of in the delivery of services.

The Ten Parts of the Act

Part I — Preliminary
The main point in this section is that the Act defines a child as a person up to 18 years of age.

Part II — Promotion of Welfare of Children
This section covers areas such as voluntary care, adoption, provision for homeless children, the establishment of a Child Care Advisory Committee in each Health Board area. The promotion of the welfare of children and families, having regard to the principle that the **welfare of the child is of paramount importance**, underpins this whole section and indeed the entire Act.

Part III — Protection of Children in Emergencies
This covers the powers of Gardaí to remove to safety children who are in serious danger and the making of **Emergency Care Orders**.

Part IV — Care Proceedings
This covers **Interim Care Orders**, **Care Orders** and **Supervision Orders**.

Part V — Jurisdiction and Procedure
The Court is enabled to appoint solicitor and *guardian ad litem* for the child; it provides for privacy and informality and again the welfare of the child as the first and paramount consideration in any proceedings is stressed.

Part VI — Children in the Care of Health Boards
Covers regulations regarding the placement of children in foster care, residential and/or with relatives; access; reviews and aftercare.

Part VII — Supervision of Pre-School Services
Deals with regulations for pre-schools, play groups, crèches, day nurseries and other services for pre-school children.

Part VIII — Children's Residential Centres
Registration of residential centres and regulations regarding staffing, accommodation and facilities etc.

Part IX — Administration
Outlines the functions of the Minister and of chief executive officers in the Health Boards.

Part X — Miscellaneous and Supplementary
The main point here is in relation to the sale of solvents to children. Provision is made for fines and/or imprisonment.

11

THE LEGAL FRAMEWORK FOR FAMILIES AND CHILDREN

Introduction

When working with families and their children it is important for early childhood workers to have at least a rudimentary knowledge of the basic laws which govern family life in the society in which they are operating. Because the early childhood worker meets parents on a daily basis and is in a position of trust she may be approached for general advice when one or other parent has a concern. This chapter gives an overview of how Ireland is governed and how laws are enacted. It outlines some of the laws relating to families and children; laws relating to marriage, marriage breakdown, partnerships not based on marriage and domestic violence. The position of, and effects on, children will be covered.

The Constitution (Bunreacht na hEireann)

The Constitution is a document which:

▶ lays down the fundamental rules and principles for the government of Ireland

▶ imposes obligations on those in power and has a higher legal status and authority than other laws (Acts of administration or laws can be examined by Judicial Review on constitutional grounds)

▶ guarantees basic fundamental rights both personal and political.

The present constitution was adopted by referendum in 1937. Any proposed change or amendment to the Constitution must be passed by both houses of the Oireachtas and then submitted to the people by way of referendum. Among the most recent changes has been the removal of the ban on divorce in 1996.

Articles 41 and 42 of the Constitution outlines the basic principles underlying Irish law in relation to the family (see Chapter 13, page 252).

The Government

Ireland is a constitutional representational democracy governed by two houses of the **Oireachtas.** The Oireachtas is the national parliament and is made up of the **President,** the **Dáil** and the **Seanad**.

The **President** is the ceremonial Head of State who is elected by all citizens of the State and serves a seven-year term. The President can serve two terms if re-elected.

The **Dáil** led by the **Taoiseach** is comprised of 166 TDs (Teachta Dála) who are elected through a system of proportional representation (PR). The maximum term of office is five years but TDs can be re-elected any number of times. The main areas of work of the Dáil are legislation and finance; different departments have responsibility for different areas and the day-to-day work is carried out by the Minister, department secretaries and a team of civil servants. Although Governments and Ministers change, the civil servants are permanent employees of the State.

The **Seanad**, known as the second house of the Oireachtas, is made up of 60 persons, 49 of whom are elected from different areas of expertise and interest and 11 of whom are nominated by the Taoiseach. The Seanad elections are held within 90 days of a general election so the term of office is related to the duration of the Dáil.

The main functions of the Seanad are to:

▶ keep a check on the work of the Dáil

▶ represent particular areas of interest such as education and agriculture

▶ provide additional expertise for input to policy formation and legislation.

TASK

Find out:

‣ Which government departments are involved in children's affairs?

‣ Who are the TDs representing your area?

‣ Are there any Ministers from your area and what are their responsibilities?

‣ Are there any Senators from your area and what is their field of expertise or interest?

Local Government

Since it not possible to govern everything centrally, local authorities are empowered to provide, regulate and supervise local services such as housing, sanitation, roads and halting sites. Local government can also involve itself in legislation and each authority will have its own bye-laws; the area that we are most aware of is probably the planning bye-laws. Local government is administered by corporations and county councils.

ACTIVITY

Aim: To distinguish between local and central services

‣ Brainstorm: list all the services provided in your area, e.g. schools, roads, libraries.

‣ Rearrange the list into those that are provided by central government and those that are provided by the local authorities.

How Laws are Made

Laws are basically rules laid down for the regulation and controlling of the individual and society. The Irish Government makes Irish laws but these in turn are sometimes prescribed by European and/or international law, e.g. the laws relating to employment equality.

New legislation or a change to an existing law may be instigated in either the Dáil or the Seanad. The process often begins with the Minister issuing a **Green Paper** (essentially a consultation paper) suggesting a policy development or putting forward alternative policies on a particular issue, with a view to generating a debate. Submissions from interested parties are invited and are considered in the formulation of the policy. In time a White Paper may be issued which will (ideally) take into account all the views received. A **White Paper** is a policy development document. There is no connection necessarily between Green and White papers on the one hand and Bills and Acts on the other, although in particular instances they may be connected.

If the Minister decides to pursue a policy as formulated in a White Paper and legislative change is required, a Bill has to be prepared. A **Bill** is a proposal for legislation which must be passed by both houses of the Oireachtas. The essential point is that a Bill remains a Bill, i.e. a proposal for legislative change, until the President signs it into law after which it becomes an **Act**. Alternatively the President can refer it to the High Court to examine its constitutionality.

Laws are upheld or enforced through the judiciary or court system.

Irish Family Law

The laws and conditions outlined below refer to civil law unless otherwise stated. Religious denominations each have their own separate rules and regulations in regard to marriage and marriage breakdown.

Marriage

Until 1972, the minimum age for marriage in Ireland was 14 years for boys and 12 years for girls. This was based on Canon Law which is Roman Catholic Church law. Although the age was raised in 1992 there was much concern that very young people were ill-prepared for marriage and were more at risk of their marriage breaking down.

Under the **Family Law Act 1995**, in order for a marriage to be valid both parties must be 18 years old, and three months written notice of the intention to marry must have been given to the registrar where the marriage is due to take place. Most religious denominations have premises registered for the administration of civil marriages. In addition to the legal requirements outlined above, other conditions must be fulfilled in order for a marriage to be deemed valid. These are as follows:

▸   Each party must be free to marry.

▸   Each must be of sound mind and aware of what the marriage contract means.

▸   Neither party must be forced to marry against his or her will.

▸   One person must be female and one male.

▸   The parties must not be more closely related than first cousins.

▸   Regulations regarding residency and recognition of foreign divorces must be adhered to.

Marriage Breakdown: Background

The marriage rate has been dropping in Europe in recent times and Ireland reflects this trend. In 1980 approximately 22,000 couples got married in Ireland; in 1995 it had gone down to 15,500 but has risen somewhat since then to just over 19,000 in the year 2000. In countries where divorce was available, a rise in divorce rate coincided with this drop in marriage rates. Divorce has been available in Ireland since 1997 but the Irish Labour Force Surveys (ILFS) and demographic results from the Census of Population suggest that the incidence of marriage breakdown has been increasing dramatically in recent years. The increase in the number of separated people in 1986 was 37,200 — in 1996 this had more than doubled to 87,800. The increasing numbers involved in marriage breakdown are reflected in the increasing numbers who favour divorce. In a referendum in 1986 to remove the constitutional ban on divorce almost two voted against the change for every one who voted in favour of divorce. In the referendum in 1995 the 'yes' vote was carried by just over half of one per cent. Legislation enacted in the intervening years between the two referenda relating to property, social welfare and pension rights of divorced persons facilitated the acceptance of divorce among the public.

If a marriage does not work out there are now three options available in Ireland to a couple choosing to end their civil contract and to split up:

▶   Nullity
▶   Separation
▶   Divorce.

Nullity

An annulment is a declaration that the marriage never actually existed. Even now that divorce is available some people may prefer to try to establish that their marriage was null and void in the first place.

There are six grounds for establishing nullity and they are related to the regulations governing marriage. The six grounds are as follows:

1.   There was an already existing valid marriage.
2.   One or both were underage at the time of the marriage.
3.   The formalities were not adhered to, e.g. three months notice was not given.
4.   Full consent was absent — they were forced or tricked into the marriage.
5.   They were too closely related.
6.   They were both the same sex, that is two men or two women.

Marriages may also be annulled if facts emerge at a later date which would have had an influence over either party's decision at the time of the marriage, e.g. if a past psychiatric history was concealed. However, there are no hard and fast rules in many cases and it is up to the courts to judge each individual case.

Separation

Separation may be by order of a court (a judicial separation) or by agreement between the couple without recourse to any law. Many couples who are separated in Ireland did so by common agreement, which involved no court hearings. Many would have consulted a solicitor in drawing up their mutual agreement.

Either a mutual agreement or a judicial separation merely means that the husband and wife no longer have to live together. They are not free to marry another person and they are free to be reconciled. Other matters can also be considered by the courts including who will live in the family home and the maintenance of children.

The grounds for a **judicial separation** are as follows:

▶ Adultery
▶ Unreasonable behaviour
▶ One year's continuous desertion
▶ One year's separation with consent, or three years without consent
▶ No normal sexual relationship for at least a year
▶ Indisposition.

In some cases a combination of these grounds may exist.

Divorce

Divorce gives legal recognition to the fact that a marriage has irretrievably broken down and no longer exists in anything but name. It gives the right to remarry if one or both parties so wish.

In Ireland, **all four** of the following conditions must be fulfilled in order to obtain a divorce:

1. The spouses have lived apart for at least four of the preceding five years.
2. There is no reasonable prospect of reconciliation.
3. Both spouses and any dependent children have been properly provided for.
4. Either spouse lived in Ireland when the proceedings began (or lived here for at least a year before that date).

Approximately 300 divorces per year have been granted since the legislation was introduced; many couples continue to opt for judicial separation.

Children and Divorce

If a couple divorces the court will always make orders relating to the children. Matters such as **custody**, **access** and **guardianship** (see below) of children will invariably have been dealt with in some manner by the couple, given that they must be living apart for at least four years before a divorce can be granted. When the couple divorces the court will not normally disturb whatever agreements have been made if they properly provide for and protect the welfare of the children. If a dispute exists about the custody of the children or access by either parent then the court will decide on such questions, and in such cases the welfare of the children will be the primary consideration. The court may request reports to be made about any issues which affect the children's welfare. Legal Aid is available to couples who cannot afford to pay legal fees.

Marriage Breakdown: Consequences for Children

Marital breakdown has serious consequences for children. It is generally recognised that it is not the separation or the divorce which causes problems for the children, it is rather the problems and friction that preceded it, combined with how the parents deal with the split afterwards. How children react to, and cope with, the disruption to family life depends on how their needs have been met prior to and during the upheaval. It also depends on the nature of the marital split, i.e. whether it was reasonable and amicable or whether violent rows and animosity preceded it. Research indicates that all children are affected by the separation of their parents and some children are severely damaged by the experience. Children may experience some or all of the following, depending on their personality, the nature of the split and their age and stage of development:

▶   Grief

▶   Anger

▶   Resentment

▶   Denial

▶   Sadness and loss

▶   Insecurity

▶   Relief.

Children may exhibit emotional distress and experience behavioural difficulties prior to and after the breakdown. The effects may be long lasting, resulting in poor performance at school and work. Children may also have difficulties in their future relationships as adults. On the practical side, the 'absent' parent (i.e. the parent who no longer lives with the children on a daily basis) is more likely to lose contact and the family is likely to be poorer as a result of the breakdown.

When parents are helped to manage their problems, conflicts and separation in a positive way, it is more likely that the children will be better able to cope with the situation. Some recent studies would seem to suggest that it is less harmful for children to live with two parents who are not getting on than for those two parents to separate; however, other studies suggest just as strongly that it very much depends on the nature of the family relationships.

Minimising the Negative Effects of Divorce and Separation

The government is committed to providing support for couples and their families who are separating and the following measures are in place:

▶   A Commission on the Family has been set up to advise on family issues in the general economic and social framework.

▶   Since 1995, the government has greatly increased funding for groups involved in marriage counselling.

▶   Legal Aid has been increased, both in terms of expansion of the numbers of centres and of eligibility bands.

▶   A Family Mediation Service is available free to separating couples to help them sort out their affairs agreeably so that the trauma and disruption to the children can be kept to a minimum.

The Family Mediation Service has been expanded and made more accessible particularly to those who live in rural areas. There are now 12 mediation centres across the State and this accessibility is reflected in the increasing numbers of couples using the service. In 2000, the number of couples involved in mediation was 1,225 compared to 250 in 1997. The positive outcome for children whose parents have taken advantage of mediation services, and who have subsequently been less acrimonious in their dealings with one another, has been shown in various research studies.

Unmarried Parents

When a child's parents are not married to each other the child has rights pertaining to both parents, including rights to maintenance and inheritance. These rights are laid out in the **Guardianship of Infants Act 1964** which was the first piece of modern legislation to address the needs of children born outside of marriage or in the event of marriage breakdown. The **Status of Children Act 1987** equalised in law the status of children born in or out of wedlock. The important points of the 1987 Act were:

▶   to abolish the concept of illegitimacy

▶ to give unmarried fathers legal rights to be appointed guardians or to seek access and/or custody

▶ to provide for the establishment of paternity through presumption, declaration or blood test

▶ to update and extend the law in relation to maintenance payments.

The **Children Act 1997** further amended and expanded the law with regard to maintenance, guardianship, custody and access.

Guardianship

A guardian is a person who has **legal** rights and duties in respect of a child. The guardian is entitled to have a say in all decisions relating to the child's upbringing — choice of school, medical treatment, acquiring a passport, religious upbringing. The guardian also has a responsibility to ensure the provision of adequate care. Under the Children Act 1997, an unmarried father can become guardian of his child without going to court providing the mother and father are in agreement. Otherwise the father must apply to the courts for guardianship and this might involve proof of paternity (i.e. proving that he is the father). Where a marriage breaks down both parents may retain joint guardianship; or the court may appoint just one parent or an independent guardian. (Note: Not to be confused with *guardian ad litem* see Chapter 12.)

Custody

The person or persons who have custody of a child have charge and care of the child on a day-to-day basis. The mother of a child who is born outside marriage has sole custody of the child and the father must apply to the courts for custody. The 1997 Act allows for joint custody orders to be made.

Access

Where one parent has full custody of the child the other parent can apply for access to visit the child regularly or at specified times. The 1997 Act allows that other persons such as grandparents may also apply to the courts for access.

Maintenance

Maintenance refers to the payments made by one person to another for that person's own and the children's cost of living. Maintenance can be voluntary or by order of the court. Orders made by the courts will take into consideration the earnings of the person against whom the order is being made. Paying maintenance does not give any rights of access or guardianship.

Except where parents are in agreement, all decisions about guardianship, custody and access are made by the court with the first and primary consideration being given to the child's interests and welfare. While the mother's views will be considered in making a decision about any of the above, the court may grant an order in favour of the father without the mother's agreement.

ACTIVITY

Aim: To explore the role of the early years professional in a changing social/legal environment

Read the case study of the reconstructed family in Chapter 13, pages 251.
Imagine that Sam is attending a pre-school service where you work.

What impact might Sam's family situation have on:

▸ your work with Sam

▸ your contact with his parents/step-parents

▸ the administrative work which would be involved for the early childhood worker.

Checklist: Have you considered the following?

▸ Sam's feelings and possible confusions

▸ the possibility that he may be spending nights/weekends with a different parent

▸ Sam's need to feel that his family situation is acceptable

▸ issues of guardianship/access/custody

▸ the parents' need for support and counselling

▸ contact numbers in case of emergency

▸ consent forms

▸ who can collect Sam

▸ reporting progress and meetings to all concerned parties.

Draw up an outline plan of activities that you would use to work with Sam in relation to his family situation.

Registration of Births

When a woman is married there is a presumption in law that her husband is the father of the child and the birth can be registered in both parents' names automatically. If the parents are not married to each other both parents can go together to the registrar's office to place the father's name in the Births' Register. Alternatively, one parent can bring along a statutory declaration which names the father of the child. If the child has been registered in the mother's name alone it is possible to re-register at any date in order to place the father's name on the birth certificate.

The entering of the father's name on the birth certificate does not confer guardianship, access or custodial rights.

Where parents subsequently marry the child automatically becomes a child of the marriage and there is no requirement to re-register if the father's name is already entered into the Register.

If the mother subsequently marries another man, any orders made in favour of the father will remain in force. If the couple want the husband to adopt the child then the father's consent will be required if he has been appointed guardian/custodian.

Domestic Violence

Domestic violence refers to violence in the home perpetrated by adults on their partners and/or children. The most common forms of violence are physical and sexual assault and it occurs across all social classes. The incidence of domestic violence is difficult to gauge as it is grossly under-reported. Women are slow to report incidents, often because of fear of reprisals but also because there is often no escape, and the attitude until recently was for the authorities to encourage the partners to resolve their own difficulties. Men may be slow to report for the same reasons, but also because of fear of ridicule. Domestic violence may also be under-reported because people find it difficult to admit that there is violence in their relationship.

In contrast to previous research results some recent studies suggest that men are as likely as women to experience violence at the hands of their partners. However, there seems to be evidence to support the thinking that women experience more severe forms of violent domestic abuse than men. In Ireland, in the Dublin area alone, 12 barring orders a week are granted against violent partners (virtually all men). Of the 65 women murdered in Ireland in the six years since 1996 over a third were murdered by a partner or ex-partner in their own home. In the same years not one women was charged with the murder of her partner.

Women's Aid Helpline received 58,000 calls between 1992 and 1997, i.e. about 25 calls per day. In 1999, 9,000 women used the services provided by Women's Aid and in the same year 11,000 calls for help were received by The National Network of Refuges and Support Services. A 1996 survey of the general population revealed that 18% of women had suffered violence at the hands of their partner. Over half the women reported that they knew a woman who had experienced such violence.

These figures are conservative by international standards. In Sweden (population 8.8 million) where there are 115 refuges which are always full, one woman is battered to death by her partner every 10 days. Closer to home, 25% of women in Britain are reported to have been physically assaulted by their male partners.

Impact of Domestic Violence on Children
Each child will react differently whether emotionally, behaviourally and/or physically. The following are general reactions:

▶   Fearfulness and nervousness

▶   Low self-esteem

▶   Anger

▶   Helplessness and guilt

▶   Stress

▶   Insecurity

▶   Secrecy and shame

▶   Depression

▶   Imitation of violent and abusive behaviour.

Strategies for Change
Any attempt to reduce the incidence of domestic violence must address gender issues and power imbalance in society. On a practical level there needs to be a safe place where victims can escape to with their children, and they also need to be able to obtain counselling and support. In Ireland family accommodation in refuges has risen marginally from 90 rooms in 1998 to 93 in 2002 in 17 refuges countrywide. These are always stretched to the limit.

To adequately meet the need, one refuge place per 10,000 population is recommended (that would mean 300–400 refuge places in Ireland). There is also a need for an integrated and combined effort on the part of all the services and agencies involved.

Agencies involved:

▶   **Department of Justice, Equality and Law Reform/Gardaí**: A Woman and Child Unit has been established in Harcourt Street Garda Station, Dublin to deal specifically with violence against women and children. Special training for Garda personnel is now also provided.

▸ **Department of the Environment and Local Government**: There is some provision of emergency accommodation but not nearly enough to meet the need. This results in families staying in refuges and hostels much longer than is necessary.

▸ **Department of Social and Family Affairs**: Financial assistance and social services are available; separate and emergency payments can be arranged fairly promptly.

▸ **Department of Health and Children**: Accident and Emergency Department Personnel and GPs are more aware of the implications of domestic violence.

The **Domestic Violence Act 1996** has gone some way to providing increasing protection for adults and children who experience violence. The main provisions of the Act are as follows:

▸ The law has been extended to cover any adult with whom the person shares residence, not just the spouse.

▸ Power has been given to the Health Boards to apply for protection on behalf of a person.

▸ Persons who break the law can now be arrested without a warrant. This is a vast improvement on the 1981 Act, which left the onus on the victim to report and to follow-up.

Under the 1996 Act, four types of court order could be obtained to protect a spouse, partner, dependent child or persons in other domestic relationships.

Safety Order — prevents the person from using or threatening to use violence against the applicant, or molesting or frightening her. If they live in the same house, the respondent (the defendant in law) does not have to leave. It is effective for five years.

Protection Order — has the same effect as a safety order. It is an interim order which is effective until a decision on another order can be made.

The **Interim Barring Order** and **Barring Order** which required the respondant to leave home but which did not necessitate hearing any evidence from the person against whom the order was being made was deemed unconstitutional by the Supreme Court in October 2002. Legislation in this regard will have to be redrafted.

Application by Health Boards

The Domestic Violence Act 1996 empowers Health Board personnel to apply for an order to protect a person of any age if they believe that person to be in danger and unable to pursue an application for a barring or safety order, perhaps because of fear.

ACTIVITY

Aim: To reflect on the extent and nature of domestic violence

BREAKING SILENCE ON SONS' VIOLENCE:
The Domestic Violence Act allowed parents for the first time to take a barring, protection or safety order against their adult children who lived with them. A barring order can be used to exclude violent children from the family home, while a safety order allows them to remain there, but prevents them from threatening or using violence against their mother. The law, which was widened to include cohabitees and people in same-sex relationships, does not, however, include children under 18. About 170 of the 2,145 barring orders granted in the year ending last July were to parents, according to provisional figures from the Department of Justice.

(*The Irish Times*, 1 May 1998)

Discuss:
What are the usual assumptions when we refer to domestic violence?
Who else besides spouses, according to this article, might inflict violence?
Why do you think a child might use violence against his/her parent?

SUMMARY

▶ The Constitution lays down the fundamental rules and principles by which Ireland is governed.

▶ The government provides central services and makes laws. Local government enacts bye-laws and provides local services.

▶ Marriage breakdown has serious consequences for all children and the marriage laws reflect this, both in the marriage regulations themselves and in the divorce regulations.

▶ Whether parents are married or unmarried the law is designed to protect the best interests of the child and to ensure that all children are treated equally.

▶ Domestic violence is a serious problem in our society and the legislation recognises that violence is inflicted by others apart from spouses.

12
CHILD PROTECTION

Introduction

Increasing concern about child protection is rooted in profound changes in Irish society. In the past, abuse and neglect of some children were often accepted as hard facts of life. More recently, the idea that children have a fundamental right to protection, whether there is obvious risk of abuse or not, has grown and is now reflected in the Child Care Act 1991 and in *Children First: The National Guidelines for the Protection and Welfare of Children 1999* (hereafter referred to as 'The National Guidelines'). This chapter aims to familiarise early childhood workers with the issues and the procedures involved in child protection.

The Child Care Act 1991

The Child Care Act 1991 has affirmed children's rights and needs and the concept of 'the best interests of the child'. The enshrinement in the Act of the principle that parental responsibilities are at least as important as parental rights points to a significant shift in focus in terms of child protection.

The Act has now been implemented in full and it is generally accepted that the basic needs of children should be met. In medical terms this acceptance of the need to protect as well as cure has long been accepted; out of this acceptance has grown protective programmes such as ante-natal care programmes and vaccination programmes. Great efforts are made on a daily basis to protect children from all sorts of dangers. No-one waits until a child has been burned by fire or run down by a car to teach him about fires or road safety.

Historical Perspective

Under the Provisions of the Poor Law Acts 1834 children in Ireland were rescued from utter starvation or from moral degradation (particularly if mothers were unmarried). Under this law the help offered to children and families who were in need was minimal and the aim of the administration was to deter people from seeking benefit because it was a soft option. There was also the concept of the 'deserving' poor; in short this meant that when people's needs were being assessed part of that assessment was about whether they had brought the hardship on themselves through laziness or lack of morals. If they were considered to be undeserving then they did not receive help. Children who were mistreated by parents were often considered undeserving because they must have deserved the punishment! If parents were considered to be undeserving, as unmarried mothers were, then their children would suffer the same judgment. Such harsh conditions and negative attitudes persisted in Ireland until well into the second half of the twentieth century.

It is not so long ago since it was often accepted in Ireland that it was necessary to literally beat the badness out of children. In law, children were the property of their parents, particularly the father, so parents could decide in what manner they would treat their children.

Change began toward the end of the nineteenth century. In 1874, a scandal culminated in the setting up of the New York Society for the Prevention of Cruelty to Children. (The NSPCC in Britain and the ISPCC in Ireland are direct descendants.) Mary Ellen was an adopted child who was severely ill-treated, abused and neglected. Neighbours were concerned but there was little that could be done because the parents 'owned' her; that is until an enlightened lawyer decided to take a case against the parents under the laws relating to the ill-treatment of animals; he won the case.

Soon the NSPCC in Britain was established and through their campaigning, attitudes to child abuse and child protection slowly began to change. In Ireland during the early part of the twentieth century, most child protection work was carried out by ISPCC officers and most residential care facilities for children were run by religious orders.

Child Abuse and Protection

1908 — The Children's Act (Britain and Ireland) was enacted. This was the principal legislation governing child protection until 1991.

1937 — The Irish Constitution was written and strongly upheld parental rights. The 'inalienable and imprescriptible rights' in Article 1.1 led to an extreme reluctance of the State to interfere in family affairs, even to the extent of being unwilling to promote family welfare.

1968 — Drs Kempe and Kempe coined the term 'Battered Baby Syndrome' to describe babies and young children who presented repeatedly for medical attention with non-accidental injuries.

1970 — The Health Boards were established and given responsibility for some children's affairs. Most services established under the Department of Health were reactive in nature, i.e. they reacted to issues and controversial cases of abuse rather than actively promoting child welfare and protection.

1970s and 1980s — A number of tragedies and child murders in Britain at the hands of parents/carers gave rise to a lot of concern and publicity. Public enquiries and policy appraisals led to changes in practices.

Ireland had its own well-publicised tragedies which came to light much later. Some of the more prominent ones listed below related to abuse that had been on-going for decades.

1990s

1992 — The X Case. Controversy continues to reverberate in debates around protection of the unborn.

1993 — The Kilkenny Incest Case and its subsequent investigation gave impetus to significant improvements in child protection services.

1994 — The Kelly Fitzgerald tragedy brought to light the shortcomings in communications between departments and personnel.

1993-6 — Madonna House, Goldenbridge Orphanage and Trudder House were the forerunners in bringing to light extensive abuse, collusion and cover-ups of child abuse in childcare institutions.

1994 to present — Cases of abuse of children by members of the Roman Catholic clergy and religious orders, with yet more collusion and cover-ups, are still coming to light.

1998 — McColgan v. North Western Health Board set a precedent because a survivor of abuse successfully sued the Health Board for neglect of its duty to protect her.

While tragedies and enquiries pushed policy-makers into action, other influences were probably also at play. Civil rights and human rights were brought to people's attention across America, Britain, Europe and Ireland in the late 1960s/early 1970s. The feminist movement and women took some of the darker issues from behind closed doors. Certainly the growing ability and freedom of women to speak out about physical and sexual violence within marriage had a direct bearing on the exposure of child abuse in all its forms.

Although the Child Care Act was passed in 1991 it was slow to be implemented because the necessary resources and machinery needed to be put in place. *The Report of the Kilkenny Incest Investigation* published in 1993 resulted in the allocation of funds for the implementation of the Act. The child protection provisions of the Act were implemented by the end of 1995, but difficulties remain in relation to scarcity of resources and how they are deployed.

Incidence of Abuse

Table 12.1: Child Abuse Statistics

	1992	1993	1994	1995	1986	1997	1998	1999
Reported	3,812	4,110	5,152	6,415	7,732	7,312	9,649	10,031
Confirmed	1,701	1,609	1,868	2,276	2,279	2,659	3,367	3,318
Confirmed cases as % of reported cases	45%	40%	36%	35%	29%	36%	35%	33%

Source: Department of Health Boards various reports.

The question of whether child abuse is more prevalent now than in the past is a difficult one to answer. Definitions of abuse have changed over time and there are variations in definitions between different countries today. Definitions in their turn have an effect on record-keeping and therefore on statistics and how they might be interpreted. If the present-day definition that beating children in school amounts to child abuse, then according to this definition it was rampant in Ireland prior to the change which outlawed corporal punishment in schools in 1982. However, records of child abuse in schools would show that it hardly existed at all.

Additionally there was little openness surrounding the whole topic of abuse so that even those who were being abused, according to the legal definitions of the time, had little chance of being heard or of having the courage to speak out.

Organisations and resources have now been established to deal with the whole area of abuse and to facilitate people who want to get help for themselves or for others. The

National Guidelines set out clearly and in detail what action is required when abuse is suspected or uncovered. **Childline** was set up by the ISPCC with the specific purpose of providing a freephone service to children who wished to talk about their situations. The media, while being sensationalist at times, have also played their part in the broadcasting and publication of material in relation to child abuse.

There is no doubt that, today, more cases of abuse are being reported and dealt with by the courts; more people who are being abused, or at risk of being abused, are receiving help. Child abuse statistics (in Table 12.1) show that the number of cases that have been reported to the Health Boards have more than doubled between 1992 and 1999. There has also been an increase in the number of cases that have been confirmed although the percentage of cases being confirmed has fallen from 45% of reported cases in 1992 down to 33% of those reported in 1999.

Definitions of Child Abuse

Different types of abuse are defined separately below but in reality they are less easy to separate. Where a child is being physically abused within a family, that child is also being emotionally abused. Likewise a child who is experiencing sexual abuse is being emotionally abused and physically abused. The following definitions are those set out in The National Guidelines 1999.

Physical abuse is any form of non-accidental injury, or injury which results from wilful or neglectful failure to protect a child. Examples include shaking, hitting, punching, use of excessive force, poisoning, suffocating, allowing or creating substantial risk of significant harm to the child and Munchausen's Syndrome by Proxy.

Emotional abuse is normally to be found in the relationship between a caregiver and a child rather than in a specific event or pattern of events. It occurs when a child's needs for affection, approval, consistency and security are not met. Examples would include persistent criticism, sarcasm, hostility, conditional parenting, unresponsiveness, inconsistency, unrealistic expectations, under- and over-protection, or rejection of the child.

Neglect is normally defined in terms of an omission, where a child suffers significant harm or impairment of development by being deprived of food, clothing, warmth, hygiene, intellectual stimulation, supervision and safety, attachment to and affection from adults, or medical care.

Sexual abuse occurs when a child is used by another person for his or her gratification or sexual arousal, or for that of others, e.g. masturbation or exposure in the presence of a child, inappropriate touching, intercourse, sexual exploitation as in the taking of photographs for sexual gratification purposes.

Signs and Indicators of Abuse

Indicators of Physical Abuse

Physical

▶ Bruising in areas where bruises are not readily sustained, i.e. soft tissue areas (see Figure 12.1, page 216)

▶ Explanations for injuries where the explanation is not consistent with the injury

▶ Facial bruising

▶ Hand or finger marks/pressure bruises

▶ Bite marks

▶ Burns (especially cigarette), scalds

▶ Unexplained and frequent fractures

▶ Frequent and severe lacerations and abrasions

▶ Failure to thrive.

Behavioural

▶ Fearful and shying away from physical contact

▶ Frozen watchfulness

▶ Withdrawn or aggressive behaviour

▶ Sudden changes in behaviour.

Indicators of Emotional Abuse

Behavioural

▶ Attention-seeking behaviour

▶ Withdrawn or aggressive behaviour

▶ Telling frequent lies

▶ Inability to have fun

▶ Low self-esteem

▶ Tantrums — beyond normal developmental age for same

▶ Speech disorders, particularly stammering

▶ Indiscriminately affectionate.

Indicators of Child Neglect

Physical

▶   Poor hygiene

▶   Inadequate, dirty, torn or inappropriate clothing

▶   Untreated medical problems

▶   Poor nourishment/failure to thrive

▶   Emaciation

▶   Being left at home alone.

Behavioural

▶   Tiredness/listlessness.

▶   Low self-esteem.

▶   Inability to concentrate or be involved.

▶   Always hungry.

Indicators of Sexual Abuse

Physical

▶   Bruises and scratches to genital area

▶   Soreness when walking, sitting, going to the toilet

▶   Pain or itching

▶   Sexually transmitted diseases

▶   Torn and stained underclothes

▶   Bedwetting, sleep disturbances

▶   Loss of appetite.

Behavioural

▶   Hints of sexual activity through words, drawings or play

▶   Sexually precocious behaviour

▶   Use of sexually explicit language

▶   Preoccupation with sexual matters

▶   Informed knowledge of adult sexual behaviour

▶   Low self-esteem

▶   Withdrawn or isolated from other children.

(These indicators are not exhaustive.)

Figure 12.1: Bruising on Soft Tissues Areas

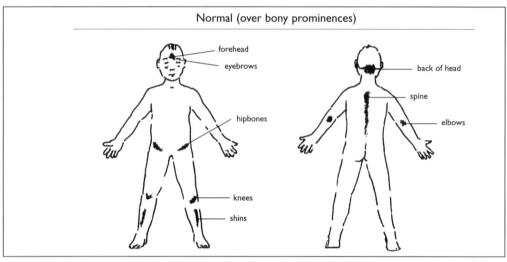

Normal (over bony prominences)

forehead
eyebrows
back of head
spine
hipbones
elbows
knees
shins

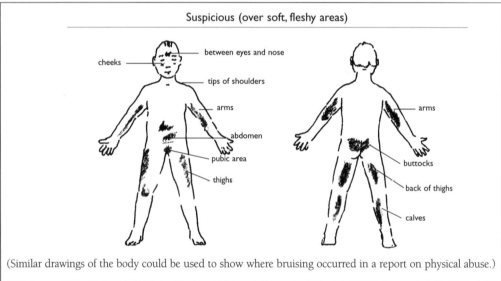

Suspicious (over soft, fleshy areas)

cheeks
between eyes and nose
tips of shoulders
arms
arms
abdomen
pubic area
buttocks
thighs
back of thighs
calves

(Similar drawings of the body could be used to show where bruising occurred in a report on physical abuse.)

It is important not to jump to conclusions: a burn may be caused by a genuine accident; a sudden change in behaviour could be because an elderly relative who requires a lot of care has moved in with the family. Mongolian blue spots which resemble a series of bruises appear naturally on the back and buttocks of some black babies. Circular bruising may be the result of 'cupping', a Chinese medical treatment.

Predisposing Factors

Some factors have been found consistently (predictive indicators) in family characteristics and/or circumstances where abuse has occurred. However, the same factors can also be found in families where there is no abuse — so predictive indicators of child abuse must be used with **extreme caution**. Statistics of child abuse show that child abuse occurs in all social classes and they also show that the people most likely to abuse children are parents, partners of parents who are not the child's natural parent, relatives and neighbours, in that order.

Parental Factors Associated with Child Abuse

Parents who Were Abused Themselves

A combination of factors are at work here, for example:

▸ Cultural — 'It didn't do me any harm so it won't do my children any harm'.

▸ Past experience — Love and violence are confused because of the parent's own experiences of being abused by parents/carers.

▸ Poor role models for the parents — parents do not know other ways of disciplining and controlling their children because this is how their parents did it.

▸ Low self-esteem — parents may be emotionally damaged and inadequate.

▸ Parents may be unable to control themselves.

▸ Parents may be unable to respond with warmth and affection.

▸ Parents may demand affection from their children in order to fulfil their own needs.

Very Young Parents

▸ Emotionally immature parents may not be able to cope with the physical and emotional demands of a young baby.

▸ There may be conflict between their own needs and the needs of their child.

▸ There may be a lack of support, or negative reactions from their own parents.

▸ There may be an inability to recognise the needs of a baby/young child because of youth and inexperience.

▸ There may be resentment of a baby where there is a new and growing relationship between parents.

▸ The reality of caring for a baby does not fit in with the 'dream' that is reinforced by society, e.g. that babies bring happiness, smiles, fulfilment and that parents are never tired, frustrated or worn out with anxiety and worry.

Parents who Expect too much of their Children

▸ Approval and love are conditional on good behaviour and positive achievements.

▸ Skills and behaviour are expected from a child that are way beyond the child's age and stage of development.

▸ A child who fails to match up to expectations is seen by parents as bold, lazy or resistant.

Parents who Abuse Substances

▸ Alcohol is often associated with violence; the adult may be predisposed to violent actions and reactions.

▸ Abuse of other substances is more often associated with neglect where money is spent on substances/drugs rather than on basic necessities such as food, clothing and heating. Abuse of substances may also lead to a general lack of responsiveness (inertia) on the part of the adult to the children and their needs.

Parents who are Under Stress

▸ Parents may be overwhelmed by any problem such as debt, grief, trauma or fear, the demands of a child may elicit an unreasonable response.

▸ Parents may blame the child partially or wholly for the stress.

▸ Parents may simply 'forget' to feed, clothe or show affection to the child — such is the level of their stress.

The reason for a person's stress may not be obvious to an outsider. It is important to remember that what is extremely stressful for one person may only constitute a minor problem for another. **We must never judge the actions or reactions of another according to our own abilities to deal with stressful situations.**

Parents who Suffer from Psychiatric Illness/Mental Health Problems

▸ Mood swings and unpredictable and bizarre behaviour patterns can be very distressful and traumatic for children.

▸ Depression in a parent can lead to a total neglect of children and a total inability to respond to a child's needs.

▸ Post-natal depression can disrupt the bonding process and the mother's response to her baby in the early weeks and months.

Child Factors Associated with Child Abuse

Children in the Age Range 1-4 Years

▸ It is during this period that children are at their most demanding in terms of the individual attention which they need. The novelty of a new baby has worn off and besides a baby who has literally found its feet is much more demanding than one who has no option but to lie in the cot. At this period, the child is also beginning to assert his independence and individuality.

Children who are Perceived as Being 'Difficult'

▸ Disruption to the early bonding and attachment process between mother and infant; where the bonds of attachment have been weakened the care of the child may be perceived as being very difficult

▸ Children who are difficult to feed

▸ Children who are difficult to comfort; a baby who cries a lot

▸ Children who are born prematurely may have a combination of all of the above. Such situations may lead to overwhelming stress for the parent. Additionally when children are difficult to feed or comfort, parents may feel a sense of failure.

Children who are 'Different'

▸ A child who does not live up to the parents' expectations

▸ A child who is not the sex that the parents had hoped for

▸ A child who has a disability.

A child may be perceived by parents to be different without this being obvious to others; in these situations it is the perception that is significant rather than the reality. Basically these are situations where the parent has rejected the child.

The above factors may contribute to our understanding of child abuse and abusive situations but many people who lack resources and cope with highly stressful situations and/or extremely demanding children would never resort to abuse. On the other hand, abuse can and does occur in families and to individuals who would seem on the surface to have no difficulties at all. Child abuse occurs in all social classes.

An Outline of Action in the Case of Suspected Child Abuse

(Before reading the following please study Figure 12.2 on pages 220–1.) The early childhood worker will be directly involved up to the decision to inform the Health Board and may be involved in discussions, case conferences and a court hearing if one takes place.

A student who is on placement should discuss his concerns with his supervisor and tutor. He will probably not be involved beyond this.

Figure 12.2: Child Protection Assessment/Investigation Process

PHASE ONE	**ALLEGATION OF CHILD ABUSE** ↓ **REFERRAL TO HEALTH BOARD SOCIAL WORK DEPARTMENT** ↓ **SOCIAL WORKER CONSULTS RECORDS & MAKES INITIAL ENQUIRIES** (both internal and external enquiries) ↓ **SOCIAL WORKER CONSULTS WITH LINE MANAGER** (Team Leader or Senior Social Worker) Matters to be considered at this point include: • Co-ordination of information • Contact and discussion with child and parents/carers • Contact with person who first reported concern • Assessment of risk and protective factors* • Emergency action/reception into care • Medical examination • Referral to services, including support services for children and families • Immediate intervention • Further information gathering • No further action • Feedback to reporters
PHASE TWO	**NOTIFICATION TO CHILD CARE MANAGER** Options to be considered at this point include the following

Notification to An Garda Síochána	Strategy meeting Consult with:	*Health Board Assessment*
• Garda investigation • Key interviews and review • Prepare file for Director of Public Prosecutions (DPP) • DPP reviews file • DPP decision due	• Family • Team Leader/Senior Social Worker • Child Care Manager • Legal advisor • An Garda Síochána-Health Board Liaison Team Assess risks and protective factors: • medical input • legal input • psychosocial input	• Assessment by health board social worker or other professional • Placement on Child Protection Notification System • Referral to other specialist assessment teams • Ongoing contact with child and parents/carers • Continued liaison with relevant professionals • Emergency action/court; reception into care • Record everything

PHASE THREE	CHILDREN PROTECTION CONFERENCE
	• Further evaluation of risk • Negotiation of a comprehensive inter-agency child protection plan between professionals and family • Allocation of tasks • Treatment intervention • Review of progress **CHILD PROTECTION REVIEW**

*	If it appears that a Garda investigation may be likely, consultation should be held with An Garda Síochána at this stage.

The Law — Orders, Terms and Roles

Orders and Terms

Emergency Care Order

An Emergency Care Order is an order which authorises the placement of a child in the care of the Health Board in cases where there is reasonable cause to believe that a child will suffer significant harm if not removed immediately from his place of residence. An order may also be made if the child is likely to be removed from the present situation placing him at risk, e.g. if a child is in hospital and might be at serious risk if returned home.

The Gardaí, without a warrant, may remove a child to safety where they consider the child's health or welfare to be at risk.

Interim Order

An Interim Order maintains a child in the care of the Health Board until an application for a Care Order has been processed and a decision made.

Supervision Order

A Supervision Order authorises the local Health Board to have a child's health and welfare checked out and supervised, where there is reasonable grounds for believing that the child is at risk.

Care Order

A Care Order places a child under the care of the local Health Board. The Health Board takes over the rights and the responsibilities of the parents and has legal responsibility to look after the health and welfare of the child.

SCENARIO

Sean aged 4 yrs and his sister Maria aged 2 yrs attend an early childhood service. It is Friday at around 6.15 p.m. You and another member of staff are in the centre with these two children, waiting for them to be collected. Their parents, prominent people in the community, arrive to collect their children and both are visibly drunk.

Write down in about 200 words a sequence to this scenario outlining what might happen.

Checklist
In your sequence consider the following:

▶   What might be the children's reactions?

▶   What might be the parents' reactions?

▶   What might you be feeling?

▶   What would be the correct procedure to follow in this situation?

Duties and Roles in Relation to Child Protection ▶

Role of the Early Childhood Worker

▶   To provide care and stimulation to each child according to each child's needs

▶   To monitor the overall progress of each child

▶   To maintain regular, accurate, impartial, dated and signed records of each child's progress. Observations are particularly useful in this area

▶   To maintain a close but professional relationship with parents/carers

▶   To be aware of signs and symptoms of abuse in all its forms

▶   To keep the best interests of the child in mind at all times

▶   In times of doubt to be prepared to err on the side of caution.

Role of the Manager/Director of the Early Years Setting

▶   To ensure that professional standards are maintained

▶   To ensure that records of all notes, logs and correspondence are dated, signed and maintained

▶   To be aware of procedures to be followed in the case of suspected abuse

▶   To liaise with the Health Boards and any other relevant personnel

▶   To provide support and in-service training for staff

▸ To be prepared to take action in the case of suspected abuse

▸ To provide direct support and counselling for any staff member involved in an ongoing case.

Role of the Health Board Social Worker

▸ To investigate reports of child abuse

▸ To assess the risk involved and what action, if any, is required to be taken

▸ To keep relevant authorities informed of developments in the case

▸ To liaise with all relevant personnel, i.e. Gardaí, medical and referring personnel

▸ To maintain supportive and ongoing contact with parents

▸ To form a relationship with the child and to maintain supportive contact

▸ To provide reports for case conferences and court hearings.

Role of the Gardaí

▸ To investigate whether a crime has been committed

▸ To institute criminal proceedings against alleged abusers

▸ To provide back-up support for social workers, doctors etc. if their investigations are being hampered or resisted

▸ To remove a child/children from immediate harm under Section Twelve of the Act if the need arises

▸ To participate in strategy meetings, case conference and reviews.

The Role of the Child Care Manager

▸ To take ultimate responsibility for the care and protection of all children in his area

▸ To convene and chair the Child Protection Case Conference at which decisions about particular children are made

▸ To negotiate a Child Protection Plan involving all key people including parents/carers

▸ To ensure that decisions are followed through and that Child Protection Reviews take place

▸ To establish and maintain the Child Protection Notification System.

The Child Protection Notification System

This is managed and maintained by the childcare manager. A child's name may be submitted for notification following a preliminary assessment where abuse is suspected or where it has actually happened. It should be constantly updated. There should be 24-hour access to the system; individual Health Boards should have agreed on who may have access to the system and also set up procedures for identifying these people.

The Case Conference

The case conference brings together any professionals who have been involved and who have relevant information to share. It may include all or some of the above in addition to specialists, legal representatives and, increasingly, the family itself. The aim of the conference is to make decisions and draw up a Child Protection Plan.

The Guardian Ad Litem

The *guardian ad litem* is appointed by the court to look after the best interests of the child in difficult cases. The *guardian ad litem* does not necessarily have any relationship with the child but will read all files and case notes and provide an independent opinion for the judge as to what might best serve the interests of the child in the case.

Case History

Surname:	Murphy	
Mother's Name:	Sarah	Age: 21yrs
Father's Name:	Thomas	Age: 24yrs
Children:	Joseph	Age: 4yrs
	Annie	Age: 2yrs 6 mths
	Stephen	Age: 15 mths

Income: Social welfare
Sarah's part-time job
(3hours x 3 days cleaning)

Accommodation: Privately rented two-bedroom fourth-floor flat. Toilet and bathroom facilities are shared with other tenants.

Other relevant factors: Sarah and Thomas are no longer in a relationship and Sarah now shares her life with a new partner, Mark who is also 21 years old. Mark has been accused of child abuse in the past but a case has never been proved. He looks after the children on the three evenings on which Sarah works. The children's father maintains contact with the children whenever he can; this is neither regular nor often. Stephen is not thriving very well and is a poor feeder and poor sleeper.

List what you consider to be the risks to:

▸ the welfare of the family as a whole

▸ each individual child.

If this family lived in your area:

▸ list the support and services which could be offered to them in order to reduce the risk of breakdown and/or abuse

▸ outline the approach which should be taken by an Early Childhood Centre if these children were admitted.

The Role of the Early Childhood Worker Where Abuse is Suspected

▸ Keep meticulous records at all times; these records must be dated and signed.

▸ Record only facts and direct observations; hearsay and hunches will not be admitted as evidence in a court of law.

▸ Discuss concerns with senior staff/experienced colleagues.

▸ Interview the parents/guardians regarding those concerns unless there is reason to believe that this would place the child at further risk. The supervisor or manager may prefer to do this either with, or without, the member of staff being present. It is important for early childhood workers to be aware that the source of the allegation will be revealed to the parents/guardians. If the case comes to court the person who discovered the abuse will have to give evidence. It is almost impossible for the authorities to investigate, pursue and prove cases of abuse when those who have the evidence are not willing to be identified.

▸ Refer to the local childcare manager/social work team.

If there is direct evidence of abuse, or if a child or someone else discloses facts of abuse to the early childhood worker:

▸ don't panic; remain calm

▸ reassure the child/person that he was right to tell

▸ give the child time and opportunity to say what he has to say. He may not do this all at once

▸ avoid shock/horror responses

▶ explain to the child what action will be taken — keep it simple

▶ report the matter to the person in charge

▶ the person in charge should report the matter to the local childcare team/Gardaí.

Remember:

▶ Leave verification and examinations to those who are professionally trained in the area.

   When physical injury or sexual abuse has occurred the child will be subjected to at least one physical examination, whether you have tried to look for evidence or not. It is good, professional practice to keep intrusion, questioning and stressful situations to a minimum.

▶ Do not offer false reassurance.

   'I will make sure that everything will be all right now.' 'I will never let anyone hurt you again.' (These are examples of promises that nobody can ever guarantee.)

▶ Do not promise to keep secrets.

   In this way you will not find yourself in a situation of being unable to obtain help for a person unless you break your promise. You can reassure him that you will not do anything without his knowing or without discussing it with him first.

▶ Avoid 'guilt-creating'/blaming responses.

   Questioning why the person did not act in a particular way, e.g. run away, shout, or tell sooner. Making suggestions as to how he could have acted is of little use after something has happened and only serves to help the person feel that somehow he was partially to blame. Survivors are too ready to blame themselves anyway without your help.

▶ Avoid telling the person how to feel.

   Horrified responses are often difficult to suppress but such responses are telling the other person what you think he should have felt — 'Oh, how horrible.' 'You must feel terrible.' 'What a monster!'

   A child may feel confused, hurt, betrayed and indeed terrible but you should enable him to express his feelings rather than putting words into his mouth.

Your expertise lies in the area of being able to communicate with and comfort the child. You can provide an environment which will support the child at such a difficult time. You will be able to explain or interpret what is going on in a way that the child can understand because you will be familiar with his level of functioning, his understanding and his vocabulary.

Record as soon as possible, and in the child's exact words if you can, what has been said.

Supporting the Early Childhood Worker

Only about a third of cases which are reported result in court cases and care proceedings, (see child abuse statistics in Table 12.1). For the most part, children who are at risk continue to attend their local schools and early years services. On the surface, it may seem that very few changes occur as a result of making a report, but the worker must continue to work with the child and family. If professionalism and impartiality are maintained at all times and the 'bests interests of the child' are always kept in mind then it will be possible to re-establish working relationships with the parent, which may have suffered because of the abuse allegations being made by the early years worker.

For the person working directly with children and parents the stress and anxiety which is provoked in situations where abuse occurs cannot and should not be underestimated. If this person does not take action a child may suffer further abuse, and if he does take action he should receive adequate support from colleagues, management and other professionals.

Allegations of Abuse Against Early Childhood Workers

When allegations of abuse are made against staff it can be a very traumatic time for all those involved. Nevertheless, it is equally important that the procedures which are in place for dealing with allegations of abuse by any adult are also adhered to in relation to allegations against staff. If the allegations are serious then the worker will be suspended pending investigation. In the case of an allegation against a staff member there is even more need for support for the staff of the setting. The reasons for such support include the following:

▶ When abuse involves an outsider there will probably be one or maybe two children involved; if abuse occurs within the setting there may be several children involved.

▶ The staff member involved may be well known or may even be a friend.

▶ Guilt feelings and feelings of anger may be very strong.

Because of the increased awareness of child abuse generally, people, especially men, who work with young children are often fearful that they will be wrongly accused and this will damage them irreparably even if the allegations are not true. If workers adhere strictly to principles of good practice then this is most unlikely to happen and the worker, if accused, will have the confidence that he has done nothing wrong.

Poor professional practices such as shouting at children, ridiculing them or imposing extreme 'time out' should be dealt with through supervision, and the member of staff should be helped through extra training and support to enable him to develop appropriate practices. Bad practice should never be condoned for any reason.

Principles for Best Practice in Child Protection

The following principles should inform best practice in child protection:

▸ The welfare of the child is of paramount importance.

▸ A balance must be struck between protecting children and respecting the rights and needs of parents/carers and families, but the child's welfare must come first.

▸ Children have a right to be taken seriously.

▸ Children should be consulted and involved in relation to all matters and decisions that affect them, taking into account their age and stage of development.

▸ Early intervention and support should be made available to children and families in order to minimise risk.

▸ Parents and carers have a right to respect and to be consulted about matters which affect their families.

▸ Actions taken to protect a child should not be intrusive and should minimise distress.

▸ Intervention should not deal with the child in isolation. The child has to be seen in a family context.

▸ The criminal dimension which may be involved must be acknowledged.

▸ Children should only be separated from their parents and family when all other possibilities have been exhausted. Reunion with families from whom children have been separated should always be a consideration.

▸ Effective prevention, detection and treatment of child abuse require a co-ordinated multidisciplinary approach.

▸ Any intervention should take account of diversity in families and lifestyles.

▸ Training for effective child protection should be mandatory in all establishments which care for children.

▸ Roles and responsibilities should be clearly defined and understood within organisations and services for children.

(Adapted from *Guidelines for the Protection of Children in Early Childhood Services*, 2000, Barnardos et al.)

Empowering the Child

The encouragement and promotion of healthy social and emotional development is vital for the well-being of all children whatever their circumstances. Promoting confidence and independence and a sense of self-worth in children may help them to tell about some abusive situation or to avoid it altogether. Although it is essential that children learn some skills of self-protection it is important to keep in mind that this in no way exonerates the adult from the responsibility of protecting them. Children cannot be expected to protect themselves and there is no conclusive research showing that children who have avoided abuse did so because they had any particular skills. Being skilled in any, or all, of the areas mentioned below gives children a greater feeling of control and perhaps assertiveness; research seems to indicate that in the area of sexual abuse it is often, although by no means always, the timid, unsure child who is targeted.

The ability of children to cope in different situations is greatly enhanced if they have been helped to:

▶   increase their self-awareness

▶   build up self-esteem

▶   develop an ability to express themselves (language skills)

▶   take control where it is age and stage appropriate

▶   cope with the unexpected

▶   identify their champions/people who will stand up for them

▶   develop problem-solving skills.

ACTIVITY

Aim: To clarify ways in which the early years worker can help to empower children

Form small groups.
▶   Review the role of the adult/carer in promoting all-round, healthy, social and emotional development.
▶   Plan a range of activities for children of different ages, which would help them to master some of the skills listed above. Different groups could focus on different age groups and feed back to the whole group.

Example of Activity: 'What if' games — 'What if you fell and hurt your knee? This type of activity will help children to learn problem-solving skills and to cope with the unexpected.

continued overleaf

When working with children **do not** focus on abusive or dangerous situations since children will learn more easily from situations that are familiar to them.

Checklist

In the activities above include some that cover the fact that **children need to know how**:

▶ to be safe

▶ to protect their own bodies

▶ to say 'no'

▶ to get help

▶ to tell

▶ to be believed

▶ not to keep secrets

▶ to refuse touches

▶ to cope with strangers

▶ to break rules.

Services for Abused Children

The main services provided fall into the following broad categories:

▶ Prevention

▶ Support

▶ Investigation

▶ Therapy.

Prevention and Support

The role of the adult in early childhood services in support and prevention has already been outlined and must be emphasised. The legal or statutory responsibility of supporting children and families who are at risk and in the prevention of abuse lies with the Health Boards and childcare managers.

Under the Child Care Act 1991 the Health Boards have a duty:

▶ to provide for children in need

▶ to prevent ill-treatment and neglect

▶ to promote the welfare of all children.

The services of the Health Board are outlined in more detail in Chapter 14. The following services are particularly relevant in the area of child protection: domiciliary support, accommodation, day care, family centres.

Investigation

The statutory/legal duty to investigate cases of reported abuse lies with the Health Board and the procedure has been outlined earlier in the chapter. In addition to the work of the social worker, other specialists in the area of psychology and paediatrics may be involved in establishing the nature and extent of the abuse both physically and mentally. Specialist units in the children's hospitals — Crumlin, Temple Street and Tallaght (all in Dublin) — deal with the investigation and treatment of child sexual abuse.

Therapy

Depending on the nature and the extent of the abuse there are many specialists who can help children and families to overcome the trauma of abuse. Social workers and psychologists will provide support and counselling. Qualified play therapists may help children deal with their difficulties through play. A psychiatrist may be involved if there are severe psychiatric difficulties. A family therapist may work with the whole family to help restore healthy family relationships. As indicated earlier, for the vast majority of pre-school children the best therapy will be to remain in the early childhood service which is familiar to the child and the family — indeed in some areas there may not be any other options. When this happens it is important that the early childhood worker liaises closely with any specialist therapist. It is equally important that the worker recognises the effects of stress and trauma on children and is able to provide the appropriate support, care, attention, stimulation and environment.

Every child is an individual with a distinct personality and therefore reactions to abuse will vary from child to child. Children may become aggressive and anti-social (fight) or they may become withdrawn, timid and sad (flight). Certainly the child's sense of himself as a worthy human being is damaged as is his ability to form relationships, because abuse has meant that his trust in adults has been betrayed both by the adults who abused him as well as by all the adults around who did nothing to protect him.

In general, children who are troubled are difficult rather than easy to work with; the anger of one or the unresponsiveness of another may try the patience of the most professional of workers. Children who are severely damaged may need specialist therapeutic help but this will not be of great benefit unless the child also has contact with caring, consistent adults on a daily basis.

The overriding need of troubled children is the need for their self-image and self-respect to be restored. This may take a long time.

Although the Health Boards have the ultimate statutory responsibility, voluntary agencies also play a big part in the area of child protection throughout Ireland. Barnardos Child and Family Services and the Irish Society for the Prevention of Cruelty to Children (ISPCC) are the two main national organisations who work in the area of child support and protection (see Chapter 14).

 TASK

Aim: To become familiar with child support and protection services in your area. Services and facilities vary greatly from place to place and from Health Board to Health Board.

▸ What are the child support and protection services provided by your local (a) Health Board, and (b) voluntary agencies?

▸ Do you have child protection policies and procedures in your place of work? Are they written?

▸ What is the name of the senior social worker responsible for child protection services in your area?

SUMMARY

▸ The definition and understanding of child abuse and protection has changed over time and it is only since the 1970s that laws, procedures and policies for dealing with child abuse have been developed.

▸ Research indicates that some factors predispose persons toward abuse but these must be used with **extreme caution**; it is most important never to make assumptions or to jump to conclusions.

▸ Good professional practice includes being aware of signs of abuse, drawing up policies and procedures and following these in all cases of suspected abuse whether allegations are against unknown adults, family members or staff.

▸ All early childhood workers should be familiar with The National Guidelines for the Protection and Welfare of Children

▸ The early childhood worker must be aware of the needs of all children and strive to empower them generally. When children have been abused the worker must take their additional needs into account, especially their damaged self-esteem and the fact that their trust in adults has been betrayed.

> ▶ Ultimate responsibility for child welfare, child protection and investigation lies with the Health Board but voluntary agencies also provide important services in the area. It is important to be familiar with the local services.

References

Department of Health and Children, 1999, *Children First: The National Guidelines for the Protection and Welfare of Children,* Dublin: Stationery Office

Barnardos, 2000, *Guidelines for the Protection of Children in Early Years Services*, An Comhchoiste Réamhscolaíochta Teo, Barnardos, NCRC, Childminding Ireland, IPPA, NCNA

McGuinneas, C., 1993, *Report of the Kilkenny Incest Investigation*, Dublin: Stationery Office

Key Terms — Section Five

Chapter 11

Constitution

Judicial Review

Oireachtas

Dáil

Seanad

Taoiseach

Local Government

Bill

White Paper

Green Paper

Marriage breakdown

Nullity

Annulment

Separation

Judicial separation

Divorce

Custody

Access

Guardianship

Maintenance

Paternity
Family mediation
Illegitimacy
Domestic violence
Safety Order
Protection Order
Barring Order
Interim barring Order

Chapter 12

Protection
Poor Law Acts 1834
Battered Baby Syndrome
Incidence of abuse
Predisposing factors
Physical abuse
Emotional abuse
Neglect
Sexual abuse
Indicators
Care Order
Emergency Care Order
Interim Care Order
Supervision Order
Guardian Ad Litem
Allegations
Verification
Empowerment

SECTION SIX

SOCIAL ISSUES

This section covers relevant aspects of the social framework for families and children in Ireland. Chapter 13 focuses on sociological concepts relevant to early childhood care and education placing them within the context of the modern Irish family. Chapter 14 gives an overview of the Irish social services — housing, health, income maintenance, family support and education services.

13

SOCIOLOGY: KEY CONCEPTS FOR EARLY CHILDHOOD WORKERS

AREAS COVERED

▶ Socialisation

▶ Culture

▶ Social Roles

▶ The Family

Introduction

The word sociology was coined by Auguste Comte (1798–1857). Sociology is the scientific study of society, the causes and consequences of social change and the principles of social order and stability. It takes a look at the obvious from a not so obvious angle.

This chapter defines sociological concepts relevant to social development in early childhood. It describes varying forms and structures of families and partnerships, with particular reference to the modern Irish family. The focus taken is quite narrow and ignores to a large extent historical, economic and other influences.

Socialisation

Socialisation is the process by which human beings learn to live according to the values, rules and expectations of their society. The process involves learning through experience and through relationships. During the process children learn how to behave in different situations and they grow into adults who can function in a variety of social roles in that particular society.

Socialisation is divided into two stages: primary and secondary.

Primary socialisation refers to the first stage when the child learns basic patterns of acceptable behaviour, language and social skills. They are learned from those people who are closest to the child, i.e. parents, close family and main carers. These are referred to as the **primary agents** of socialisation. Early childhood experts consider that at this stage the child should have a small number of carers to relate to, and it is also important that these carers are working in partnership with each other so that the child receives consistent messages about appropriate ways to behave. The Child Care Act 1991 takes account of this important stage of socialisation and has provided guidelines for staff-child ratios in early years settings (see Chapter 2).

Secondary socialisation takes place when children begin to have contact with the wider community, e.g. neighbours, friends, schools, clubs and churches. At this stage children begin to adapt to the wider world and learn to relate to a variety of people in a variety of different ways. Peers or friends have a huge influence on children from quite an early age, and they exert pressure on each other to conform and be part of the group. The media (television, radio and print) are also very important as **secondary agents** of socialisation.

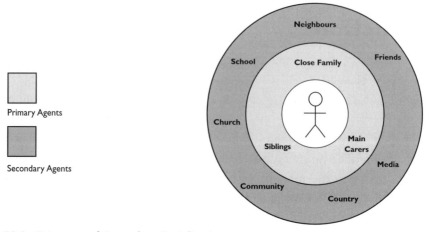

Figure 13.1: Primary and Secondary Socialisation

Culture

A **society** is a group of people who share the same culture, e.g. Irish people. Societies usually organise themselves in response to their environment. For example, the weather, economics and natural resources are factors which influence society. People in other cultures do things in a way that may seem weird and strange to us; equally the way that we do things may seem weird and strange to others. Neither are weird or strange — just different.

Culture is the set of beliefs, values and norms that shapes the way individuals behave in a society. Aspects of culture change over time. Irish people share the same culture. Culture is complex and there are some differences in the way life is conducted. These differences might, for instance, reflect regional or social class variations.

Beliefs are a general set of opinions about how things should be. *In our society, we believe that children should be protected and cared for until they reach adulthood.*

Values are ideas that derive from beliefs and are about what is thought to be just, correct and proper. *It is considered wrong to take another person's life but, in times of war and conflict, a person may be rewarded for killing people.*

Norms are patterns of behaviour that are expected, what is considered 'normal' conduct in any given situation. Norms are basically 'social manners'. *It is the norm in Ireland to shake hands when introduced to someone. In some Islamic societies shaking hands with a person of the opposite sex is considered highly improper.*

Customs refer to patterns of behaviour that are in common practice. *It is a custom in rural Ireland when someone dies to have a wake, with people coming to the deceased's home to pay their respects.*

Social Roles

A **role** is a pattern of behaviour that is associated with a particular position or status. Family roles are, for example, those of father, mother, brother, sister, grandparent. Occupational roles might be early childhood worker, teacher, plumber, doctor, waiter, bank manager or construction worker. Most people play more than one role in society. One may be a student but also be a mother, a sister, a daughter, a best friend and a member of the soccer team.

Sometimes there is **role conflict** and the person can be pulled in two ways. In the example above the student's role may involve study and this conflicts with the demand of the soccer team to practise and to be available to play matches. When parents become old and infirm the son/daughter may have to provide care; their earlier roles are reversed; this is known as **role reversal**.

Children become aware of roles at a very early age and in this way they learn what to expect from people in different roles. This provides structure in the social world and adds to one's sense of security.

A small child who has a minor fall while in junior infants class may just pick himself up and keep going. The same experience in his mother's or father's presence may bring on a deluge of tears because he expects comfort from the parent but not from the teacher.

People who do not abide by the general rules and expectations of the society in which they live are disciplined. This is called '**social control**' and can be informal and/or formal. Social control which is informal is expressed in the disapproval of others, and a person may be considered difficult, different or odd. Social control is formal when it is backed up by the law, the courts and the police. For example, killing and stealing are punishable by law.

ACTIVITY

Aim: The aim of this activity is to clarify how roles and values work out in practice in society and to draw attention to the complexity of the issues involved.

Read the extract below from an account of growing up in a small town in Ireland in the 1950s.

'Sergeant Moran was sergeant of the guards in Finea for a long period. His family and ours became very close. He had a large family. The older ones were friends of my sisters, but a number of the younger ones were dreadfully handicapped. The story of their suffering made a huge impression on the Slacke ladies.

The mother often spoke with grief of Mrs Moran. After each birth she grew more and more reclusive. Each pregnancy brought on terrible fits of depression, my mother told me. And at the thought of another pregnancy ahead her spirits would wilt. She prayed, my mother said, to pass childbearing age as others prayed to enter heaven.

She braved the sympathy of the village with a heavy heart and eventually never went up the village to shop. Maurice, one of the older sons, grew fond of my father, and my father, in turn, began looking after the Morans. He'd arrive on duty in the morning carrying loaves and potatoes and boiling bacon and eggs and butter. Mrs Moran stayed in the married quarters.

Bless you, Guard Healy, she'd say and retire.

Maurice clung to my father while Sergeant Moran sat in full uniform by his desk going over and over lists, frantically scribbling events of note in Kilcogy, Togher, Castletown and Finea.

For long periods of silence the two men sat hunched over the fire in the dayroom. They stood in the dark opposite dance halls, and walked the village through storms in their greatcoats till they were foundered. Then they'd return and sit by the fire again, water running from their caps and coats onto the hearth.

From the private quarters the healthy children and the distraught younger ones made their way into the dayroom. And lo and behold, said my mother, if he didn't do there what he didn't do at home! My father helped the older girls feed the infants, scalded nappies on the stove, changed underpants and warmed their milk bottles. Often the sad sergeant would stand in the doorway watching his underling rear his children. My mother would saunter up the village with my father's dinner under a cloth on a hot plate. She'd come in she often told us, to find her husband playing with the Moran children in one of the cells while Maurice, wearing my father's garda hat, was sitting up on duty on the Sergeant's high stool.

He spent more time with them than he did with us, she'd recall. It was a terrible cross.

In the evenings the Sergeant and the Guard would stroll the village, part at the monument and meet again at the bridge, each with a bicycle lamp cupped in his hands. Swans careered overhead on a journey from Lough Kinale to Lough Sheelin. A shotgun went off. They'd return in time to put the children to bed, then look into the fire in the dayroom and toe the ash.

There'd be a shout from the married quarters. An infant would stand on the threshold.

None of the handicapped was long for this world, my mother told me years later. Not one of them reached the age of reason.

They were carried off to the graveyard in homemade coffins on the shoulders of policemen. Neighbours shied away. The names of the dead children were read out at Sunday mass and their names sounded strange to the ears of the villagers. They were people who had never been seen and yet had lived among them for a few short years. They were phantoms when they lived, but when they died, they suddenly became real live human beings.'

(Healy, 1996: 10–12)

Consider the following questions:

▶   What behaviour is associated with the role of a Guard?

▶   What other roles does Guard Healy fulfil besides policing?

▶   Are there any signs of role conflict and, if so, what are they?

▶ Why does Guard Healy do things for the Moran children that he would not do at home?

▶ What does the extract reveal about the role of women?

▶ What does the extract reveal about how disability was viewed in Ireland at the time?

▶ Are there any values evident in the extract? What are they?

▶ What skills are the children learning?

▶ List at least five skills that young children in our society learn within their families during the process of socialisation.

The Family

What Is a Family?

The definition of the Family used by the UN is as follows: 'Any combination of two or more persons who are bound together by ties of mutual consent, birth and/or adoption or placement and who, together, assume responsibility for, inter alia, the care and maintenance of group members through procreation or adoption, the socialisation of children and the social control of members.'

This description includes families based on married and unmarried partnerships; the constitutional definition of families in Ireland includes only those based on marriage. The 1996 Census in Ireland reveals that households with no children (whether made up of married or cohabiting couples) was the fastest growing type of household between 1991 and 1996. In line with this trend the average number of children per family in Ireland as in Europe is declining steadily, having fallen from 2.2 per family in 1981 to 1.8 per family in 1996 (CSO, 1996).

Functions of the Family

In pre-industrial societies, family functions evolved in response to needs, their own and that of the community in which the family lived. These functions were primarily concerned with survival (production — making goods; and reproduction — making children!) and each family's contribution was essential to that survival.

The main functions of the pre-industrial family were as follows:

Socialisation: Children required a group of dedicated carers to socialise them into society. The family were also the educators of the children.

Economic Support: While some people, usually women, were preoccupied with childbearing and childrearing, other committed members of the family were required to provide the basic necessities like food and accommodation. Family members were more dependant on each other economically when there was no social welfare system and the state did not provide support.

Regulation of Sexual Behaviour: Almost all societies had some rules and regulations in this area. Unregulated sexual behaviour tended to cause lots of conflict. Contraception and family planning were not an option and it was necessary to provide a stable situation prior to the birth of children. In some societies the regulation of sexual activity was essential to the maintenance of family wealth and was tied into laws governing property and inheritance. Many churches reinforced such regulations on moral grounds.

Reproduction: Societies needed to maintain their populations and families were seen, for the most part, to be the best place to rear children whatever the family structure.

Emotional Support: Very little is known about the amount and origin of emotional support for family members in pre-industrial times. It is presumed that the mother was close to her children while they were young. In extended family situations she also probably supported her children when they had children if she survived long enough.

The Family Today

In modern times many of the traditional functions of the family have been transferred to other social systems. The family has changed from being primarily a unit of production and reproduction to being a consumer of goods.

While most children probably spend their first few years being cared for by close family this period of primary socialisation can be very short. Crèches, nurseries and pre-schools can provide full day care from the age of three months, and later on schools provide education.

The social services system can provide all the basics necessary for survival — housing, food and clothing. In extreme cases, the State can take over the parenting role by taking children into care. The Gardaí can provide protection.

Sexual behaviour no longer needs to be regulated in the same way because contraception has given people greater ability to separate reproduction from sexual activity. Relationships and the quality of the emotional bonds have taken centre stage to some extent. The relatively modern westernised notion of romantic love which tends to drive relationships in Irish society defines and sets standards for the emotional relationship. If the emotional bond breaks down then the partnership often breaks down, regardless of the needs of the children or the economic circumstances of the family members.

Figure 13.2: The Family and Industrialisation: A Summary

	The pre-industrial family	Industrialisation and the family	The family today
Structure	Mainly nuclear families, but the better-off had larger households, as people came to stay with them; late marriage; small families because of the high death-rate of children.	Working-class families — became extended as numbers of children increased because of higher child survival rates (results of medical improvements) and people crowded into limited housing available in towns. Middle-class families — became extended as younger generation remained at home until they were economically free to leave and set up own house.	Nuclear families, with connections by telephone/car to wider kin.
Relationships	Not very close or warm, marriage and child-rearing mainly for economic reasons; idea of love was unusual.	Working-class — children close to mother; father and mother not close at all; women oppressed by men. Middle-class — children not close to parents, father and mother, cold relationship; women oppressed by men.	Close family relationships, the 'privatised' family: husband and wife fairly equal but women still expected to be responsible for domestic matters; children are seen as extremely important.
Functions	Families very important as all worked together in the home or on the farm; family looked after its members if they survived to old age.	Working-class — families very important for survival; pooling of economic resources, helped each other where possible in all matters; older generation looked after by younger generation.	Mainly emotional but still practical and financial help (loans etc.) when needed; state and voluntary services assist or replace the family in many of its functions.
Wider setting	Agricultural society, people living in the countryside in small villages.	Industrialised society, people living in large towns.	A mobile family moving for promotion and to take job opportunities: people living in suburbs: light industry and offices are places of work.

(*Source*: Moore, 1996)

Although the family unit continues to be an important and valuable factor in our society there are some negative aspects to family life which cannot be ignored.

Violence: Violence within families is probably as old as families themselves. In Ireland, violence against women and children in the home has gained increasing recognition since the 1970s and refuges and services have grown accordingly (see Chapter 11).

Sexual Abuse: Most sexual abuse of children occurs within families and this aspect has only been highlighted in Ireland since about the 1980s. Sexual abuse seems to be generally perpetrated by male relatives and the full extent of this is not known (see Chapter 12).

The Unequal Position of Women: Women had less economic independence in the past, now they have more opportunities for economic independence but their unequal position within the family continues because they tend to have more responsibility for the rearing of children.

The Economic Burden of Children: In pre-industrial societies children were an asset. They provided labour so that the family production unit could produce more and in this way accumulate wealth. Today children consume the family wealth because of the length of their dependence and their protracted education.

ACTIVITY

Aim: To explore changes in family structures and definitions during the last half of the twentieth century

In 1949, the family was defined as follows: 'A family is a social group characterised by common residence, economic co-operation and reproduction. It includes adults of both sexes, at least two of whom maintain a socially approved sexual relationship and one or more children owned or adopted by the sexually co-habiting adults.'

▶   List points that you think are still valid in Irish society today.

▶   List points that you think are no longer valid today.

Types of Families

Figure 13.3: Types of Family

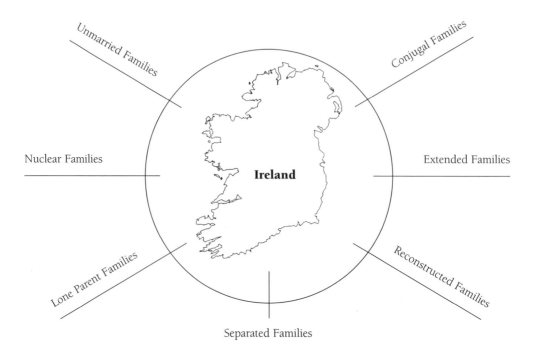

Separated Families

In most societies, different family structures and marriage patterns have grown in response to economic or population structures. **Polygamy** (where a man or a woman can have more than one spouse) gives rise to different types of extended family structures. In a society such as Ireland, whose laws only allow **monogamy** (which means one person in partnership with another), these other forms of marriage are known as **bigamy** which is a crime. A family organised around a married couple and their children is known as a **conjugal family**.

A large group of people who are living together and who are not closely related may be just friends, but if they are dependent on each other in their social and economic organisation then they are referred to as a **commune**.

There are three main types of family organisation in the modern Western world all of which are based on monogamy. These are:

(a)   the nuclear family
(b)   the extended family
(c)   the reconstructed family.

The Nuclear Family

The nuclear family consists of parents and their children living in a unit that is separate from the wider family. Within this arrangement, partners and children depend on each other for support and are mostly independent of relatives.

The nuclear family also includes the **one-parent family** which consists of one parent and a child/children living together. One-parent families occur because the parent has never lived in a partnership or because of death, separation or divorce. One-parent families have become more common in many Western, industrialised societies. The latest census figures available (1996) showed that there were approximately 130,000 lone parent families (15% of all family units) in Ireland and more than four-fifths of them were headed by women.

One-parent families resulting from separation/divorce have been steadily increasing and account for over a quarter (28%) of all one-parent families in this country. There were over twice as many marriages which had broken down in 1996 than ten years previously, up from 37,200 in 1986 to 87,800 separated (including divorced) people in 1996 (CSO, 1996).

Figure 13.4 — One-Parent Families

One-Parent Families

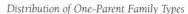

Fig 8.4 One-Parent Families as % of all Families   *Distribution of One-Parent Family Types*

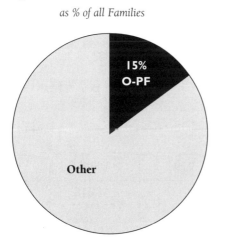
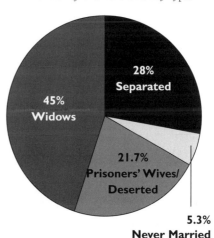

15%
O-PF

Other

28%
Separated

45%
Widows

21.7%
Prisoners' Wives/
Deserted

5.3%
Never Married

Total Number One-Parent Families 1996: 130,000

The number of never married parents has also greatly increased. The introduction of the Unmarried Mother's Allowance in 1973 gave a means of supporting children outside of marriage without family approval or support being necessary. The number of births outside of marriage increased steadily from this time, as can be seen from Table 13.2. However, the greatest increase in the number of births outside of marriage has taken place since 1990, from 12.8% of all births in 1989 to 30.9% in 1999 (Department of Health and Children, 2000). This suggests that economics alone is not the sole reason for the increase; other factors may include changes in social values and a decrease in adherence to religious regulations.

Families where parents are gay or lesbian are also increasing in some countries, with children conceived through donors or being adopted. In Ireland gay men and lesbians have difficulty being accepted generally but recent Equality Legislation should address some of the difficulties which they face at present.

Table 13.1: Marriage and Birth Rates in Ireland 1950–2000

	Marriages		Births	
Year	No.	Rates	No.	Rates
1950	16,018	5.4	63,565	21.4
1960	15,465	5.5	60,735	21.5
1970	20,778	7.1	64,092	21.8
1980	21,792	6.4	74,064	21.8
1990	17,838	5.1	53,044	15.1
2000	19,168	5.1	54,239	14.3
2001	19,246	5.0	57,882	15.1

Source: Dept of Health and Children

Table 13.2: Births Outside Marriage 1969-99

	1969	1979	1989	1999
Total No. of live Births	62,912	72,539	52,018	53,354
Total No. of Births outside marriage	1,642	3,337	6,671	16,461
Births outside marriage as % of total births	2.6%	4.6%	12.8%	30.9%

Source: Dept of Health and Children

Table 13.3: Birth rates and Births Outside Marriage — EU Countries 1998

Country	Birth Rate	% of births outside marriage
Austria	10.1	29.5
Belgium	11.2*	17.5
Denmark	12.5*	45.1
Finland	11.1	37.2
France	12.6*	40.1
Germany	9.6*	19.3
Greece	9.6*	3.7
Ireland	**14.5***	**28.3**
Italy	9.0*	9.0
Luxembourg	12.6	17.5
Netherlands	12.7	20.5
Portugal	11.4*	20.1
Spain	9.2*	11.7
Sweden	10.1	54.6
United Kingdom	12.1*	37.6
EU average	**10.7***	**25.2**

* Indicates that figures from these countries are estimated or provisional

Source: Demographic Statistics Eurostat 1999

The Extended Family

This type of family consists of the nuclear unit plus other relatives living with, or in very close proximity to, each other. Other relatives may mean grandparents, aunts or uncles. The extended family is more common where living together in large groups is necessary for economic survival, as in agricultural societies or where family industries exist. This type of family also predominates where there is extreme poverty, as the members may supply mutual support and aid to each other in the form of clothing, cooking utensils and sleeping accommodation. The extended family is also important among Travellers and Asian families. The notion that many generations lived together in mutual contentment and support in Ireland in the past is probably mistaken as people died younger, many people never married and those who did so, married at an older age than at present.

ACTIVITY

Aim: To introduce the 'family tree' as a tool for representing family structure

Figure 13.5: A Family Tree

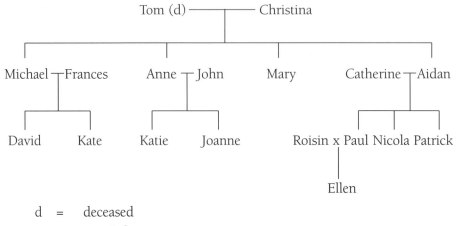

d	=	deceased
—	=	married
x	=	unmarried partners

Study the depiction of the family tree above and answer the following questions:

▶ How many grandchildren does Christina have?

▶ If they all live separately, how many nuclear family units are there?

▶ What is the relationship between Mary and Ellen?

▶ If the grandmother, Christina, lives with her daughter Anne how many people would be living in that extended household?

▶ Draw your own family tree.

The Reconstructed Family

A reconstructed family formerly known as the stepfamily is one where two people who have had children within a previous relationship, marry or cohabit and each bring their children to live together and have more children together. Divorce and separation is on the increase and research in Britain and the US indicates that the majority of divorced men and women form another partnership within five years. This practice is known as **serial monogamy**. Reconstructed families may pose many problems in defining who our relatives are, as the following case illustration shows.

CASE STUDY

Sarah divorced her first husband Youenn when their three children were quite young; Shareen was 6 years, Ali was 4 years and Áine was 2 years. Two years later Sarah formed a relationship with Andy and he moved in to live with her and the children; with him was his daughter Amanda (11 years) from his previous marriage to Mairéad. They did not get married until three years later when Sarah was pregnant with Sam. Sam was only 3 years when Sarah and Andy split up. Shareen, Ali and Áine maintain contact with their father, Youenn, who has a new partner called Alice, and they have two children, Marcus 5 years and Anna 3 years.

Consider the following questions:

▶ When did Andy become a stepfather to the children?

▶ Can he become a stepfather without being married?

▶ Do Andy's parents become the children's grandparents and his siblings their aunts and uncles?

▶ Does Andy remain their stepfather after he has split up with Sarah?

▶ Shareen, Ali and Áine are step-siblings to Sam, Marcus and Anna — are Marcus and Anna related to Sam?

▶ Draw a family tree depicting the above reconstructed family.

The Family in the Irish Constitution
ARTICLES 41 AND 42 — THE FAMILY

41.1.1.   The State recognises the Family as the natural primary and fundamental unit group of Society, and as a moral institution possessing inalienable and imprescriptible rights, antecedent and superior to all positive law.

41.1.2.   The State, therefore, guarantees to protect the Family in its constitution and authority, as the necessary basis of social order and as indispensable to the welfare of the Nation and the State.

41.2.1.   In particular, the State recognises that by her life within the home, woman gives to the State a support without which the common good cannot be achieved.

41.2.2.   The State shall, therefore, endeavour to ensure that mothers shall not be obliged by economic necessity to engage in labour to the neglect of their duties in the home.

41.3.1.   The State pledges itself to guard with special care the institution of Marriage, on which the Family is founded, and to protect it against attack.

42.1.1.   The State acknowledges that the primary and natural educator of the child is the Family and guarantees to respect the inalienable right and duty of parents to provide, according to their means, for the religious and moral, intellectual, physical and social education of their children.

(*Bunreacht na hÉireann*, 1937)

ACTIVITY

Aim: To explore the ideas of family structure and organisation which are promoted by the Irish Constitution

Read the Articles of the Constitution above in full.
In small groups discuss the following questions:

▶   What do you think is meant by Article 41.1.1?

▶   What is the role of women in the family as envisioned by the Constitution?

▶   Why is it in the interest of the State to guard marriage against attack?

▶   Are there any issues in Irish society today which you feel are undermining family and family life?

Since the Constitution was written there have been many social and legal changes which have had profound effects on family life in Ireland. Most of these have taken place from 1970 onwards. The impact of EU membership on our social and economic policies has been significant. The increase in the economic independence for women and the removal of the stigma of out-of-wedlock births not only changed patterns of family life but paved the way for women to have greater influence in Irish life generally.

SUMMARY

▸ Society passes on its culture, values, beliefs, norms and customs through the socialisation process.

▸ Children learn how to expect others to behave and how to behave themselves in society by learning social roles.

▸ The family is the primary socialising agent and therefore is a very important element in practically all societies.

▸ The structures and functions of the family have changed greatly since the industrial revolution.

▸ Many of the traditional functions of the family are now undertaken by the State.

▸ Since the foundation of the Irish State and particularly since joining the European Union there have been major changes in social and economic policies which have affected the family.

References

Bunreacht na hÉireann, 1937, Dublin: Stationery Office

Commission on the Family, 1998, *Strengthening Families for Life*, Final Report, Dublin: Stationery Office

Department of Health, 2000, *Vital Statistics*, Dublin: Stationery Office

Healy, Dermot, 1997, *The Bend for Home*, London: The Harvill Press

Moore, Stephen, 1996, *Sociology Alive*, 2nd edn., Cheltenham: Stanley Thornes

Census of Population, 1996, *Principal Demographic Results*, Dublin: CSO Government Publications

14

SOCIAL SERVICES

AREAS COVERED

▶ Overview of Social Services in Ireland

▶ Housing

▶ Health Services

▶ Income Maintenance

▶ Family Support and Child Welfare Services

▶ Education

▶ Voluntary Services

Introduction

The main areas of social service provision are housing, health, income maintenance, personal social services and education. In Ireland they have developed in a piecemeal and haphazard fashion but they do affect, and are used by, almost the entire population at some time in their lives. Almost one half of government spending is on social services. Everyone benefits from the system at some level — education is free and compulsory and all families are entitled to claim the child benefit. Hospital and healthcare services are available at varying costs to all. However, the greater the stresses on the person/family/group, the more they are going to need to use the social services that are available to them.

This chapter outlines services provision in each sector — except early education which is covered in Chapter 1. A brief history of the development of the service in Ireland and an examination of social problems related to the service will be included.

Overview of Social Services in Ireland

Social services are shaped by social policy and one of the principal aims of social policy is to alleviate poverty. There are two types of poverty:

1. **Absolute** poverty is easy to define as it means that people do not have enough to live on and some will literally die from starvation and lack of shelter.

2. **Relative** poverty is less easy to define; it means that some people are poor compared to others, or are poor in terms of what is acceptable as a basic standard of living in the country in which they live. In Ireland today the working definition used is that of relative poverty. Poverty lines are drawn using different measurements of basic or acceptable standards of living. The Report of the Commission of Social Welfare 1986 set the poverty line at 60% of the national average income. Put simply this means that if the average income per week is €100.00 then anyone who receives €60.00 or less per week is considered to be living in poverty. (Other issues relating to poverty and inequality are covered in Chapter 5.)

The provision of health and social care in Ireland is through a combination of **statutory**, **voluntary** and **private** services. Informal services provided by families, friends and social networks also play an important part.

Statutory Services

These services are provided by the State and are covered by State law. The State is responsible for funding such services although that does not necessarily mean that they are free to everyone; some are public and some are private. This is referred to as a two-tiered system.

Statutory Services are provided in the following areas:

1. Housing – Department of the Environment and Local Government
2. Health – Department of Health and Children
3. Income Maintenance (Social Welfare) – Department of Social and Family Affairs
4. Personal Social Services – Department of Health and Children
5. Education – Department of Education and Science.

Voluntary Services

These services are provided by voluntary bodies, charities and volunteers. A service is described as voluntary when it has been set up by people who identify a need and who organise the resources to meet that need without being required to do so by law. Voluntary agencies or groups may receive government grants but usually that falls far short of their full financial requirements so a lot of fundraising and voluntary work is often involved.

Voluntary organisations can have a number of different functions and sometimes all these functions are fulfilled by a single organisation.

▶   Providing information, e.g. Threshold (housing and accomodation)

▶ Supporting individuals or families through services and/or counselling, e.g. Barnardos (Child and Family Services)

▶ Campaigning for change in State provision or in laws, e.g.Children's Rights Alliance

▶ Providing money/material for people in need, e.g. St Vincent de Paul.

Private Services

These services are primarily set up to make a profit whilst meeting an identified need. A large number of pre-school services in Ireland are private services as are the majority of caring institutions for the elderly.

TASK

Aim: To become acquainted with the voluntary services in your local area.

Find out:
▶ What are the voluntary agencies in your area?
▶ What kind of service do they provide?
▶ What is their target population?
▶ Where do they get funding (government grants/fundraising)?
▶ How many staff are salaried and how many are volunteers?
▶ What level of training do staff and volunteers receive?
▶ Which of these services are specific to children?

Housing
Sectors in Irish Housing 1946-91

Table 14.1 Sectors in Irish Society

Sector	1946	1961	1971	1981	1991
Local Authority	16.5%	18.4%	15.5%	12.7%	9.7%
Private Rented	26.1%	17.2%	13.3%	8.1%	7.0%
Other (Social Housing)	4.7%	4.6%	2.4%	3.1%	–
Total Housing Stock	662,654	676,402	726,363	896,000	1,006,506

(Sources: Census of Population — Various Years)

Whilst the main aim of Irish government policy has been that every family should have access to adequate housing, one of the central features of its policy has been the encouragement of owner occupation. Those who own their own houses are more secure, both financially (each mortgage payment is an investment) and in the sense that they have some more choice about where they live.

Discrimination may flourish in the private rented sector because the owner has complete control in terms of choice of tenant to whom he rents. Tenant rights are very few and difficult to enforce. Under the Housing Miscellaneous Provisions Act 1992 regulations were introduced in relation to rent books, standards for rented dwellings and registration of rented houses. Subsidies for tenants in this sector include the Rent Allowance Scheme and tax relief for some people, e.g. those aged 55 and over.

Local authority (public) housing accounts for just under 10% of Irish housing stock. Housing policy aims to meet the needs of those who:

▸ are living in unfit or overcrowded conditions

▸ do not have sufficient finances to buy their own house

▸ have special needs, e.g. elderly people or those who have a disability

▸ have become homeless.

A **differential rents scheme** operates in public housing provision which means that rent is related to income. A **tenant purchase scheme** allows tenants to buy their houses through a combination of rent, reduced mortgage and preferential loans from the local authority involved. While this is in line with the preference for owner occupation, it has been criticised for depleting the stocks of public housing that is left available for those in need.

A less desirable characteristic of public housing provision has been the tendency to build large estates or flat complexes where people are isolated, often without proper amenities and services. There is now a commitment to adopt new approaches in the provision of public housing, and the foremost of these is not to build any more large estates and to improve and refurbish existing houses.

Social Housing, also called voluntary housing, accounts for a very small portion of houses in Ireland today. Initially, social housing was provided by businesses to encourage and provide for workers who migrated to the city, e.g. Guinness was one of the first. Social housing today is aimed at vulnerable groups who might not be able to get housing on their own. Ireland has one of the least developed social housing movements in the EU.

Some of the main Social/Voluntary Housing groups concerned with the accommodation needs of families are:

▸   The Iveagh Trust

▸   St Vincent de Paul

▸   Religious Orders

▸   Focus Ireland

▸   Social Service Councils

▸   The Rural Housing Organisation.

Homelessness

Homelessness has been highlighted by a number of voluntary agencies over the past few decades, most notably Focus Ireland and the Simon Community. With rising unemployment, increase in marriage breakdown and soaring house prices the number of homeless people has been steadily increasing.

The following groups are at the greatest risk of becoming homeless:

▸   Long-term unemployed

▸   One parent families

▸   People who are discharged from long-stay institutions

▸   Children out of long-term care

▸   Youths who run away from, or are rejected by, their families.

Because of a lack of an accepted definition of homelessness, there has been disagreement on the incidence. However, the Housing Act 1988 and the Child Care Act 1991 both address the problem.

The **Housing Act 1988** broadened the definition of homelessness to include people residing in night shelters, hospitals and hostels who were only there because of a lack of accommodation. The Act, while not placing a statutory duty on local authorities to accommodate homeless people, did empower them to provide a range of suitable options in conjunction with other agencies. The Department of the Environment issued guidelines to this effect.

The **Child Care Act 1991** addressed the needs of homeless youths for the first time in legislation.

The implications of being homeless are many, including:

▸   discrimination

▸   risk of exploitation

▸   difficulty in acquiring social welfare, a medical card etc. without a fixed address

▸   the near impossibility of getting a job

▸   deterioration of physical and mental health.

Effects of Homelessness on Children

It is difficult to consider the effects of homelessness and poor housing on children in isolation as the problems are usually compounded by other adverse circumstances, e.g. poverty and marital breakdown. Many families who become homeless are accommodated by Health Boards in bed and breakfasts because of lack of suitable housing.

Poor housing, inadequate household amenities and overcrowded conditions are associated with:

▶ poor social and emotional adjustment and lower educational attainments

▶ a higher incidence of physical illnesses because of damp, infestation, lack of hygiene facilities and accidents. The family may be confined to one room where space is at a premium and it may be difficult for the children to get to sleep

▶ stress — adults who are trying to rear children in such adverse conditions may become worn out from the everyday effort to survive and may not have the physical, mental or emotional energy to cater adequately for the children's overall needs

▶ overly strict parenting — overcrowding, lack of privacy, lack of space and the sheer pressure on parents to keep the children quiet and out of other people's way can lead to parents having to be very strict. There are often rules about noise and running in corridors, all of which culminate in an extremely restrictive experience for the child. This in turn leads to understimulation, pent-up energy and frustration. Children who have to live in such conditions may be more aggressive and impulsive and have a greater difficulty concentrating.

▶ security — the family may be moving around from hostel to hostel or between bed and breakfast accomodation, and typically this can go on for some time before the family's housing needs are met. Their familiar environment and routines will have totally changed. Schooling may be disrupted and the family isolated from neighbours and friends. Parents will not be able to prepare children for changes because the parents themselves will not know what is going to happen.

▶ powerlessness — if parents feel powerless in this situation children will feel even more so.

Development in every area at all stages can be severely affected. In such situations the provision of good childcare services can be a lifeline.

Health Services

Ireland has a two-tiered health service — a private service for those who can afford to pay the fees or who can afford to pay for health insurance each year, and a public service which is available to everyone and provided free for those whose income falls below a certain threshold. The public service is inadequate to meet the demands at present and waiting lists are invariably long. The environments in which private services are offered are generally more comfortable, less stressful and offer more privacy than the public service environment.

Health Boards were established under the Health Act 1970 for the administration of the health services of the State. There are currently ten established Health Boards: three area Health Boards in the eastern region under the umbrella of the Eastern Regional Health Authority (ERHA) and seven regional Health Boards covering the rest of the country.

Figure 14.1: Health Board Areas

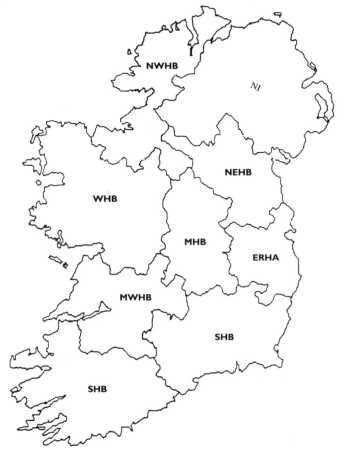

Table 14.2: Eastern Regional Health Authority

East Coast Area Health Board	South eastern Dublin and east Wicklow
Northern Area Health Board	Dublin city and county north of the Liffey
South Western Area Health Board	Dublin inner city south of the Liffey, South Dublin, Kildare and the Baltinglass areas of Wicklow

Table 14.3: Regional Health Boards

Midland Health Board	Laois, Offaly, Longford and Westmeath
Mid Western Health Board	Clare, Limerick and Tipperary North
North Eastern Health Board	Cavan, Monaghan, Meath and Louth
North Western Health Board	Donegal, Sligo and Leitrim
South Eastern Health Board	Wexford, Carlow, Kilkenny, Waterford and Tipperary South
Southern Health Board	Cork and Kerry
Western Health Board	Galway, Mayo and Roscommon

The health services are delivered under three programmes:

▸ The General Hospital Programme
▸ The Special Hospital Programme
▸ The Community Care Programme.

The general hospital programme provides for inpatient and outpatient hospital treatment. These are available free to all (public service) or privately if the person chooses a private hospital.

The special hospital programme covers services for people who are in need of psychiatric treatment and for people who have a disability.

The community care programme has three sub-programmes:

(a) Community Protection	*(b) Community Health Service*	*(c) Community Welfare Service*
This covers control and prevention of infectious diseases, child health examinations, immunisations and health education.	This covers general practitioner, dental, aural, ophthalmic, home nursing services and the refund of expenditure on drugs scheme.	This covers child care services, home help services, grants to voluntary organisations and the administration of special allowances.

Briefly, since the Health Act 1970 under the general medical services eligible persons (i.e. people who have a medical card) are allowed to:

▸ attend, for free, the doctor of their choice who is participating in the medical card scheme

▸ obtain free medicines on prescription

▸ obtain free hospital services in a public ward.

Eligibility for a medical card is assessed by way of a means test, and if eligible it covers healthcare for the cardholder, his spouse and any children under the age of 16 years.

Medical card holders are entitled to:

▸ general practitioner services

▸ prescribed drugs and medicines

▸ all inpatient public hospital services in public wards

▸ all outpatient public hospital services

▸ all consultant services within public hospital services

▸ dental, ophthalmic and aural services and appliances

▸ a maternity and infant care service

▸ a maternity cash grant.

People who exceed the income limit and are not eligible for a medical card are entitled to some subsidised services as follows:

▸ all inpatient public services in public wards (including consultant's fees) subject to set public hospital charges

▸ outpatient public hospital services, subject to a set charge excluding dental, aural and ophthalmic services

▸ free maternity and infant care services

▸ a refund on prescribed drugs when over a specified amount is spent in any given quarter. These amounts are revised from time to time

▸ free drugs and medicines under the Long-Term Illness Scheme.

Details of public hospital charges, Drugs Refund Scheme and medical card guidelines are revised regularly and up-to-date details are available from the Department of Health and Children or from the local Health Board.

A number of other schemes govern eligibility for access to services for certain groups of the population. These include the Long-Term Illness Scheme, Infectious Diseases Regulations, Maternity and Infant Care Scheme, School Medical Service, Nursing Home

Subvention Scheme, Public Dental Service, preventive services such as immunisation schemes and early detection services such as breast cancer screening.

Long-Term Illness Scheme

People who have any of the following long-term conditions can obtain drugs and medicines free, regardless of their income: mental handicap, mental illness (for children under 16 years only), phenylketonuria, cystic fibrosis, spina bifida, hydrocephalus, diabetes mellitus, diabetes insipidus, haemophilia, cerebral palsy, epilepsy, multiple sclerosis, muscular dystrophy, parkinsonism and acute leukaemia.

Health Services for Children

The following services are available free to all regardless of income:

▶ A mother and infant care service which includes the services of a family doctor, inpatient and outpatient services in a maternity unit/hospital for the mother during pregnancy and for the mother and baby for up to six weeks after the birth

▶ Free dental treatment for pregnant women

▶ A health examination service for pre-school and primary school children

▶ All necessary follow-up services for problems discovered during these examinations, including dental, optical and aural problems

▶ A national screening service for scoliosis from Our Lady's Hospital, Crumlin, Dublin

▶ Inpatient and outpatient hospital services for all children under 16 years who have: mental handicap, mental illness, phenylketonuria, cystic fibrosis, spina bifida, hydrocephalus, haemophilia and cerebral palsy

▶ Immunisation against a number of infectious diseases.

Table 14.4: Approximate Timing of Immunisations

The approximate timing of these immunisations is as follows:	
At birth	BCG (anti-tuberculosis)
At 2 months	Diphtheria, Whooping Cough, Tetanus, Polio, Hib (5-in-1)
At 4 months	5-in-1 is repeated
At 6 months	5-in-1 is repeated
At 15 months	Measles, mumps, rubella (MMR)

About 5 years	Whooping Cough, Diphtheria, Tetanus, Polio (boosters)
12-14 years	Tuberculosis (BCG), tetanus and low-dose diptheria, rubella to males and females
All under 22 years	National immunisation programme against meningitis C

A health screening service is provided free of charge to all children at all local health centres. Services for pre-school children are provided by public health nurses and area medical officers. Public health nurses are notified of all births in their area and visit the mother and baby at home soon after the birth, and afterwards as necessary. The PHN provides both general health and specific developmental advice and monitors the overall development of the child. Developmental paediatric examinations are offered at regular intervals up until 4 years by appointment at the local health centre. The Health Strategy 2001 'Quality and Fairness', which has been published by the Department of Health and Children, sets out detailed plans for the development and improvement of the health services over ten years until 2011. It sets out an action plan which includes target dates.

The strategy sets out four main goals:

1.   Policies which promote health, reduce inequalities and ensure a better health service for all
2.   Fair access, which aims to ensure equality of access
3.   Responsive and appropriate care delivery
4.   High performance.

Income Maintenance (Social Welfare)

In Ireland, 'income maintenance' is more commonly referred to as 'social welfare'. It is the system by which the State aims to provide a basic income for all individuals, families and their children at times when, e.g. due to illness, unemployment, disability or old age, they are unable to earn an income from employment.

The Irish social welfare system embraces three types of income maintenance schemes:

1.   Social Insurance
2.   Social Assistance
3.   Universal Allowances.

1. Social Insurance

Social Insurance (contributory benefits) is based on social insurance (PRSI) contributions. Entitlement to social insurance benefits is conditional on the claimants having a certain number of contributions paid or credited in a specific period of time.

2. Social Assistance

Social Assistance (non-contributory allowances or assistance). One of the basic requirements to qualify for payment under the social assistance schemes is that persons claiming must satisfy a means test, which shows that they have insufficient income to cover the basic necessities of life. The system of the means test here is different to that used for assessing eligibility for the medical card; it is highly complex and a Deciding Officer makes decisions about eligibility.

The Social Welfare Appeals Office was set up in 1991 to deal with all appeals against decisions made by Deciding Officers.

The Supplementary Welfare Allowance is payable to those who do not qualify for assistance or benefits. Social Welfare Officers who are attached to health centres administer this allowance. There are also special grants and supplements available under this scheme such as:

▸ Rent and Mortgage Interest Supplements

▸ Back To School Clothing and Footwear Allowance

▸ Supplements for Special Housing and Dietary Needs

▸ Exceptional Needs Payments

▸ Urgent Needs Payments.

The amount of payment, conditions and eligibility regarding social insurance, social assistance and supplementary welfare payments change regularly (typically after the annual budget), so it is advisable to get an up-to-date copy of the Guide to Social Welfare Services from the local office.

3. Universal Allowances

Child Benefit is one example in Ireland. It is paid in respect of all children regardless of income or PRSI contributions.

Table 14.5: The Main Benefits and Allowances Payable under Income Maintenance Schemes

Unemployment Payments

Unemployment Benefit
Unemployment Assistance
Part-Time Job Incentive Scheme

Family Income Support Payments

Child Benefit
Maternity Benefit
Adoptive Benefit
Health & Safety Benefit
Family Income Supplement
Supplementary Welfare Allowance
Orphan's (Contributory) Allowance
Carer's Allowance
Survivor's (Non-Contributory) Pension
Deserted Wife's Allowance
Prisoner's Wife's Allowance
One-Parent Family Payment
Survivor's (Contributory) Pension
Deserted Wife's Benefit
Orphan's (Non-Contributory) Pension

Occupational Injuries Benefits Payments

Injury Benefit
Disablement Benefit
Unemployability Supplement
Medical Care
Constant Attendance Allowance
Death Benefits (Survivor's Benefits)

Payments for Ill or Incapacitated People

Disability Benefit
  (to be known as Sickness Benefit)
Invalidity Pension
  (to be known as Disability Pension)
Disability Allowance
Blind Person's Pension

Payment for Retired or Elderly People

Retirement Pension
Old Age (Contributory) Pension
Pre-Retirement Allowance
Old Age (Non-Contributory) Pension

Payments from Health Boards

Blind Welfare Allowance
Infectious Disease Maintenance
  Allowance
Other Allowances and Grants
Charges in Public Hospitals
Income Guidelines for Medical Card
Drugs Refunds Scheme

Extra Benefit

Butter Vouchers
Fuel Allowance
Smokeless Fuel Allowance
Free Electricity Allowance
Free Natural Gas Allowance
Free Bottled Gas Refill Allowance
Free Television Licence
Free Telephone Rental Allowance
Back to School Clothing and
  Footwear Allowance
Death Grant

Other Services Provided Under the Department of Social and Family Affairs

Employment Support Services facilitates, advises and assists unemployed people and lone parents to take advantage of the full range of options for employment, education, training and self-employment.

Voluntary and Community Services administer a range of grant schemes and programmes supporting community development. They provide financial assistance toward the staffing and equipping of local resource centres, grants to locally based groups and voluntary organisations. They also provide funding for projects which tackle the problems of indebtedness and moneylending.

The Combat Poverty Agency advises and makes recommendations to the Minister on all aspects of economic and social planning in relation to poverty in the State. It also initiates and evaluates pilot measures aimed at overcoming poverty and examines the nature, causes and extent of poverty in the State while promoting greater public understanding.

Comhairle, established in 2000, combines all aspects of the work of the National Social Service Board (NSSB) and the National Rehabilitation Board (NRB). It is responsible for the provision of independent information, advice and advocacy services and its establishment is part of the government commitment to the overall mainstreaming of services for people with disabilities. Comhairle provides information and advice mainly through a network of Citizen's Information Centres and through the Citizen's Information Database at http://www.cidb.ie. The 85 information centres are locally based, nationwide, and provide information on a range of services including social welfare, health and taxation.

The Commission on Social Welfare undertook a comprehensive and fundamental review of the social welfare system in 1983, and published its report in 1986. In the report, three main objectives were identified for the social welfare system:

▸ the abolition of poverty and an improvement in the basic rates of payment
▸ an equitable redistribution of income
▸ the protection of the standard of living of claimants.

The National Anti-Poverty Strategy (NAPS) (see Chapter 5) is the driving force which has given impetus to developments in some areas related to income maintenance.

Family Support and Child Welfare Services

The Child Care Act 1991 empowers all Health Boards to develop their services in the following areas:

1.   Family Support
2.   Alternative Care (foster care, residential care and provision for homeless children)
3.   Adoption Services
4.   Child Protection Services (see Chapter 12).

1. Family Support

Central to the Child Care Act 1991 is the idea that it is best for a child to grow up in his own family if at all possible. Family support, therefore, is about promoting the welfare and healthy development of all children but particularly those who are living in adverse and stressful situations. Of course, family support cannot be divorced from support provided in all the other social service areas, namely housing, health, income and education.

Ferguson and Kenny (1995) identify three types of family support:

Developmental Family Support
These services build on the social supports and strengths which already exist in the family and community, e.g. community groups, personal development groups, recreational projects and parent education.

Compensatory Family Support
These services seek to compensate for the effects of living in situations of disadvantage and stress, e.g. through the provision of high quality pre-school services and parents support groups.

Protective Family Support
These services seek to strengthen the ability of individuals within families to survive identified risks. Direct support to individuals and families is provided through the social work service; because of the heavy demand on limited resources most of these services are problem focused, which means that priority is given to families who are most seriously at risk of complete breakdown or where a child is seriously at risk of neglect or abuse. Some examples of protective family support services are:

▸   Social Work Services
▸   Family Resource Centres

▶   Domiciliary Support Services

▶   Day Care Services

▶   Day Fostering

▶   Community Mothers Scheme.

Social Work Services

Social workers are employed in all Health Board areas to provide supportive counselling and child protection services; they also intervene where child abuse is suspected. Apart from individual support they will recommend families to other supportive services and make referrals.

Family Resource Centres

In these centres, families can take advantage of many services under one roof, i.e. supportive counselling, parenting programmes, self-help groups, courses in self-development, early childhood education and after-school services; specialist services such as speech therapy, play therapy, child and family guidance services. Different centres may offer different services depending on the resources and needs of the local population.

Domiciliary Support Services

Domiciliary childcare worker, home maker and home help services can be offered to families in their own home where day-to-day care of the home and the children is causing intolerable stress and strain for the family, e.g. perhaps where a parent is recovering from an illness. A *domiciliary childcare worker* will help the parents to develop parenting skills and will model ways of responding to children's needs.

The *home maker* helps the parent(s) to establish routines, budgets and general organisation

The *home help* is employed to help with housework.

Day Care Services

This means children are looked after in a pre-school or after-school service.

Day Fostering

This means children will spend each day with a foster family but will return home in the evenings. This is another option for families who are seriously stressed and unable to cope. It gives the family a chance to tackle their problems and children are spared the trauma of complete separation.

Community Mothers Scheme/Homestart

The Community Mothers Scheme is aimed at new mothers and operates in the Eastern Regional Health Authority. Homestart is aimed at families with children under five years and operates in the Southern and Eastern Health Board areas. They are both examples of domiciliary support which is given by trained volunteers with the services being administered by Health Board personnel. Volunteers, with training and supervision, offer support, friendship and practical help to families with babies and very young children.

2. Alternative Care

Children come into care in three ways:

Abandonment: The child becomes the legal responsibility of the Health Board concerned.

Compulsory Care: The child is taken into care for her own protection and well-being by the authorities and legal responsibility is taken by the Health Board.

Voluntary Care: Children may be placed in the care of the Health Board with the parents' consent. Indeed the parents may request it until they can sort out their difficulty. (For more details of Child Care and Protection see Chapter 12.)

There were a total of 4,216 children in the care of the Health Boards at the beginning of 2000; this was up from a reported 750 children in the care of the Health Boards in 1996.

Having been received into care, arrangements for the child's care is then organised through (a) foster care, or (b) residential care.

Foster Care

This means that the child is placed with a family who then share home and family life with that child. Foster care can be **short term** when, for example, a lone parent is hospitalised and has no family back-up. With short-term foster care, maintaining contact with the child's natural family is usually important. When children come into long-term care, and returning to their natural family is not possible in the foreseeable future, a **long-term foster** family will be sought for the child. Contact with his own family may or may not be possible. All foster parents are assessed by a social worker prior to placement. A social worker also provides support for the child and family for the duration of the placement. Foster parents have a support group. The Health Board pays a weekly maintenance allowance for each foster child and extra allowances as required.

Residential Care

In the past, residential homes were large, impersonal and institutional places; today residential care is provided in small group homes with the emphasis on personal care and individual attention.

Foster care is generally considered to be the preferred option but sometimes there are no foster families available, and sometimes trained and expert childcare staff can be in a better position to cater for the special needs of a particular child.

Of those in care in 2000, the majority (60% or 2,535 children) were placed in foster care.

Provisions for the regulation of foster care and residential care are laid down in Part VI of the Child Care Act and the regulations were implemented in 1995.

3. Adoption Services

All the Health Boards make provision for a full range of adoption services. This includes professional and counselling services to pregnant women, birth mothers, adoptive families and adoptees. Adoption services are also provided through voluntary adoption agencies in each Health Board area. An Bord Úcthála (The Adoption Board) is the statutory body which ratifies all adoption placements.

When a child is adopted, this means that the birth mother/natural mother relinquishes all legal rights to her child and these rights are passed in full to the adoptive parents. This does not happen overnight but involves a lengthy assessment of the adoptive parents and in-depth counselling with the birth mother/parents. There is also a considerable time lapse (at least three to six months) between the placement of a child for adoption and the mother's signing of the final consent form. Maintaining links between the child, the birth mother and the adoptive parents is now also a feature of adoption work

Foreign Adoptions: Under the Adoption Act 1991, Health Boards have a statutory responsibility to carry out assessments for couples/families planning to adopt abroad. The number of Irish children being adopted has been steadily decreasing but the number of adoptions of children overseas has been increasing.

Tracing of birth parents is an area of adoptive work that is steadily increasing.

Education

Education is compulsory for all children between the ages of six and fifteen years. In practice the majority of children start school between the ages of four and five. Parents can choose to educate their children outside the school system but have to show that their children are receiving an appropriate education. Official and practical support for this is limited.

Formal education in Ireland is provided by the Department of Education and Science at primary, secondary and third level and is free at all levels. However, there are considerable costs attached to education apart from tuition fees, e.g. books, uniforms and so-called 'voluntary contributions'. At primary and secondary level supplementary welfare grants are available for those who are on long-term benefit or who can prove that the costs involved would cause undue hardship. At third level a grant is available to individual students but this is means tested.

(Details of early childhood education services provision are given in Chapter 1.)

Voluntary Services

The provision of services and support through voluntary agencies has always been very important in Ireland and there is a large number of voluntary organisations in operation. It is not possible to cover all those which provide services to families with young children. Some voluntary services have already been outlined. Two nationwide organisations that provide a range of services to families and children are described below.

Barnardos

In consultation with statutory and other agencies, Barnardos provides and develops selected services for disadvantaged children and their families. These services include:

▸   Pre-school Services

▸   Toy Library

▸   Counselling and Support

▸   Adoption Advisory Service

▸   Advisory service for people who are setting up early services

▸   Children's Resource Centre which includes a library and reference section

▸   Training Services

▸   Family Centres.

The Irish Society for the Prevention of Cruelty to Children (ISPCC)

The ISPCC offers child-centred services aimed at improving child/parent relationships and reducing levels of violence in families. These services include:

▸   National Childline Service

▸   Children's Centres

- Family Centres
- Children's Resource Centre
- Child and Parenting Centre
- Children's Rights Campaign
- Services for teenagers.

ACTIVITY

Services and facilities available in different areas of the country will vary greatly. This activity aims to help you to identify those that are available in your local area.

SCENARIO 1

Anne is a young mother who has arrived in your area with her two children aged two and five years. After years of suffering domestic violence she has decided to make a clean break and start life afresh for herself and her children. Unfortunately, a refuge does not exist in your area.

- Make a list of the needs of Anne and her family.
- Identify the support services resources available to them.

SCENARIO 2

Michael and Sheila have five young children; the age range is 10 years, twins aged 7 years, 3 years and a baby aged 9 months. Michael has been unemployed for a long time. The family income is unemployment assistance and they are heavily in debt to a moneylender. The old family house in which they lived has been deemed unfit for habitation and they must move. On top of this the twins are about to make their first communion and Sheila has to go into hospital for a hysterectomy. The family, besides having financial difficulties, is at breaking point and Michael does not feel that he will be able to cope when Sheila goes into hospital.

- Make a list of this family's needs.
- Prioritise the items on this list.
- Identify resources that are available to help the family through this crisis.

In carrying out this task, find out exactly what would be available for both these families in your own area. Include all statutory and voluntary social services.

SUMMARY

▶   Services for families and children are provided through State, voluntary and private bodies.

▶   The system of service provision in Ireland is two-tiered — private and public.

▶   The main areas of social service provision are housing, health, income maintenance, family support services and education.

▶   Services may vary from area to area.

References

Curry, John, 1998, *Irish Social Services*, 3rd edn., Dublin: Institute of Public Administration

Ferguson H. and P. Kenny, 1995, *On Behalf of the Child: Child Welfare, Child Protection and the Child Care Act (1991)*, Dublin: A & A Farmar

Report of the Commission on Social Welfare, 1986, Dublin: Stationery Office

Key Terms — Section Six

Chapter 13

Socialisation
Primary socialisation
Secondary socialisation
Peers
Culture
Beliefs
Values
Norms
Customs
Social roles
Role conflict
Role reversal
Formal social control
Informal social control
Production
Reproduction

Monogamy

Bigamy

Polygamy

Commune

Conjugal family

Nuclear family

One-parent family

Extended family

Reconstructed family

Serial monogamy

Chapter 14

Absolute poverty

Relative poverty

Statutory services

Voluntary services

Private services

Private rented housing

Local authority

Differential rents

Tenant purchase schemes

Social housing

Homelessness

Community care

General hospital

Special hospital

Eligibility

Means test

Medical card

Long-Term Illness Scheme

Income maintenance

Two-tiered system

Social insurance

Social assistance

Universal benefit

Contributory

Non-contributory

Supplementary welfare allowance

Developmental family support

Compensatory family support

Protective family support

Social work support

Family resource centre

Day care

Community mothers

Homestart

Domiciliary support

Compulsory care

Voluntary care

Alternative care

Foster care

Residential care

Adoption

Birth mother

Tracing

Appendix 1

UN Convention on the Rights of the Child — Unofficial Summary

The United Nations Convention on the Rights of the Child
Unofficial Summary of Main Provisions

Article 5
Parental guidance and the child's evolving capacities

The State's duty to respect the rights and responsibilities of parents and the wider family to provide guidance appropriate to the child's evolving capacities.

Article 6
Survival and development

The inherent right to life, and the State's obligation to ensure the child's survival and development.

Article 7
Name and nationality

The right to have a name from birth and to be granted a nationality.

Article 8
Preservation of identity

The State's obligation to protect and, if necessary, re-establish the basic aspects of a child's identity (name, nationality and family ties).

Article 9
Separation from parents

The child's right to live with his/her parents unless this is deemed incompatible with his/her best interests; the right to maintain contact with both parents if separated from one or both; the duties of States in cases where such separation results from State action.

Article 12
The child's opinion

The child's right to express an opinion, and to have that opinion taken into account, in any matter or procedure affecting the child.

Article 13
Freedom of expression

The child's right to obtain and make known information, and to express his or her views, unless this would violate the rights of others.

Article 14
Freedom of thought, conscience and religion

The child's right to freedom of thought, conscience and religion, subject to appropriate parental guidance and national law.

Article 18
Parental responsibilities

The principle that both parents have joint primary responsibility for bringing up their children, and that the State should support them in this task.

Article 19
Protection from abuse and neglect

The State's obligation to protect children from all forms of maltreatment perpetrated by parents or others responsible for their care, and to undertake preventive and treatment programmes in this regard.

Article 20
Protection of children without families

The State's obligation to provide special protection for children deprived of their family environment and to ensure that appropriate alternative family care or institutional placement is made available to them, taking into account the child's cultural background.

Article 25
Periodic review of placement

The right of children placed by the State for reasons of care, protection or treatment to have all aspects of that placement evaluated regularly.

Article 26
Social security

The right of children to benefit from social security.

Article 27
Standard of living

The right of children to benefit from an adequate standard of living, the primary responsibility of parents to provide this, and the State's duty to ensure that this responsibility is first fulfillable and then fulfilled, where necessary through the recovery of maintenance.

Article 37

Torture and deprivation of liberty

The prohibition of torture, cruel treatment or punishment, capital punishment, life imprisonment, and unlawful arrest or deprivation of liberty. The principles of appropriate treatment, separation from detained adults, contact with family and access to legal and other assistance.

From: Williams, K. and R. Gardner, 1993, *Caring for Children*, London: Pitman Publishing

Appendix 2

Doing a Research Project

Glossary of Terms

Administer:	to direct or conduct an interview, questionnaire or test.
Atypical:	irregular, not usual.
Bias:	a slant or point of view. A study is said to be biased if the researcher has been subjective and influenced the outcome. To prejudice the outcome.
Bibliography:	a list and description of all books, articles and other sources that the researcher has read and which have informed the study.
Case study:	a detailed examination of a person, a group, an organisation or even a country.
Checklist:	a list which shows at a glance items that are arranged in a logical order, and against which the researcher can check.
Citation:	a passage referred to, or words quoted from, the work of another author.
Classify:	to arrange in sets according to common characteristics.
Closed questions:	have pre-set answers. The researcher limits the range of answers. (See also **questionnaire** and **open questions**.)
Confidentiality:	adherence to principles of trust and privacy.
Content analysis:	an examination and classification of the subject and approach of a piece of communication such as an individual document, media article or programme, book, letter or report.
Data:	facts, quantities or conditions which are given or known.
Ethics:	relating to morals and obligation.
Experiments:	a trial where the researcher sets up conditions in order to study the effects of one or more factors on a subject(s).
Hypothesis:	a theory; a speculation on what might be.

Interview:	a conversation between a researcher and a respondent, the purpose of which is to elicit information on a certain topic/area.
Longitudinal survey:	a study undertaken over a period of time; it could be weeks or years.
Non-participant:	no involvement with, or influence on, the subject.
Objective:	external to the researcher's own mind, feelings or values.
Official statistics:	facts and figures contained in authorised public sources.
Open question:	allows respondents to give a broad, informative and in-depth answer if they wish to do so.
Opinion poll:	a survey of people's opinions.
Participant:	the researcher is part of the group.
Primary research/source:	all the information and data that the researcher has found out for himself/herself.
Qualitative research:	pertaining to quality, it aims to gain insight through the study of individuals.
Quantitative research:	pertaining to quantity; it aims to study the relationship of one set of facts to another using scientific methods.
Questionnaire:	a list or series of questions designed to elicit certain information. (See also **open questions** and **closed questions**.)
Quotation:	the use of an author's exact words.
References:	a list and description of all the works (books, articles, CD-ROMs) which have either been quoted or mentioned in a text.
Reliability:	the research method used will produce the same or similar results every time it is carried out in the same conditions.
Representative sample:	a section of the population which is typical of the general population.
Respondent:	a person who replies to questions or who allows himself/herself to be interviewed.
Response rate:	the number or percentage of people who participate in the research.

Sample: The numbers of people/groups about whom facts are gathered.

Secondary sources: all sources of information, other than primary sources, which may be used to support primary research or may be used exclusively in a study.

Structured interviews: a very tightly organised interview with set questions. (See also **interview** and **unstructured interview**.)

Subjective: relating to the researcher's own mind and thoughts.

Survey: aims to gain information from a representative selection of the population. Questionnaires, interviews or checklists are common tools used.

Unstructured interviews: an open interview with the interviewer given scope to rephrase questions or to ask extra ones. (See also **interview**, **structured interview** and **open questions**.)

Doing a Research Project

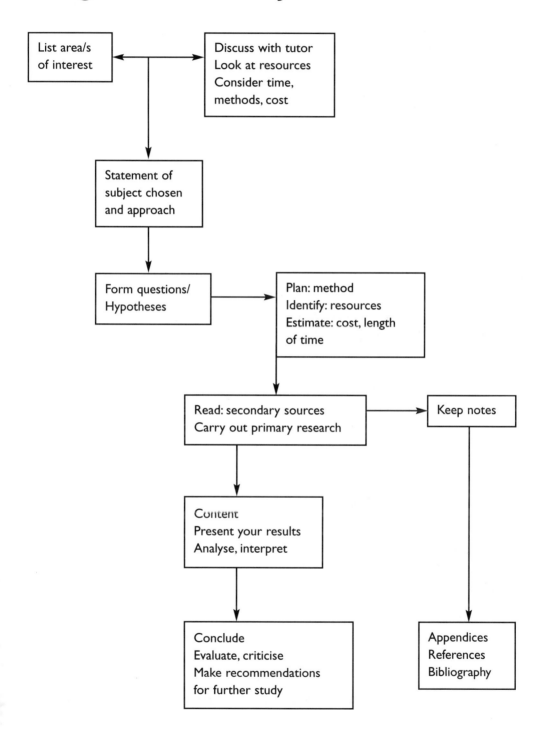

Choosing a Topic

Choose your topic early and avoid the urge to keep changing. List your areas of interest.

Several exercises and tasks are set throughout this book which would be ideal to take on as a project but you may prefer to choose a topic about which you know absolutely nothing, or a topic about which you feel very strongly or have a particular interest. The choice should be an individual one. If a group undertake a project together careful planning, close co-operation and regular reviews are required.

Narrowing the Subject Area

Discuss your choice of topic with your tutor. Your tutor will pose many questions which will help you to narrow your focus.

Inevitably, whether you are doing a school project or a Ph.D. you will begin with a broad idea, which then has to be narrowed down. For example, you might be interested in considering the impact of television on children; the following questions would help to narrow the focus of the topic:

▶ Which programmes am I going to consider?

▶ What age group will I focus on? There will be a vast difference between the content of a study that has 2- to 3-year-olds rather than teenagers as a focus.

▶ What slant will you take:
  — effects of violence
  — effects on general knowledge
  — effects on social interaction
  — effects on literacy?

Statement of Subject Chosen

Write down a broad outline of the topic you are going to cover, your aims and your hypotheses.

Identify Sources

Where and how you are going to get your information? Be realistic. Start with your textbooks (secondary research). List all other possible sources — local libraries, facilities, services, newspapers, TV, local representatives, tutors, other students, staff at your work placement, children. Do not be discouraged if there appears to be a lack of secondary material on your chosen topic. If there is very little already, then your project will be all the more interesting.

Using the Library

In a library it is useful to be familiar with the arrangements and divisions. Most libraries are divided into three main areas:

▶ Fiction: this is usually arranged by author in alphabetical order; it may also be subdivided into different categories e.g. Romance, adventure, science fiction.

▶ Non-fiction.

▶ Reference — dictionaries, thesaurus etc.

If you know the name of the book or the author you can locate it using the author or subject index, but if you want to browse a subject area refer to the 'Dewey Decimal Classification' system. The main divisions are:

000–099	Generalities
100–199	Philosophy
200–299	Religion
300–399	The Social Sciences
400–499	Language
500–599	Pure Sciences
600–699	Applied Sciences
700–799	Fine Arts
800–899	Literature
900–999	Geography, Biography and History

Librarians will help you to locate books on a particular subject.

If a particular title is not available in the library, the Librarian may be able to tell which library nearby will be able to help. Many libraries are now computerised and you will be able to locate the books on this system.

When you have located a book, use the following approach to find out if it contains material which might be relevant or useful in your research.

Check:
▶ contents page
▶ date of publication
▶ Introduction
▶ conclusion
▶ index.

What Research Methods to Use?

If you are going to do some primary research decide what primary method suits your purpose. For example if you are doing a survey:

▶   Are you going to use a questionnaire/interview?

▶   What questions will you ask?

▶   How many people will be included in your research?

▶   Are you going to approach organisations?

▶   How much is it going to cost?

▶   How much time will you need for your primary research?

▶   Is all this possible?

Designing and Using a Questionnaire

Decide	—	what information you want.
Design	—	the question that will help obtain the information.
Write	—	the questions down in logical sequence on a 'form'.
Select	—	the people that you are going to question.
Ask	—	these people the questions.
Record	—	the answers, using tick boxes, graphs or other suitable methods which make them easy to read.
Present	—	the findings in an appropriate way.
Conclude	—	with statements drawn from the analysis.

Writing Up Your Report

Your project will contain the following sections: Title page, Contents page, Introduction, Description of methodology, Main body of text, Conclusion, Appendices, References and Bibliography.

Keep a record of all your planning notes. This is part of the research. Sometimes you will do a lot of background work, which will not be evident in your written submission, and it is recommended to provide evidence of all your project work.

Introduction

Your introduction should be brief and clear; it should give a broad overview of the general area, which might include a definition of subject area identifying size and context. For example if you are going to do a study on Traveller children and their participation in early education, your introduction would include a definition of

'Traveller', how many Travellers there are, percentage of the population as a whole, percentage that are aged 5 or under, an overview of Traveller participation in education generally and a comment on literacy levels.

Your introduction should then state clearly what you are going to examine in your project and what you expect (or hope) to find out. In the example above you may write — *'I am going to look at the participation levels of Traveller children of pre-school age in integrated early education settings. Participation levels have always been very low, so I will try to identify the main barriers and difficulties as well as the factors which contribute to successful integration.'*

Definition of Methodology

This can be fairly brief. You should outline how you conducted your study. State what type of research you used (primary/secondary) and include a brief description of this, giving numbers covered and time spent if applicable. What did you read? You should point out the strengths and weaknesses in your methodology.

Main Body of Text

This is the main part of your written project in which you:

▶   present

▶   analyse

▶   relate to theory.

Experiment with different ways of presenting your findings. Data taken from surveys and questionnaires need to be put into categories and groups so that the reader will easily be able to see patterns of difference or similarity and extract significant information. Numerical data can be presented in many ways — tables, bar charts, histograms, graphs These are the simplest methods of presenting your data. If you have access to a computer then you may be able to produce very elaborate presentations.

Photographs, video or audio recordings may be used. When you have presented your findings, describe what you have found drawing attention to significant points, what surprised you, which results were predictable. How did your findings relate to the literature? For example, if you study a group of five-years-olds playing with construction toys then you should be able to relate this to what is said about children's development in your text books.

Example of a Table
Expenditure per Student

	1990	1991	1992	1993	1994	1995	1996	1997	1998
Primary	1072	1136	1260	1350	1438	1477	1552	1690	1786
2nd Level	1811	1892	1963	2136	2254	2290	2376	2604	2645
3rd level	4130	3887	3898	3932	3947	3905	4209	4749	4016
Ratio of 3rd to Primary	3.9:1	3.4:1	3.1:1	2.9:1	2.7:1	2.6:1	2.7:1	2.8:1	2.2:1

Source: Cantillon, Corrigan, Kirby and O'Flynn, 2001. *Rich and Poor*, Dublin: Oak Tree Press

Example of a Graph

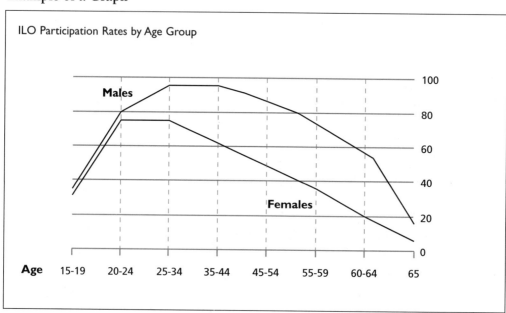

ILO Participation Rates by Age Group

Source: CSO Statistical Release, Sept–Nov 1997

Example 1 of a Bar Chart

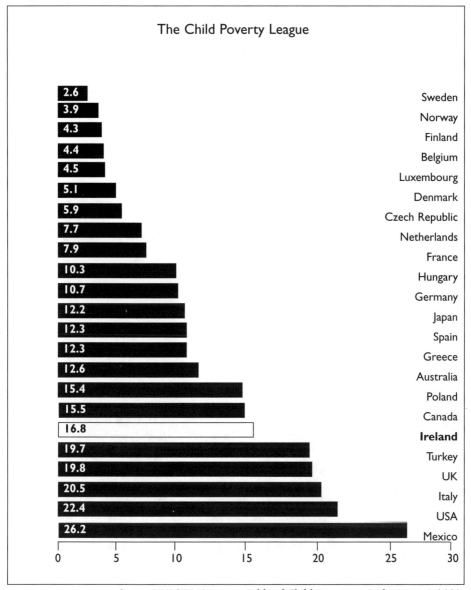

The Child Poverty League

Value	Country
2.6	Sweden
3.9	Norway
4.3	Finland
4.4	Belgium
4.5	Luxembourg
5.1	Denmark
5.9	Czech Republic
7.7	Netherlands
7.9	France
10.3	Hungary
10.7	Germany
12.2	Japan
12.3	Spain
12.3	Greece
12.6	Australia
15.4	Poland
15.5	Canada
16.8	**Ireland**
19.7	Turkey
19.8	UK
20.5	Italy
22.4	USA
26.2	Mexico

Source: UNICEF, 'A League Table of Child Poverty in Rich Nations', 2000.

Example 2 of Bar Chart

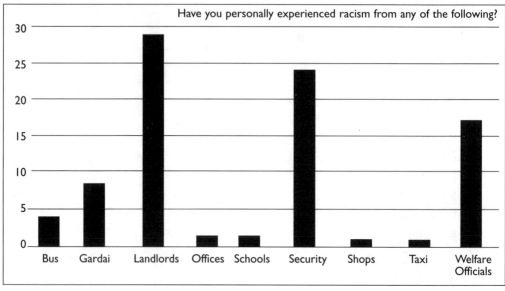

Frm ARN, 1999: *African Refugees and Need Analysis*

Example of a Pie Chart

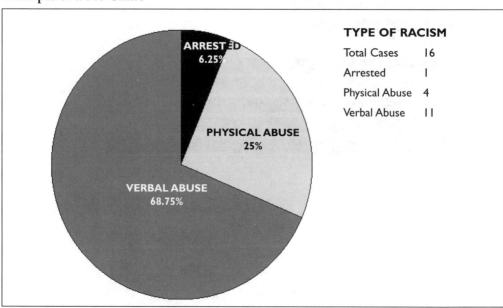

Source: African Refugees Need and Analysis

Conclusion

▸ Summarise

▸ Clarify

▸ Evaluate

▸ Recommend.

Summarise and clarify the main points but do not go into long repetitions of what you have already said. Do not be tempted to include opinions and hunches here that were not evident in your research.

Be critical of yourself and your methodology and indicate improvements you could make if undertaking the project again. Were you surprised by anything you discovered while doing your project? Comment on bias, and any ethical issues that have arisen. Suggest ways that you feel the research area could be extended. In your evaluation do not be afraid to be negative, e.g. admitting 'In my questionnaire, answers given to No. X revealed nothing material to the study because I had phrased the question badly'. You will demonstrate by admitting this that you have acquired an insight into the skill of devising questions. However, if you try to cover up the fact that some part was not a success or if you do not mention it, hoping that it will not be noticed, you will be showing that you have gained little skill or that you are a dishonest researcher!

Appendices

In the appendix, include material not suitable for the main part of your study, e.g. newspaper cuttings, the questionnaire that you used, a copy of a table of statistics. Label them clearly, as the purpose of appendices is that you can refer to them in the main text.

References and Bibliography
How to Compile References and a Bibliography

An outline of the 'Harvard System' of referencing is given below. There are other systems and this is why you will notice that references and bibliographies may be presented differently. All methods are broadly similar but whatever one you adopt you should stick to it, or both you and your readers will be totally confused.

Referencing

▸ Quotations must be taken word for word from the original text.

▸ Short quotations begin and end with a single inverted comma, e.g. 'Early childhood learns by playing and therefore optimal learning means freedom to play' (Leach, 1994: 138).

▶ Longer quotations (three or more lines) are set out separately from the enclosing paragraph; they are usually indented and do not have quotation marks, e.g.

Early childhood learns by playing and therefore optimal learning means freedom to play: to choose what to do, with whom, when and for how long; to touch, manipulate and experiment as well as to look and listen... (Leach, 1994: 138).

▶ If you do not quote a sentence in full you indicate this by use of an **ellipsis** as in the example above.

▶ Please note in the example that the reference is placed in brackets at the end of the quote and consists of the author's surname and the year of publication, followed by the page number.

▶ Citations: if the author's name is part of the sentence you should put the year of publication in brackets (parentheses), e.g. Leach (1994) argues that post-industrial society is not good for children. It neither caters for their basic needs nor furthers children's rights.

▶ At the end of your project, essay or report you should list the references by author surname alphabetically.

For Books

Author's surname, followed by initials, Year of publication, *Title*, Place of publication: Publisher

EXAMPLE:

Hobart, C. and J. Frankel, 1994, *A Practical Guide to Child Observation*, Cheltenham: Stanley Thornes

For Journal Articles

Author's surname, followed by initials, Date of publication, 'Title of article', *Name of journal*, Volume number, Issue number: Pages

Examples:

Clarke, B., 1994, 'Drug Using Parents: The Child Care Issues', *The Irish Social Worker*, Vol. 12, No. 2: 9

Mouatt, K., 1998, 'Good Management', *Nursery World*, 23 April: 14–5

For Edited Collections

Author's surname, followed by initials, Year of publication, Title of essay/chapter, in *Title of publication*, ed. Name of editor, Place of publication: Publisher

Example:
Robinson, M., 1993, 'Women and the Law in Ireland', in *Irish Women's Studies Reader,* ed. Ailbhe Smyth, Dublin: Attic Press

Electronic Sources
Surname of author, name, title of web page, website address, date last accessed

Example
Berkeley Carroll, Sample Bibliography or Works cited, Available: *http://www.berkelycarroll.org/bis/tour, September 1998*
Crane, Nancy, Electronic sources: MLA Style of Citation, University of Vermont, Available: *http://www.uvm.edu/~ncrane/estyles/mla.html, September 1998.*

Note: These two sources use a method slightly different from the Harvard method in referencing written sources.

CD-ROMs
Author, Title of article, *Name of magazine or publication*: Name of database, Format, Name of company

Example:
Angier, Natlaie, *Chemists Learn Why Vegetables Are Good for You*, *New York Times*, 13 Apr. 1993, late ed.: C1. New York Times On disc, CD-ROM, UMI-Proquest, October, 1993

Please note:
▶ Punctuation marks are used specifically — commas, full stops, colons and quotation marks (the latter in relation to journal articles).
▶ The second line of the reference is indented so that the surname of the first author is easily identified.
▶ If there are more than three authors, the citation lists the first surname followed by 'et al.', e.g. Beaver et al. 1999.
▶ Second and subsequent author's initials come before the surname.
▶ If you refer to the same author and book twice (or more) in a row with no reference between them you can use the abbreviation 'ibid' — i.e. 'the work referred to above'.

There are many finer points to be learned about referencing; only the basics are included here. Probably the best way to learn is to note how references are handled in your textbooks and other books that you will read.

Appendix 3

Sample Narrative Observation

OBSERVATION OF A CHILD'S EMOTIONAL DEVELOPMENT

Observation Number	One
Date	29 March 2003
Method and Media Used	Narrative method, using pen and paper
Start Time	11.07 am
Finish Time	11.14 am
Number of Children Present	12
Number of Adults Present	4
Permission From	Child's parent and nursery manager

Setting

The observation took place in a workplace nursery providing crèche and Montessori pre-school services for employees of a local company. It is located within five minutes walk of the parents' workplace. The service is open from 8.15 a.m. to 6.15 p.m., Monday to Friday.

Immediate Context

The children are playing in the garden. A small group of four or five are playing in toy cars, while others are pushing the cars. The other children are playing with various other toys and the adults are supervising the group. TC is sitting on a toy car.

Child Observed TC

Description of Child

TC is female, aged 1 year and 6 months. She is an only child whose parents commute to work every day. She has been attending the centre on a full-time basis since she was 11 months old. She is very well settled here, and has a close attachment with one member of staff. She eats well, and takes a nap every day for about one and a half hours. She is in the toddler group; this consists of eight children aged between 15 months and two and a half years. There are two full-time staff members with this group.

Aim and Rationale

To observe TC at outdoor play in the garden, and to assess her emotional development. I am doing this because I am interested to discover how she plays in an unstructured environment and in a larger group than she is used to. This is the first time I have observed her playing outdoors.

The Observation

TC is sitting on a toy car, both feet flat on the ground and both hands grasping the steering wheel. She is looking in my direction. She is moving her body forward over the steering wheel and turning her head around toward the left. Pushing with both feet at the same time, she begins to move the car backwards. Looking down toward the steering wheel, she stoops and looks in A's direction (the adult). She then looks back toward the steering-wheel and begins to push again with both feet, moving the car. Looking toward TC2 she sits still for a moment with her mouth open.

A says 'hi' to TC.

TC smiles and turns her head in A's direction, looks away still smiling and turns her head back again. Again she turns her head down toward the steering wheel and begins to move the car backwards. She stops and starts this movement several times, looking around her and then looking in my direction. She is now standing up, sitting down and moving backwards in the car again. Pushing with both feet, she is moving until she backs into the climbing frame/slide. Putting her right arm on the climbing frame and turning her head to the right she is looking through a slot in the climbing frame. Putting her right hand back on the steering-wheel, she is again moving the car backwards and forwards a few inches, while facing forwards.

She is now putting her right arm on the climbing frame and her left arm on the slide. She replaces both hands on the steering-wheel and moves the car backwards, again using both feet on the ground to push. She is standing up and sitting down quickly. Again her right hand is going onto the climbing frame and her left hand on to the slide. Turning and looking toward A she says 'hiya', sticking out her tongue and beginning to laugh.

TC passes her left hand over the steering wheel a few times and then brings it to rest. She stands up and looks in the direction of TC3. Now she is sitting down, looking around her and beginning to laugh again.

Evaluation

The aim of this observation was to observe TC and to assess her emotional development. I wish to examine her stage of development as well as her temperament.

Stage of Development

In terms of her stage of development, TC showed that she was trying out new, developing physical skills and enjoying it. She was cautious on the toy car, but stuck with it, moving it carefully backwards and forwards. According to Bruce and Meggitt (1999: 187), this trying out of new skills is an important feature of this stage. It is part of the development of autonomy, doing things for herself. TC showed evidence of this in the observation, playing on the car, using her legs and physical strength to move the car backwards, '...trying out new, developing physical skills' (ibid).

In this type of activity, there are no unrealistic expectations of what she can manage; this is important in terms of developing her self-esteem (ibid: 186).

Her stage of social play is apparent in the observation. She is playing alone, but from the amount of looking around she does she is very aware of the other children around her, and also of A. She is in the stage of parallel play, which means that she is not interacting with other children (Beaver et al., 1999: 74). This fits in with the above comment on her trying out new skills — she needs to focus right now on practising her developing skills, and appears more interested in A than in the other children. She does stand by the slide watching through the slot in the climbing frame for a few moments, but turns her attention back to the toy car fairly quickly.

Temperament

Temperament is defined by Bruce and Meggitt (1999: 189) as:

▶ Emotionality: the child's feelings
▶ Activity: whether the child does things impulsively or slowly
▶ Sociability: whether the child likes company or not
▶ Variations in concentrating on something.

Her confidence in the environment and in her caregivers is evident in that she plays quite happily and explores what she could do with the car. In the observation we see her responding to A, saying 'hi', smiling and laughing. She appears calm and content in the observation.

The level and type of activity seen in the observation is a good indicator of TC's temperament. She behaves with a certain amount of caution on the car, looking around her frequently, but is neither totally impulsive or slow. Overall, she is probably more inclined to be slow than impulsive — taking her time, moving slowly, stopping frequently and looking around.

Sociability is relevant to her stage of development. She is interacting with the adult and looks toward her several times.

She stays involved in what she is doing for the length of the observation, apart from saying 'hi' to the adult.

The overall picture of her temperament is of a balanced, content and focused child. We also get a picture of her style of doing things — consistent and focused.

Personal Learning Gained

I learned something about the emotional development of TC, and how this is connected to other areas of development — in this observation that was physical development. Separating out the areas of development is useful from the point of view of studying each one individually, but in the child it is apparent that they influence each other. In the case of TC, her use of physical skills showed me something about her emotional development.

Recommendations

Continuing to practices new skills will develop TC's autonomy and ability to do things for herself. This in turn will develop her self-esteem. Since she seemed to enjoy the toy car, she could try out some other ride-on toys in the garden. She could also be encouraged to try out the climbing frame with help from the adult.

References

Beaver, M., J. Brewster, P. Jones, A. Keene, S. Neaum and J. Tallack, 1999, Babies and Young Children Book 2: Early Years Education and Care, 2nd ed., Cheltenham: Stanley Thornes

Bruce, T. and C. Meggitt, 1999, Child Care and Education, 2nd ed., London: Hodder & Stoughton

Bibliography

Beaver, M., J. Brewster, P. Jones, A. Keene, S. Neaum and J. Tallack, 1999, *Babies and Young Children Book 2: Early Years Education and Care*, 2nd ed., Cheltenham: Stanley Thornes

Bee, H., 2000, THE DEVELOPING CHILD, 9TH EDN., MA: Allyn and Bacon

Bruce, T. and C. Meggitt, 1999, *Child Care and Education*, 2nd ed., London: Hodder & Stoughton

Harding, J. and L. Meldon-Smith, 1999, *Helping Young Children to Develop, a Step-by-Step Guide*, London: Hodder & Stoughton

Signatures

Learner   —————————————   Date   —————————————

Supervisor/Parent —————————————   Date   —————————————

Tutor   —————————————   Date   —————————————

Appendix 4

FETAC Modules and Related Chapters

FETAC Modules	Chapter
Child Development	**9**, **10**, 3, 6, 8, 12, **Appendix 3**, **Appendix 5**
Early Childhood Education	**7**, **8**, 6, 3
Working in Childcare	**1**, **2**, **3**, **4**, 5, 6, 12, Appendix 1
Caring for Children 0–6 years	**2**, **7**, 12
Social Studies	**11**, **12**, **13**, **14**, 5, 6, Appendix 2

Note: Chapter numbers in bold highlight the main sources of information for that module.

Appendix 5

Sample FETAC Examination Questions

Social Studies

Question 1
(a) What is the difference between foster care and adoption?
(b) Write brief notes on two of the following, outlining services that they provide: ISPCC; Barnardos; Community Mothers Scheme; Department of Social and Family Affairs.
(c) A lone parent and her three children (ages 5 years, 2 years, and 3 months) arrive in Dublin with no means of support. Outline the support services that could be offered.

Question 2
(a) What is the term used for a family which includes only:
    (i) Father, mother and children?
    (ii) Mother and child?
(b) List two other types of family groupings.
(c) Outline two major changes which have affected the Irish family in the last fifty years.
(d) Describe the possible effects of marital breakdown on children.

Question 3
(a) List five factors which contribute to the measurement of one's social class.
(b) Lone parents are at greater risk of living in poverty. Give three reasons why this is so.
(c) A child who comes from a poor family can be disadvantaged in many ways. Explain how disadvantage can be compounded within the education setting.

Question 4
(a) In the box below, study questions V, W, X, Y and indicate which are open and which are closed questions. (NB You do not have to answer the questions V, W, X, and Y.)

V   What do you think about racism?

W   Do you agree or disagree with the following statement:

'The influence of the Catholic Church is weakening in Ireland today.'

X   How many cigarettes do you smoke per day?

None

5–10

11–20

21–30

Y   Why do you think people commit crime?

(b)   You have studied theory and carried out research while on this course. Give two examples of areas on which you might do research in an early childhood setting. (Examples may be child focused, parent focused or staff focused.)

(c)   You want to find out if parents are satisfied with the service offered in your early childhood centre. Name one method of research you would use. What are the advantages and disadvantages of the method chosen?

Question 5

(a)   Write a short note on one the following:
  (i)   Health Board Social Worker
  (ii)   Domiciliary Services
  (iii) Care Order
  (iv)   ISPCC.

(b)   Where would you advise parents to go for help if lack of finance is leading to family stress and neglect of children?

(c)   Outline the role of voluntary agencies in family support.

Question 6

(a)   List three signs indicating that a child is being neglected.

(b)   Give five examples of circumstances which research has shown may lead to child abuse.

(c)   Discuss the advantages and disadvantages of one of the following:
  (i)   Foster Care
  (ii)   Residential Care.

Question 7

(a)   According to research, children in the age range 1–4 years are the most likely of all age groups to be abused. List three reasons for this.

(b)   Write short notes on two of the following in relation to child protection:

▶   The Early Services Manager

▶   The Gardaí

▶   The Social Worker

▶   The Child Care Manager.

(c)   Although adults are primarily responsible for child protection, children also need to learn some self-protection skills. Describe in detail two activities which could be carried out with 1–4 year olds that would increase their ability to cope in difficult situations.

Question 8

(a)   What do you understand by the term 'Equality'?

(b)   With reference to the following:

▶   People with physical/sensory disabilities

▶   Travellers

▶   People who have a mental illness

▶   Refugees.

(i)   Give examples of prejudice and discrimination which they might experience.

(ii)   Outline how individuals could enhance positive images in early childhood services.

(iii) Outline, briefly, strategies which could be implemented at governmental level (laws and policies) to combat prejudice and discrimination.

Child Development

Short answer questions

1.   How could a childcare worker encourage a pre-school child's creativity?

2.   List two mathematical skills that children could learn when playing with water.

3.   You have €10.00 to spend on a toy for a baby aged three months. What toy would you purchase and why?

4.   List four items of outdoor equipment that would help to promote the gross motor development of a group of young children aged 3–5 years.

5.   What is a child-centred activity?

6.   Name two skills that a pre-school child could develop when playing with playdough.

7.   Explain the difference between process and product in relation to a child's creative development.

Structured Questions

Question 1

(a)   State five reasons why it is important for pre-schools to keep accurate records of how children are progressing developmentally.

(b)   Describe any two methods of observation that a pre-school or nursery might use to gain specific information about the developmental progress of a child.

(c)   Outline how your course has prepared you to participate in observation and record-keeping roles in the workplace.

Question 2

(a)   Select two of the following observation techniques:
   (i)   Checklist
   (ii)   Time Sampling
   (iii)   Event Sampling.

Write about each technique that you have selected under the following headings:

▸   A brief description of the technique

▸   When the technique should be used

▸   The advantages of the technique

▸   The disadvantages of the technique.

(b)   Why is it important to carry out observations in an early childhood setting?

Resources

READING RESOURCES

Beaver, M., J. Brewster, P. Jones, A. Keane, S. Neaum and J. Tallack, 1999, *Babies and Young Children, Books 1 and 2*, 2nd ed,. London: Stanley Thornes

Bell, Judith, 1993, *Doing Your Research Project: A Guide for First Time Researchers in Education and Social Science*, 2nd edn., Buckingham: Open University Press

Brown, B., 2001, *Combating Discrimination: Persona Dolls in Action*, Staffs: Trentham Books

Bruce, T. and C. Meggitt, 2002, *Child Care and Education*, 3rd edn., London: Hodder & Stoughton

Carswell, D., 2002, *Child's Play, An Exploration into the Quality of Childcare Processes*, Dublin: IPPA, the Early Childhood Organisation.

Children's Rights Alliance, 2000, *A Country is Judged on How it treats its Children. An Information Pack on the importance of the UN Convention on the Rights of the Child*, Dublin: Children's Rights Alliance

Cleary, A., M. Nic Ghiolla Phádraig, and S. Quinn (eds), 2001, *Understanding Children, Vol. 1: State, Education and Economy*, Dublin: Oak Tree Press

Comhairle, 2000, *Employment Rights Explained*, Dublin: Comhairle

Commission on the Family, 1998, *Strengthening Families for Life. Final Report*, Dublin. Stationery Office

Creaser, B. and E. Dau (eds), 1996, *The Anti-bias Approach in Early Childhood*, Sydney: Harper Educational Publishers

Department of Education and Science, 1999, *Ready to Learn — White Paper on Early Childhood Education*, Dublin: Stationery Office

Department of Health and Children, 1999, *Children First: National Guidelines for the Protection of Children*, Dublin: Stationery Office

Department of Health and Children, 1997, *Child Care (Pre-school Services) Regulations 1996 and Explanatory Guide to Requirements and Procedures for Notification and Inspection*, Dublin: Stationery Office

Department of Health and Children, 2000, *Our Children — Their Lives: The National Children's Strategy*, Dublin: Stationery Office

Department of Justice, Equality and Law Reform, 1999, *The National Childcare Strategy; Report of the Partnership 2000 Expert Working Group on Childcare*, Dublin: Stationery Office

Derman-Sparks, L., 1989, *Anti-bias Curriculum: Tools for Empowering Young Children*, Washington DC: National Association for the Education of Young Children

Dodge, Diane T., L.J. Colker and C. Heroman, 2002, *The Creative Curriculum for Preschool, 4th ed.*, Washington: Teaching Strategies Inc.

Dombro, A.L., L.T. Colker and D.T. Dodge, 1999, *The Creative Curriculum for Infants and Toddlers, 2nd ed.*, Washington: Teaching Strategies Inc.

Douglas, F., M. Horgan and C. O'Brien (eds), 2000, *Project E.Y.E.: An Irish Curriculum for the Three to Four Year Old Child*, Cork: The Early Years Unit, UCC

Drummond, M.J. and D. Rouse, 1992, *Making Assessment Work*, London: NCB

Environmental Health Standards for Full-time Pre-school Services, 1996, Sligo: EHOA

Equality Authority, The, 2000, *Equality Information Pack*

French, Geraldine, 2000, *Supporting Quality: Guidelines for Best Practice in Early Childhood Services*, Dublin: Barnardos National Children's Resource Centre

Gura, P., 1996, *Resources for Early Learning: Children, Adults and Stuff*, London: Hodder & Stoughton

Harding, J. and Melon-Smith, 1996, *How to Make Observations and Assessments*, London: Hodder and Stoughton

Irish Congress of Trades Unions, *Citizens First — Equal Rights and Opportunities for Women and Men in the European Union*, Dublin: ICTU

IPPA, the Early Childhood Organisation 'Quality Discussion Paper' presented to the National Co-ordinating Childcare Committee, March 2001, revised April 2002

Lindon, Jennie, 1998, *Child Protection and Early Years Work*, London: Hodder & Stoughton

National Children's Resource Centre, 2002, *Child and Family Directory*

National Children's Nurseries Association, 1998, *Towards Quality Daycare*, Dublin: NCNA

O'Doherty, A. and P. O'Doherty, 2000, *A Career in Childcare?*, Dublin: National Children's Nursery Association

Pavee Point, 2002, *éist: Respect for Diversity in Early Childhood Care, Education and Training*, Dublin: Pavee Point Travellers' Centre

Purcell, B., 2001, *For Our Own Good: Childcare Issues in Ireland*, Cork: Collins Press

Siraj-Blatchford, I. (ed), 1998, *A Curriculum Development Handbook for Early Childhood Educators*, Staffs: Trentham Books

Treoir, 2001, *Information Pack for Unmarried Parents*, Dublin: Federation of Services for Unmarried Parents

Yeo, A. and T. Lovell, 2002, *Sociology and Social Policy for the Early Years*, London: Hodder & Stoughton

USEFUL ADDRESSES

AIM Family Services, Family Law Information, Mediation and Counselling Centre, 6 D'Olier Street, Dublin 2. Tel: 01 670 8363

Amnesty International, Seán McBride House, 48 Fleet Street, Dublin 2. Tel: 01 677 6361, http//www.amnesty.ie

Association of Refugees and Asylum Seekers in Ireland (ARASI), 213 North Circular Road, Dublin 7. Tel: 01 838 1142

Barnardos National Children's Resource Centre, Christchurch Square, Dublin 8. Tel: 01 453 0355, http://www.barnardos.ie

Childline, Tel: 1800 666 660

Childminding Ireland, 10 Marlborough Court, Dublin 1. Tel: 01 287 5619

Children's Rights Alliance, 13 Harcourt Street, Dublin 2. Tel: 01 405 4823, http://www.childrensrights.ie

Combat Poverty Agency, Bridgewater Centre, Conyngham Road, Islandbridge, Dublin 8. Tel: 01 670 6746, http://www.combatpoverty.ie

Comhairle, 7th Floor, Hume House, Ballsbridge, Dublin 4. Tel: 01 605 9000, http://www.comhairle.ie

Comhchoiste Réamhscolaíochta Teo, An, 7 Cearnóg Mhuirfean, Baile Átha Cliath 2. Tel: 01 639 8441

Department of Justice, Equality and Law Reform, 72–76 St Stephen's Green, Dublin 2. Tel: 01 602 8202, http://www.justice.ie

Department of Education and Science, Marlborough Street, Dublin 1. Tel: 01 873 4700, http://www.education.ie

Department of the Environment and Local Government, Head Office, Custom House, Dublin 1. Tel: 01 888 2000, http://www.environ.ie

Department of Health and Children, Hawkins House, Hawkins Street, Dublin 2. Tel:01 635 4000, http://www.doh.ie

Department of Social, Community and Family Affairs, Áras Mhic Dhiarmada, Store Street, Dublin 1.Tel: 01 874 8444, http://www.welfare.ie

Dublin Islamic Centre, 19 Roebuck Road, Clonskeagh, Dublin 14. Tel: 01 260 3740

Equality Authority, The, 3 Clonmel Street, Dublin 1. Tel: 01 417 3333, http://www.equality.ie

Equality Services Galway, 26 Clareview Park, Ballybane, Galway. Tel: 091 773434. kwiotek@oceanfree.net

Family Mediation Service Floor, St Stephen's Green House, Earlsfort Tce, Dublin 2. Tel: 01 872 8277, e-mail: fmsearlsfort@oceanfree.net

FETAC, The Further Education and Training Awards Council, East Point Plaza, East Point Business Park, Dublin 3. Tel: 01 888 1400, http://www.fetac.ie

Health and Safety Authority, 10 Hogan Place, Dublin 2. Tel: 01 614 7000, http://www.hsa.ie

IMPACT (Trade Union for Early Childhood Workers), Nerney's Court, Dublin 1. Tel: 01 817 1500, http://www.impact.ie

IPPA, the Early Childhood Organisation, Unit 4, Broomhill Business Complex, Broomhill Road, Tallaght, Dublin 24. Tel: 01 463 0010, http://www.ippa.ie

Irish Congress of Trade Unions (ICTU), 31–32 Parnell Square, Dublin 1. Tel: 01 889 7777, http://www.ictu.ie

Irish Society for the Prevention of Cruelty to Children (ISPCC), Head Office, 20 Molesworth Street, Dublin 2. Tel: 01 679 4944, http://www.ispcc.ie

Know Racism, 43–49 Mespil Road, Dublin 4. Tel: 01 663 2694, e-mail: info@antiracism.gov.ie

National Association for the Education of Young Children (NAEYC), 1509 16th Street NW, Washington DC 200 36. http://www.naeyc.org

National Children's Nurseries Association (NCNA), Unit 12c, Bluebell Business Park, Old Naas Road, Bluebell, Dublin 12. Tel: 01 460 1138, http://www.ncna.net

National Children's Office, St Stephen's Green, Dublin 2. Tel: 01 480582.

National Consultative Committee on Racism and Interculturalism (NCCRI), 26 Harcourt St, Dublin 2. Tel: 01 478 5777, e-mail: nccri@eircom.net

National Women's Council of Ireland (NWCI), 16–20 Cumberland St Street, Dublin 2. Tel: 01 661 5268, http://www.nwci.ie

Office of the Director of Equality Investigations, 3 Clonmel Street, Dublin 2. Tel: 01 417 3333, http://www.odei.ie

Parental Equality, 54 Middle Abbey Street, Dublin 2. Tel: 01 872 5222, http://www.parentalequality.ie

Pavee Point Travellers' Centre, 46 North Great Charles Street, Dublin 1. Tel: 01 878 0255, http://www.paveepoint.ie

Refugee Agency, The, 9 Marlborough Court, Dublin 1. Tel: 01 878 7200

Treoir, National Information Centre for Unmarried Parents, 41 Gandon House, Lower Mayor St, IFSC, Dublin 1. Tel: 01 670 0120, e-mail: treoir@indigo.ie

Women's Aid, PO Box 791, Dublin 1.Tel: 01-874 5303, Helpline: 1800 341900, http://www.womensaid.ie

PRACTICAL RESOURCES

Amnesty International and Trócaire, 'The Rights Stuff'. An Education Resource on the UN Convention on the Rights of the Child.

Childsplay, 112 Tooting High Street, London SW17 ORR (Toys)

Irish Congress of Trades Unions, 2000. *Sway — Skills, Work and Youth*, Dublin: ICTU

Letterbox Library, 8 Bradbury Street, London N16 8JN (Book Club)

Mantra Publishing, 5 Alexandra Grove, London N12 8NU (Books and Tapes)

Pavee Point Travellers' Centre, 46 North Great Charles Street, Dublin 1. (Posters, Pictures, Jigsaws, Cards, 'RESPECT for Diversity in Early Childhood Care and Education' CD-ROM)

UN High Commissioner for Refugees (UNHCR), 27 Fitzwilliam St Upr, Dublin 2. Tel: 01 632 8680, e-mail: iredu@unhcr.ch

Index